TOM
HAWKINS

TOM HAWKINS

The autobiography

with
COURTNEY WALSH

Hardie Grant
BOOKS

Published in 2024 by Hardie Grant Books, an imprint of Hardie Grant Publishing

Hardie Grant Books (Melbourne)
Wurundjeri Country
Building 1, 658 Church Street
Richmond, Victoria 3121

Hardie Grant North America
2912 Telegraph Ave
Berkeley, California 94705
hardiegrant.com/books

Hardie Grant acknowledges the Traditional Owners of the Country on which we work, the Wurundjeri People of the Kulin Nation and the Gadigal People of the Eora Nation, and recognises their continuing connection to the land, waters and culture. We pay our respects to their Elders past and present.

All rights reserved. No part of this publication may be reproduced, stored in a retrieval system or transmitted in any form by any means, electronic, mechanical, photocopying, recording or otherwise, without the prior written permission of the publishers and copyright holders.

®™ The AFL logo and competing team logos, emblems and names used are all trademarks of and used under licence from the owner, the Australian Football League, by whom all copyright and other rights of reproduction are reserved.
Australian Football League, AFL House,
140 Harbour Esplanade, Docklands, Victoria, Australia, 3008
Prints of photos published can be purchased at aflphotos.com.au

The moral rights of the author have been asserted.

Copyright text © Tom Hawkins 2024

 A catalogue record for this work is available from the National Library of Australia

Tom Hawkins
ISBN 978 1 74379 887 4
ISBN 978 1 76144 257 5 (ebook)

10 9 8 7 6 5 4 3 2 1

Publishing Director Pam Brewster
Edited by Geoff Slattery
Cover design by Luke Causby, Blue Cork
Cover images AFL photos
Typeset in 11/18 pt Sabon LT Std by Kirby Jones
Printed in Australia by Griffin Press, an Accredited ISO AS/NZS 14001 Environmental Management System printer.

 The paper this book is printed on is certified against the Forest Stewardship Council® Standards. Griffin Press holds FSC® chain of custody certification SGS-COC–001185. FSC® promotes environmentally responsible, socially beneficial and economically viable management of the world's forests.

For Emma, Arabella, Primrose and Henry

Contents

Chapter 1	Hawkins Country	1
Chapter 2	A Geelong heritage	4
Chapter 3	Obsessed	7
Chapter 4	Finding my way	13
Chapter 5	Meeting my idols	21
Chapter 6	The journey begins	24
Chapter 7	A shock to the system	29
Chapter 8	Footy lessons	44
Chapter 9	A mate celebrates	61
Chapter 10	'Bomber'	75
Chapter 11	A premiership!	81
Chapter 12	Changing agents	96
Chapter 13	Bouncing around	101
Chapter 14	Overcoming doubts	112
Chapter 15	Great moments	131
Chapter 16	Old man's back	140
Chapter 17	Missing my greatest supporter	150
Chapter 18	A magnificent leader	160
Chapter 19	Committed to the Cats	167
Chapter 20	Champions come and go	173

Chapter 21	Regrets	179
Chapter 22	Copping a right whack	189
Chapter 23	A season like no other	199
Chapter 24	On it goes	225
Chapter 25	One hell of a ride	235
Chapter 26	No joy	262
Chapter 27	More milestones	277

| Milestones and statistics | 293 |
| Acknowledgements | 296 |

1

Hawkins Country

I WAS BORN AND raised in Finley, Hawkins Country, a land of farmers and footballers. It's a place I adore. Situated about 300km north of the MCG is Springfield, the Hawkins family farm I grew up on. Springfield, which covers 1400 hectares, sits to the north of Finley, a town of 2500 people, about a 30-minute drive north of the Murray River. My family has lived, worked and played and run footy in this region for close on 100 years. It truly is Hawkins Country.

The fabric of my being stems from a boyhood spent roaming around Springfield, where my dreams alternated from being a farmer or a footballer.

My grandfather Wynne bred prized cattle at Springfield for decades while raising three sons, Michael, Jack and Robb. All three boys ventured south to Geelong at some stage to play football for the Cats before coming home to build their own families and work their own farms. My father, Jack, played

182 games for Geelong in the 1970s and 80s before returning to Finley after a career-ending knee injury to forge his career in agriculture.

Returning to Finley with Dad was my mum, Jennie, also part of a Geelong footy family as a daughter of former Geelong ruckman Fred Le Deux and his wife, Pam. Finley was far away from the beautiful beaches of Barwon Heads where Mum grew up, but she took to farm life and the Finley community like she was born to it. Together they immersed themselves in the local community while raising four children including me – a kid with a big smile, big hips and even bigger dreams. Hawkins Country has given my family everything and taught me to love and respect the land. Farming paid for our tuition and our sporting endeavours, both in Finley and then at boarding schools in Melbourne – for Dad and me and my younger brother, Charlie – and Geelong – for my sisters Jane and Edwina – and Finley has provided me with lifelong mates.

Our family homestead sits at the end of a long gravel driveway not far from the Newell Highway and, typical of most farmhouses, is not the flashiest to look at. But inside it bears mementoes of many family celebrations. As a youngster I would bounce the footy all around this place, baulking chooks and cattle, weaving past the utes and the tractors and kicking for 'goal' near the cast-iron sheds. I dreamed of being Gary Ablett Snr. Of course, I barracked for the Cats. Occasionally we would jump in the car and head off to wherever Geelong was playing, to go to the footy with my grandpa Fred. But the distance between life on the farm and the dream of footy in the big smoke was daunting. I was never too sure if I could make it to the big League.

It was not until I headed off to board at Melbourne Grammar in 2003 as a 14-year-old, just as Dad had done more than three decades earlier, that I began to realise footy might just be for me. Even then I had my doubts. It was not until a breakout series for Vic Metro, winning the Larke Medal and making the All-Australian under-18 side, that I felt I might make it.

All these years on, I feel like I am one of the luckiest men alive. How could I not?

2

A Geelong heritage

I LOVED MY LIFE on the farm, but it was also clear from a young age that I was obsessed with sport and in particular footy. Making it with Geelong was my boyhood dream. The footy genes and Geelong connection run strong in my family and it is no surprise that I fell in love with the game.

It is incredible to consider, but our family links to Geelong have now run for more than a century, dating back to when my maternal grandmother's uncle Nick Brushfield made his debut for the club as a 16-year-old in 1923. He ended up playing 41 games over five seasons. He was the start of a lifelong affiliation between the Geelong Football Club and my extended family.

My grandfather Fred Le Deux's move to Ocean Grove to begin a teaching job after finishing studying in Bendigo in the mid-1950s continued the family's link to the Cats. A defender and a follower, Fred was born in Nagambie and played 18 games between 1956 and 1958 when coached by the legendary Reg Hickey. He had the great fortune to play alongside stars of the era including Bob Davis, Neil Tresize, Bernie Smith and Fred Wooller. In his final season with the Cats, Fred met my grandmother, Pam, after a dance at The Palais. The family tradition continued, with their son Rick playing for Geelong reserves before a career in the VFA and VAFA.

Pam's brother, Brian Brushfield, played 15 games for the Cats between 1962 and 1965, featuring in a couple of reserves premierships. His cousin Terry Callan also donned the hoops for the Cats, playing 61 games between 1961 and 1964, though unfortunately he missed the 1963 premiership with a knee injury. Terry's son Tim played with the Cats and the Western Bulldogs and was a great help to me during my first season in 2007 when we both played in Geelong's VFL team.

My uncle Michael, who was three years older than Dad, also played two games with the Cats – alongside Dad – in 1973, before returning to Finley. He later won the O'Dwyer Medal, the best-and-fairest player in the Murray League, playing for Finley, of course.

Dad's younger brother, Robb, also played three games with the Cats – in 1984 – as a ruckman after winning two best-and-fairest awards in his 115 games with South Adelaide in the SANFL. I'm told by Dad and others who saw Michael and Robb play that they could have played many more games for the Cats if they had desired.

Dad enjoyed the best season of his career under Rod Olsson in 1976, finishing 12th in the Brownlow Medal behind Graham Moss, polling 22 votes. This was the season – as in 1977 – when both umpires voted on a 3,2,1 basis. While I managed to win a Coleman Medal, finishing that high in a Brownlow is something I never managed, so Dad, who also represented Victoria in State of Origin, holds the bragging rights there.

In the final two seasons of his career under Bill Goggin in 1980 and 1981, the Cats fell short. After finishing on top of the ladder in 1980, winning 17 of their 22 games, the finals were a disaster, with the Cats losing the second semi-final to eventual premiers Richmond by four goals and then to Collingwood in a heartbreaking preliminary final by four points.

In 1981, the Cats finished third, with 16 wins and, after beating Collingwood in the qualifying final, the Magpies turned the tables in the preliminary final, this time by seven points, after Geelong led by four points at the last break. They were, as Dad has told me, difficult losses to stomach and I'm glad we were able to get some big wins over the Magpies in my time in footy. Goggin was full of praise for Dad's talent and he was named at centre half-back in Geelong's team of the half century (1946 to 1996). But he was stunned when Dad, whose VFL career finished at age 27 – the 1981 preliminary final was his last League game, due to a bad knee injury – missed selection for the New South Wales AFL Greatest Team of All.

'At centre half-back he just marked everything and would give it off very quickly, which got us running out of defence,' Goggin told the *Herald Sun* in 2019. 'He was so important to us that when he got injured, it arguably cost us a place in the Grand Final. It must be a very good side if Jack Hawkins can't crack a mention.'

When I played my 300th game against Port Adelaide in 2021, Granddad Fred joked that at least I had made a reasonable contribution to the family business. 'With my 18 games, Jack's 182 and you up to 300, that gives us 500 between us,' he said.

3

Obsessed

My obsession with footy was clear in the years I spent mimicking my first boyhood idol, Gary Ablett Snr, around the family farm.

My admiration for Gary as a player had been sharpened from watching him on television highlights or in video compilations. I would watch his highlights for hours at a time. There was nothing quite like the excitement of watching him flying for a screamer or listening to Rex Hunt on the radio as he yelled, 'Yaaabbbleeettttt.'

I can remember heading to Berrigan to visit friends of our family, and we would often watch a video called *One Special Season* about Gary's great deeds in 1993.

It followed the season when coach Malcolm Blight shifted Gary to full-forward from the wing in a move that reaped great results for both the team and the player. He won the Leigh Matthews Medal as the AFL Players Association's Most Valuable

Player and also his first Coleman Medal that season, kicking 124 goals. He followed that with 129 goals in 1994 (113 in the home-and-away season) and 122 (118) in 1995!

Having played in the modern era where the very best full-forwards struggle to get within 30 goals of the century – my personal best is 68 goals, in 2014 – it is incredible to consider how potent he was when playing deep in attack.

My grandparents Fred and Pam still tell the tale of how, when I was about 10, I ran around at a function celebrating their 40th wedding anniversary in Bannockburn pretending to be Gary. I only ever had the good fortune of watching him play a couple of times before he retired for good in 1997. Gary was a player blessed with a talent on the footy field that very few could ever hope to match, such was his explosive power and athleticism. His highlight reel is incredible. I doubt there will ever be a better one in footy, though I am mindful that one of my old rivals Lance 'Buddy' Franklin did some spectacular things. If a player as talented as Gary Snr comes along again, I hope it happens in my lifetime, as I'd love to see another footballer capable of producing those deeds.

When I was in primary school, I tried to connect with Gary. It was my version of a message in a bottle. I wrote a letter to the Geelong champion, telling him of my dreams to one day play the game like he did while asking his advice on how to achieve this. I then wrapped that note in a piece of string and tied the letter to a balloon, waiting for a windy day to blow it from our farm to Kardinia Park, where I thought the superstar lived. What could possibly go wrong with the plan? What seemed like a good idea at the time fell flat when Mum found the deflated balloon, my letter still attached, in the garden a couple of weeks later.

Not deterred, I continued to boot the footy around the back paddock, believing I might one day become the next Cat to wear his famous No.5 guernsey.

Footy fans might remember the time when Gary Ablett Snr and a few others – notably Travis Cloke, Adem Yze and Warren Tredrea – wore gloves to help them grip the ball. As a result, I had to have my own set and I convinced Mum to order a set for one of my early birthdays. If I could not match his leap, at the very least I could borrow from his fashion sense. I figured it could only help my footy to follow the example set by the greatest.

Every day I'd jump out of the car after Mum had picked us up from the bus stop and race to the mailbox, hoping it would be the day that my dream birthday gift arrived. The only problem was the gloves, like the letter, never arrived. I do not know what happened there. So, I had to learn to mark the footy using my bare hands. Luckily, I was born with big mitts.

Being Gary Ablett was my footy fantasy. But on the farm, it was not all about dreaming. I spent hundreds of hours trying to master the skills needed to split the middle of any target I could find.

A key to my kicking skills in general play, which I believe was a strength during my career, traced to those times when I was fumbling around with the footy. It was a rare moment when I was not handballing or kicking it to myself or booting the ball in the backyard with Dad after school.

As much fun as it was, there was a critical lesson. Dad would stand as a target and if I was able to kick it to him, the ball would come swiftly back to me, for even with his dicky knee,

Dad remained a superb kick. But if I was even a couple of metres wide, I would have to retrieve the footy. It taught me that finding the target is better than having to gallop after the footy.

It might sound like Dad was being harsh, but there was a good reason for his rule. He was exhausted after a long day working the farm and some days must have felt even longer when I was kicking the footy at the livestock and being a menace.

There is no doubt that there were times I annoyed Dad and my grandfather when I was roaming around with a footy while they were at work, rounding up sheep or cattle. This would infuriate my grandfather, who would get impatient with me and say, 'How many times have I told you?'

It must have been so frustrating for them and it was probably dangerous as well because one thing I have learnt about cattle is that you do not want to take your eyes off them for a second, because they truly know how to deliver a hip-and-shoulder.

It was not just my granddad who was driven to distraction. If I landed the footy too close to the dogs helping to round up the livestock, they would completely lose their focus, which only added to grandpa's frustration.

My Geelong teammates thought that kicking for goal was difficult when there was a gap between the stands during the redevelopment of Kardinia Park. But the swirling wind there had nothing on the challenge I faced every day in Finley.

There was a natural progression in the difficulty of my target practice as a kid. Initially I would kick a ball between some trees in the backyard of our family farm.

It was a beautiful setting. One of my 'goal posts', a superb lemon tree, still grows the juiciest lemons. Among many challenges

I faced was trying to avoid knocking the lemons off the branches. I then moved on to the sheds that housed cattle when they were brought in from the paddocks. Sitting about 100 metres apart, each shed served as a natural goalkicking target.

One shed had an open window, about a metre wide and a little longer in height, proving an ideal target for a young kid learning to kick straight. Once I had mastered that, I moved on to the other shed, for what appeared to be Mission: Impossible.

This target was an open vent, about four metres above ground level. The margin for error was far smaller than my earlier targets: the vent was about 30cm wide, just enough to skim a Sherrin through, and about 75cm in height, with a slant towards the roof of the shed.

To split the middle was a true test of skill. Particularly as I was usually wearing farm boots instead of sneakers or footy boots.

Time and again the footy would slam into the shed as I tried to find the perfect flight path. Kicking too high was a big fail. The number of times I had to climb onto the roof to retrieve the footy makes me shudder. I soon learnt the importance of weighting my kicks properly.

I'm also certain Mum was happy the back shed was far enough away for the ding and clatter to be stifled by the many other soundtracks that accompany life on the farm. Just as I was banned from booting balls around the inside of the house, my goal-kicking practice would have been short-lived had the shed been closer to our back door.

Just as I bothered Dad and Grandad when booting a footy at the cattle, there were times where my behaviour with balls got the better of me at school. If there was a bottle or some other target sitting near a ledge and I had a tennis ball, I'd treat it like trying to have a ping at the stumps. This resulted in quite a few broken windows and semi-regular trips to the principal's office at St Joseph's.

One instance in particular stands out. A couple of mates and I were booting a soccer ball around near the school chapel when I saw a target I liked.

The challenge was seeing how much risk I was prepared to take while testing out my control of the ball. Control? What control? The ball went sailing straight through a window, with the shards flying everywhere. The playground was silent. I remember feeling sick in the stomach.

There was no fun in confessing my 'sin' to Father Martin, the local parish priest. I'm told that to this day, he is waiting for my contribution to cover the cost of fixing that broken window. Perhaps that 'sin' has driven me to sponsoring Finley's under-14s since 2014! It won't fix the broken window but might help the 'Tom Hawkins' of this era to fulfil their footy dream.

4

Finding my way

RIGHT FROM THE rough-and-tumble of primary school and kick-to-kick at high school, I had been pitted against kids who not only had a serious love and appreciation for footy but could really play. I was probably pretty good in those years but I was by no means a standout and there were times I got towelled up. Even in my final full year with Finley, as an under-14, when I was playing as the ruckman, I did not win the club's best and fairest.

I was once up against Jarrod McGough – former Magpie Mark McGough's younger brother – in a junior game against Mulwala when I was asked to tag him. He was an absolute gun and I can remember thinking, 'There is no way this guy is not making it'. He was far too good for me. He didn't make the AFL, but he did enjoy success in regional and suburban football, including kicking a match-winning goal for Panton Hill in the dying stages of a Division 3 Northern Football League Grand Final against Watsonia in 2013.

Marcus Drum, who played 22 games for Fremantle after he was selected as pick #10 in the 2005 AFL National Draft, (and would join me at Geelong in 2010 after four seasons at Fremantle) was another from our region who gave me a beating as a junior. He was the year above me and dominated all year for Congupna, in the Murray Valley League, when playing centre half-forward. He kicked seven goals on me one day and I was named the best for our side, which shows you exactly how good a player he was.

It really was a good breeding ground to develop as a kid, given the strength of local players. Most of the best players made their way to the Murray Bushrangers, which fielded a really strong team in what was then the TAC Cup, against the best Victorian under-18 teams.

* * *

The first major change in my life came at the age of 14, when I followed in my father's footsteps and headed off to board at Melbourne Grammar. I was not looking forward to the move because I loved my life on the farm. The simple country life suited me, being able to roam the farm and play sport with my mates. But with my older sister, Jane, already boarding at Geelong College, the writing was on the wall for me.

I was not a shy kid, but I had never really liked being taken out of my comfort zone around Finley. I needed a push to do that. I was going to a school with a huge reputation and I was concerned as to whether I was up to the task academically. My early school reports were promising but by the time I left Finley, I was at best a C-grade student.

I was always really close to Mum and Dad, and that was the hardest part about being away, although I never really felt homesick, knowing it was not that hard to get back to Finley for the holidays, so I was able to find a reasonable balance.

The first two weeks in Melbourne were the toughest and there was one lesson in particular where I remembered thinking that I was not cut out at all to be a student. We had to choose a language in Year 9 and because Dad, as a rice grower, had partnerships with Japanese companies, we would occasionally host Japanese exchange students. With that in mind, I thought it might be a good idea if I was able to speak some Japanese. The first class I attended proved to be an eye-opening experience.

I was late to the class and it was not too long before I felt severely embarrassed as well. My teacher Ben Hanisch started the class by speaking in Japanese, which was not the best beginning for a rookie who had no idea what he was saying.

When my fellow students responded to him in what sounded like fluent Japanese, it was rather deflating. I could see he was trying to gauge the language levels of each of my classmates but sitting there and unable to understand a word, I was soon thinking, 'What am I going to do? Am I going to have to leave?' All I could imagine was my new classmates laughing at me as I bolted out the door.

Eventually Mr Hanisch got to me and asked me something and all I could say was, 'Sorry, mate. I don't understand what you mean.' He brushed me off and kept going with the class.

I was mortified, certain that the teacher hated me. I called Mum as soon as classes were over to tell her she needed to get me out of this class.

But she urged me to stick it out. As usual, her advice was sound and, in the end, it worked out well, not that I got a whole lot better at Japanese. Sandy Robinson, who was best man at my wedding, had a similar reaction in his French class and his mum allowed him to transfer to Japanese, where we became a pack of two. The fun we had in that class helped us to form such a great relationship that we are now godparents to each other's children. That may not have happened without Japanese!

* * *

It was not too long before I really took a shine to my new life at boarding school. Being able to mix with people from different regions and different countries, and with different backgrounds, was something I enjoyed and while I missed home, I soon came to love Melbourne.

My 2009 and 2011 premiership teammate Steve Johnson once told me that he believed a season spent with a group of guys at a footy club was equivalent to spending three years with them in real life. Effectively, you spend so much time with each other, from training and rehabilitation to meetings, travelling and matches that you get to know each other inside out. If that is true, I'd say attending a year of boarding school is the equivalent of spending five normal school years together because you would literally do everything with your closest mates.

I was really challenged in the classroom but, despite my anxiety at the beginning, I realised my new friends did not care whether I was an A-student or a D-student. For me, the importance of school was more about the mateship, and I found the social side of living on campus absolutely brilliant. From the moment the alarm went off, you would be with your mates, queuing for a shower, having breakfast together, heading off to classes and then finishing off the day with cricket or footy or athletics training. I loved pouring my energy into my sporting endeavours after school each day. It was always a welcome reprieve from studying. Afterwards, we would be back to the boarding house for dinner before heading off for a 90-minute study period. It might have been a 90-minute period, but I would have averaged about 20 to 30 minutes where I was actively studying.

Year 10 also marked the arrival from Gippsland of Xavier Ellis, who went on to play in a premiership with Hawthorn in 2008 and later finished his career in Perth with the West Coast Eagles. We were roommates and quickly became the closest of mates, which is not really a surprise. Neither of us was particularly academic, we both loved sport and, being from the bush, we soon found that we had plenty in common.

Not that Xavier, apparently, was particularly looking forward to it, as he told me when I asked him for some school memories for this book. He said, 'I ran into a kid called Rory on my first day and he asked me who I was boarding with and I told him, "Tom Hawkins" and he said, "Good luck", started laughing and walked off. I thought, "Shit". As I walked into our room, you were sitting on this single bed with your legs sticking off the end of it and your mum was there saying, "So, Tom, do you want your jocks in the top drawer or in the second drawer?" I was like, "This bloke is a giant softie. His mum even irons his jocks." But it probably took us about 48 hours to become the closest of mates. We knew pretty quickly where our futures lay. We were not smart enough to be out there repairing brains. We were going to be the ones kicking the footy around the park.'

* * *

Melbourne Grammar placed a premium on playing school footy above competing in the TAC Cup. If there was a clash between the fixtures, school always won out, which was fair enough, although my career in Melbourne Grammar's First XVIII squad started on an inauspicious note which left a few people scratching their heads about my discipline.

The school had a rule which prevented students who were not in Year 10 or above from playing in the senior side. As a result, I spent my first year playing with boys my own age in Year 9. But having shown some promise at that level, at the end of the season I was invited to travel with the older boys to Adelaide to play a friendly match against St Peter's College.

As luck would have it, the host family I stayed with happened to be the uncle and aunt of my 2009 premiership captain, Tom Harley. I'm not sure they would have tipped then that I would make it to the AFL, based on what happened at the end of the trip.

Quite simply, the older boys filled me up with a few beers after the match and, being full of bravado, I wanted to prove I was one of the lads and capable of holding my liquor. You can take the boy from the bush, but you can't take the bush out of the boy.

It all backfired and I had to be nursed when I got back to

my host family, who were very decent towards me, despite my inebriated state. Clearly, I loved my fun as much as I loved my footy and while that incident did not really land me in any trouble, it was just one example where my youthful exuberance got the better of me.

I soon learnt the standard of school footy was pretty good. As I noted, I had played against some really talented players at home and along the Murray River, but the depth in the city was far stronger, both in Melbourne Grammar's team and in the teams that we competed against in the Associated Grammar Schools of Victoria competition. My lack of discipline in Adelaide was a thing of the past when I started my senior school footy career in Year 10, and I managed to kick four goals in my opening game. It was another special moment for me because it meant I had followed the footy footsteps of Dad, playing for the same team. Those are the types of achievements I have appreciated more and more as the years have passed. A highlight, in Year 12, was being named as the co-captain of the First XVIII alongside my great mate Xavier Ellis. It really was a tremendous honour.

My school coach, Mr Hanisch – yes the Japanese teacher – made some observations about my school career in a feature article which ran in *The Geelong Advertiser* before my 300th game in 2021: 'I still have postcard recollections of things he did in games that were very special,' he said. 'There was one game against Haileybury. We were kicking into a strong breeze and he took a mark just outside 40 metres when the siren sounded. But he just went back and put it through post-high to put us in front at quarter-time against a really strong Haileybury team. It was a big moment, because we won that game by a couple of points. As captain, it was Tom's job at the end of each game to summarise the game in front of the team. He wasn't fantastic at that at the beginning, but it was beautiful to watch him grow, and to now see him so seasoned and such a high-level natural performer in front of the media.'

Because of the school's rule that school footy came first, during my time at Melbourne Grammar I only played a handful of games for the Sandringham Dragons, though I did kick five goals in an early outing. That effort was enough to earn me an invitation into the AIS/AFL Academy Squad, which was another highlight of my school footy career. We even had the opportunity to play an International Rules game against an Irish side. But because of my school and footy commitments in Melbourne, my parents decided to limit my travel, which ruled out representing the Allies in the national carnival.

5

Meeting my idols

It was not until I had moved to Melbourne that I understood just how strongly my family was linked with Geelong and the doors that could open up as a result.

Sourcing tickets to Cats games was never an issue, and I would regularly see them play, either in Melbourne or at Kardinia Park. My grandparents the Le Deuxs were good friends with Frank and Shirley Costa, and I was lucky enough to be introduced to the long-time Cats' president. Frank was always very fond of me and I have to say the admiration was more than mutual. What he managed to do for both the club and city of Geelong during his life was remarkable. My other connection was also a handy one. My sister Jane was then dating Jimmy Bartel and was also able to score tickets.

I always went to games with a couple of mates and after the final siren, we would head towards the race and try to make contact with Vic Fuller, the much-loved Cats staff member who tragically died while watching a training session in 2021. He was a really lovely man. Vic served as a club doorman in the latter stages of what was a long and award-winning career at the Cats and, because of Dad, knew who I was and would always welcome me into the rooms. I would then look for either Frank or Jimmy because, being a mad Cats supporter, I always wanted to get closer to the players. I loved everything about being in the rooms.

After one of the wins at the Docklands, Frank grabbed me and took me to the meeting room where Mark 'Bomber' Thompson was about to debrief the players. Usually only the players and coaches attend these meetings, so I was pinching myself at my good luck. From later experience, I've learnt these meetings can be short, particularly after a win. But simply getting a glimpse of the inner workings of the club was beyond my wildest dreams, although I did wonder whether I should be in there.

It was fascinating to watch Bomber in action as he discussed the efforts of the night. I heard him say, 'Steven King. Well played. Kane Tenace. I love what you did there.' He went around all the players until he got to me and it was not long before my cheeks were turning bright red. Bomber must have been told who I was, because he said, 'Everyone. This is Tom Hawkins. You might well be playing with this kid in a few years.'

I was feeling particularly shy and a little shocked to have been invited into the inner sanctum in the first place when suddenly I was surrounded by my idols. It felt tremendous at the time and I still can't believe how welcome they made me feel that night. Bomber had a brief chat with me afterwards. I was over the moon about the whole experience.

Now that I have the best part of two decades of experience at the club, I realise every group of players would do the same to a young kid in that situation. But it does not make what Frank and Bomber did for me that night any less special.

6

The journey begins

It was during the 2006 under-18 national carnival that the hype about my talent started to build. What is less known is that if it was not for my parents' intervention, I may not have played at all in that carnival. I was always keen to head home to Finley whenever I had holidays or a long weekend, to see Mum and Dad. I loved being able to give them a hand on the farm, to check in on the chooks and the cattle, to see some old friends and, if possible, to sneak in a junior game for the Finley Cats.

That year's carnival fell right in the middle of the winter holidays and, let's face it, winter in Finley is far milder than the brisk days in Melbourne throughout July. Heading home would have been the comfortable option. But my parents encouraged me to back my ability and test my talent against the best junior footballers in the country.

I was starting to have faith in my ability. I had been pretty good at junior level at home and then strong at school. I also felt like I matched up well alongside the AIS/AFL Academy guys. Clearly State of Origin rules did not apply. Being at school in Melbourne effectively sealed the deal for me and I was selected for Vic Metro in the Nationals. I went into the carnival feeling like there were so many better players and I had little confidence I would be a standout. My main goal was to figure out where I sat in the pecking order, given I had played so little TAC Cup footy against the guys who were likely to be drafted.

We played South Australia in the first game and it was clear their defenders were undersized. Standing alongside me in the Vic Metro team were Matthew Kreuzer, who was selected by Carlton with the first pick in the following year's draft, and Chris Dawes, who played in a premiership with Collingwood before later becoming a Demon.

I was the smallest of the three of us, but I somehow ended up being on the receiving end of a few handy passes in the opening match and managed to kick six goals in our 59-point victory. For all the quality players in our squad – which also included Bachar Houli (later a three-time Richmond premiership player), Leigh Adams (104 games with North Melbourne) and Robbie Gray (three-time best and fairest at Port Adelaide) – I could sense there was a lot of interest in my performances, given the Hawkins links to Geelong, rather than my footy talent deserved. Jon Anderson, the long-time *Herald Sun* journalist, knew Dad, and had written an article about the father–son connection when I was in Year 10. At the time, I thought that story was the best thing ever, though as I found out later once I joined Geelong, not every article would be positive through my career.

The second game of the carnival, against Western Australia, is one that sticks in my memory, with good reason because it was held at Kardinia Park. The Geelong side had trained before our game, and a few Cats players stayed behind to watch. Fortunately, I had a good day, ultimately finishing with three goals from 20 disposals, though it could have been even better – I also kicked five behinds. Despite my best efforts on the farm, there were times when my kicking for goal let me down.

When looking back through some of my records – the Le Deuxs were ardent record keepers when it came to newspaper articles early in my career – I realised Bomber Thompson was also watching that day because journalists chased him for a comment. 'He's a very impressive player for a young guy,' he said. 'He's 197cm and already quite strong and already has got a lot of muscle mass on him. He looks like a ready-made player, really.' If only that were the case. But I was really pleased with how I had played in front of those players I admired.

In my three years at Melbourne Grammar, Geelong would send me letters congratulating me for the way I had played and represented school and any other achievements they were aware of. While I was in the AIS/AFL Academy as a 16-year-old, Geelong's list manager, Stephen Wells, was among those who showed our group around the club when we visited Geelong and at the start of the 2006 season. He later called to see how I was faring ahead of Year 12 and my final season of school footy. He told me that Geelong would leave me be through the season to allow me to concentrate on my final year of school but that the Cats would be in touch. And he urged me to contact him if I ever needed anything. This relationship came in handy on the final match of the carnival.

The final game of the carnival was a wipeout from a personal sense, with the weather miserable at Princes Park for our clash against a strong Vic Country combination. I was well held by one of the Brown twins – Nathan or Mitch; Nathan subsequently went on to play for Collingwood and St Kilda and Mitch for West Coast. I cannot remember which one it was who did the job that day!

It was so wet that before that game, I called Stephen Wells to ask him if he could find me a pair of long-stopped boots. I only had a normal pair. He was able to courier me a pair of Steven King's old boots. The ex-Geelong skipper is a big boy and it turned out his size 15 boots were too large even for my feet. But they were not the reason for me getting beaten on the day. The good thing was we ended up winning, 4.10 to 2.9 – indicative of the state of the weather.

It seemed I had impressed enough in my two earlier matches for Vic Metro as I was awarded the Larke Medal as the best player of the carnival, a great honour. That sent the hype into overdrive, with my Vic Metro coach, David Dickson, telling the *Herald Sun* that I was the best junior player he had coached since West Coast and Carlton champion Chris Judd. 'Tommy Hawkins, pound for pound, is the best footballer I have seen since Chris Judd came through. He is just outstanding in all ways. You don't just look at him dominating against the kids and think he won't do it against men. That is crap,' he said. 'Even coaching him, he is just so willing to learn and improve. He just kept on stepping up and getting better. He's such a great kid to coach. He's another one that's going to be a great player. He's got everything. He's got awareness. He's got sharpness. He's got strength. He's quick off mark and, in an AFL club, he's just going to get better and better.'

I had a lot to live up to, but I didn't let the publicity go to my head. I have never been one to read much into commentary or analysis, as flattering or as critical as it may be. I prefer any directions to come from my coach. But if my head did not get too big, somewhat unfortunately, other parts of my body did, due to my love of food.

After the carnival I relaxed my training, sure I would be selected as a father–son recruit by the Cats. I started stacking on the kilograms, hitting up fast food joints whenever there was a dodgy option at school. Or, as my future teammate Steve Johnson suggests, my love for cinnamon donuts proved too tempting. It was a bad habit I took to Geelong from boarding school.

Whatever the reason, between the end of the national carnival and my arrival at Geelong in the spring of 2006, I put on at least 10 kilos, and none of that was muscle mass. I put it down to stress eating through the period leading up to my exams, but obviously I was not too anxious on the academic front, given I had a good idea as to what the future held for me. Despite that surge in weight, I somehow managed to match Dad by winning the Associated Grammar Schools high-jumping competition in the last couple of months of school. That is a feat I am proud of, though one that surprised, particularly given my fitness levels.

Either way, it was not too long before I began what felt like the longest summer of my life.

7

A shock to the system

Once in Melbourne, there was never a time when I had thoughts of playing anywhere but Geelong and those meetings with Stephen Wells and letters from the club did nothing to change that thinking. That was the message I passed on to my Melbourne Grammar headmaster, Paul Sheahan, during my first year of boarding and the links had grown stronger while attending Geelong's games with my grandparents.

During this period, I didn't have any formal conversations with Geelong, but Mum and Dad, and Flying Start, the management group we had signed with, had kept in touch with the club.

Once the 2006 APS season finished in August, I made the trip to Kardinia Park with my parents to meet formally with Wells, who asked if I wanted to join Geelong as a father–son recruit. He said the club cared about my future and felt I would succeed with the Cats. He wanted to know if I felt the same way.

Of course I said yes! Bomber Thompson was pleased with my decision. He told reporters: 'I'm glad he has agreed to play with the Cats because there would be a few clubs trying to poach him, I'd imagine.' There had been nothing officially announced, but I am sure Wells would have been aware that other clubs were keeping tabs on my performances at junior level and would have kept the club – and Bomber – abreast of any information he was receiving. Flying Start also had made contact with other clubs who were checking to see whether I would be available come the draft, or whether I had committed to Geelong under the father–son rules.

Being selected as a father–son recruit meant the club could choose me in the third round in the National Draft, at pick 41. As a consequence, I would receive less pay in my first couple of seasons. A third-round draftee got a base payment of $39,300 and $2200 per game, while first rounders received $45,600 and $2200 per game.

Whether I would have taken in the first round is something I wondered occasionally, as I am sure winning the Larke Medal as a key forward would have boosted my profile among recruiters. But perhaps if clubs had monitored my fitness as my weight started to balloon in the last couple of months in Year 12, they may not have been all that impressed. I might have slipped to No. 41 anyway. I'm also thankful that the draft then was not like it is now, where newcomers to the League are introduced onstage and made to put on the jumper of their new club straight away. That would have been embarrassing for me, though I might have made more of an effort to not stack on the kilograms.

After finishing school, the next major task was to shift from Melbourne to Geelong. Within a couple of days of my final exam, I was headed down the Princes Highway to begin my new life. While at school, knowing I would be selected by Geelong, I anticipated living with my grandparents, who had moved from Barwon Heads to Bannockburn after Granddad Fred retired. Thinking back on that idea, that may not have been a smart move as the Le Deuxs are fanatical Cats fans and I'm sure they would have been pumping me for information about the team and what was going on around the club. It was better for me to connect with my teammates at a host family's.

The club's development coach, former Cats player Ron Watt, effectively arranged everything associated with the move, including organising a host family and, after a final weekend at up Springfield, I headed to Geelong with Mum and Dad in early November to meet my new host family, the Jenners, in the Geelong suburb of Highton, about a 10-minute drive from the club. At that stage, I knew I would be joined by another draftee, though I was not sure who it would be. A few weeks later, Joel Selwood arrived.

Host families play an important role for young footballers, with clubs preferring to place draftees just out of school into a secure environment where they are looked after.

Having a family to help you settle into a new environment is a big plus. The demands of the pre-season are significant and young kids are often exhausted at the end of a hard session. Sometimes all you want to do is sleep.

Bernie and Hilary Jenner, along with their four children, Andrew, Yvette, Juliette and Felicity, were terrific people. I am so grateful for the time and effort they put into looking after me as I was settling into a new life.

That year of living together with Joel opened my eyes. I learnt so much from him. I was already aware of just how competitive a person he is. That drive relates to everything. He was also so much more prepared and ready to cope with the demands of senior footy.

The gap between us in terms of our professionalism was vast. When it came to sport, if there was a chance to go head-to-head, we would jump straight to it. It might be golf, generally at the Balyang par-three in Newton, close to the Barwon River. We would go bowling at the local Tenpin lanes or whack table tennis balls at each other whenever there was a chance. I would like to say that I was the more talented in many of our pursuits, but Joel was more than capable in every sport we played.

With his never-say-die attitude, and refusal to give an inch, he was always hard to beat, with a couple of instances standing out. One day early on, we headed to the tennis courts at Geelong West, with the temperature sitting at about 35°C. There was nothing particularly special about the way he played tennis. But he would chase every ball down and make you earn every single point. The first two sets were pretty even and by the end of the second, I'd had enough. But Joel was insistent. We had to play a deciding third set, and that was a problem for me. That gulf in professionalism between us showed. He had remembered to bring a water bottle because of the heat. I had not. With bragging rights on the line, his ruthless streak took over. No way would he share his water bottle. It proved the decisive edge.

By the end of the match, I was parched, frustrated and, to my great disappointment, also beaten.

* * *

Even though we were the same age, Joel taught me that there was far more to being a footballer than simply training or playing matches. Nearly everything you did between matches could have an impact on your performance. It took a few years for those lessons to sink in for me, but I learnt that the body of work done between matches allows you to do justice to your talent on game day.

One notable difference between me and Joel initially was the stark contrast in our diets. With my liking for Subway sangas and cinnamon donuts, the kilos I had put on since I'd played in the national under-18 carnival proved a hard habit to shake. We would have a couple of sandwiches for lunch, for example, but an hour or so later, I would be topping up again in the kitchen. A particular favourite of mine was Nutella pancakes and I would often tuck into a couple not long after we had polished off lunch.

Joel was never really one to lecture, but occasionally he would say to me things along the lines of: 'Are you kidding me? What are you doing? Is that something you really need?' It would always be said in an encouraging tone, as in: 'C'mon Tom. You can do better.'

We've had a good laugh about these times over the years. As he says: 'He just destroyed everything in the kitchen. Living with the Jenner family was a great fit for both of us. Hilary was a great cook. But 'Hawk' used to get himself in a bit of trouble because banana muffins were a regular. We would walk in the front door and you had to pass the kitchen to get to your room, so it wasn't easy for him at that stage to drop the puppy fat.'

He was right, of course. I was a big boy with a large appetite but learning to cut out unnecessary treats was part of the learning process for me. Becoming more professional in every facet of my life helped me to become the player that I became, and Joel played a big role in setting an example.

* * *

Even though I recorded my heaviest-ever weight – 113kg – not long after I joined the club, I arrived full of confidence. I now knew I was a good young player, among the best of my draft year. Sure, I could have been fitter. I could also have done with a haircut, having arrived at the club with a rat's tail dangling down the back of my neck; it was not a good look.

But my fitness, I thought, would surely improve with a couple of decent runs and I did not have a worry in the world, as I told *The Geelong Advertiser* shortly after donning the blue and white hoops for a photograph ahead of that year's draft. 'I don't really have the nerves of some other players at the moment, which is good. I know where I'm going. And it has been a good couple of weeks,' I told the journalist. 'I'm just happy to be going to Geelong, because it's the team that I grew up barracking for, and it's just fantastic to be playing alongside some of the players I've grown up supporting.'

Everyone had advised me that the pre-season would be difficult, but I thought I would be able to handle whatever challenges were posed. Not so. The wake-up call on that first day was brutal.

My lungs were burning, my chest was heaving and the torrent of sweat running down my face felt like a river of tears. I wanted to cry, so great was the pain. I was being put through my paces by Ron Watt, but I was scarcely coping. If this was day one, how would I make it through this first week of training, let alone survive the summer?

It felt as though I had sprinted 15 kilometres, yet it was probably about a third of that distance. Despite my confidence, I felt overwhelmed. It was by far the hardest training session I had endured, and I remember thinking, with the rudest of shocks, that I was so underprepared for what lay ahead.

The skinfolds test that followed showed just how unfit I was: I recorded a score of 92, which was so far above the level required to play in the AFL. Measuring skinfolds is a way of determining a person's body composition and body fat percentage. The AFL standard is around 60! At the same time, I received my VCE results and my score of 43.5 confirmed that academia was not my strength. Even now, I'll joke around with friends by offering the two numbers and asking them to guess which was which when I started my career.

Because Joel had grown up with older brothers – Adam, Troy and Scott already in the AFL system – he knew what to expect and had conditioned himself to be ready to go at whichever club selected him. He set such a high standard from day one that I was chasing my tail in a bid to keep pace with him. It was not the first time in my early years I wished I had been better prepared and more able to put together all the parts that make a good footballer. Joel was fit enough to train at the AFL level immediately, and was also able to understand the messages from the coaches and put them into practice, which is why he cemented a spot in the senior side from the opening round of 2007, proving effective from his first game.

My first big highlight as a Cat was being offered the number 26 guernsey my father had worn, a tradition I loved being able to continue. As I told the Cats yearbook: 'I was pretty excited when it came up. I was happy and honoured to take it. I never got a chance to watch Dad play, but he has helped me a lot over the years and his advice has been invaluable.'

My arrival came at an interesting time for Geelong, with the Cats about to implement a vastly different system after undergoing an intense review just weeks beforehand. The team was seen to have been underperforming given the rich talent on the list. After a torrid 2006, when they finished tenth, the club was determined to put the past behind them. The club hired the Leading Teams organisation, which had enjoyed great success with the Sydney Swans, and they implemented a program that was based on the players taking more responsibility for their performances and adopting greater honesty with each other.

Up to 400 members had attended the Fred Flanagan Room at Kardinia Park as chief executive Brian Cook and coach Bomber Thompson outlined the 15 recommendations aimed at ensuring the Cats would become the best they could be, on and off the field. Tom Harley, after 142 games with the club, was installed as the new skipper, replacing Steven King. In his relatively short time in charge before his retirement after the 2009 premiership, Tom became one of the club's most decorated captains.

Neil Balme was appointed football operations manager in place of Garry Davidson, an admired former Cats player and member of the Tasmanian Football Hall of Fame who had led Geelong's footy department between 1999 and 2006. Paul Haines and Dean 'The Weapon' Robinson were hired to run the strength and conditioning department. As a newcomer, the significance of those changes was not something I appreciated at the time, but in hindsight, these were really drastic changes from one season to the next.

The pressure everyone at the club felt at the end of the 2006 season was immense, as Bomber explained to the members. 'I think I've been under the griller all year. I've been under enormous pressure,' he said. 'But I will say from a coach's point of view that I accept the changes and recommendations and am very, very happy to go back to doing what I do best. You'll see a different game plan this year.'

Bomber was great to me from my arrival at the club, even if I was not quite the 'ready-made' proposition he had envisaged when he had watched me a few months earlier playing for Vic Metro. I am certain he gave me some games in my first couple of seasons, even if I was not quite ready, in order to try to fast-track my development. But it is also just as certain that while he hoped I would be part of the long-term solution for Geelong, at that stage, I was still a long way from being able to contribute consistently.

I think he got it right, when he said of me in the pre-season: 'He has probably just relied a lot on natural ability. But there is a lot to learn about, a lot which is not footy-related, which he isn't good at. He marks the ball. He is footy smart. He has good awareness. He is huge and we are taking the weight off, rather than putting it on. It's going to be hard for him, but that's okay. I think if he does it hard in the VFL for a few weeks and we bring him up, then he will get better support in the AFL system where there's more structure. We probably think that he is going to play and be a pretty good player this year.'

After that initial shock on the training track, the spring of 2006 proved a really exciting time as I settled in with my new host family and awaited the arrival of my fellow draftees. The Cats had selected Nathan Djerrkura with pick 25, and Simon Hogan, pick 57, along with Joel. The thinking was they would help Geelong become a quicker, more versatile team.

The Geelong Advertiser certainly had their prediction right when, for the paper's first story on Joel, after the draft, they ran the headline: 'Young gun shows early leadership potential'. It was suggested straight away that Joel would one day be captain of Geelong, though he did his best to downplay this in the humble fashion we soon become accustomed to. 'You can read too much into it. I will just come down here and hopefully play some good footy and, if it does come along one day, then I would probably grab it with two hands,' he said. He was just 18 years old.

Bomber's initial assessment of Joel was also on the money in that same article. 'He is just a quality midfielder, just someone who can play consistently high-level football, who is a great person and really footy smart,' he said. 'I think all the coaches have had a look at it and thought he might be one who could play next year.'

The next day, it was my turn to be back page news in my new hometown. The billing at the top of the paper had a photograph of Australian fast bowler Brett Lee celebrating a wicket in the first Test of the Ashes at the Gabba. Directly below it was a massive photo of me with a grin as wide as the smile at Luna Park, my hands out ready to receive a handball. The headline read: 'Thumbs up, Tom'. The story said I was, as you might have guessed, 'ready-made' and, at 197cm, I towered above my new teammates. A closer look at the stats might have told them that Brad Ottens was 202cm, and Steven King was 201cm! 'His kick is long and direct. And his hands wrap around the ball like he is picking apples,' the paper noted.

It is probably not a surprise given my lack of fitness and sudden exposure to the training standards of an AFL club, but shortly before Christmas, I began to feel pain in the lower part of my left leg. The fitness staff had been trying to strip some weight from me. I was doing a lot of running, but I did not yet have the resilience to be able to cope with the workload. A scan revealed that I had a minor crack in my tibia, which meant that I missed about four weeks of training before resuming midway through January.

* * *

Joel was selected for the opening round in a season in which he would be acclaimed as the AFL's Rising Star, but I had to wait a week to make my debut. I had shown some form in the pre-season games and, despite some physical difficulties including that leg issue, I felt I was really making inroads with my fitness.

Bomber believed I was ready to be introduced for the round 2 clash against Carlton at Docklands and the local paper went with the headline, 'Tom Punt'. Bomber said: 'I think the club has been crying out for someone who can really mark the ball and be a big imposing factor down in that forward line and I think Tom's probably going to do it for a while'

I was fortunate to be given a game so early in the season and it may not have happened if we had a full complement of forwards. Steve Johnson, who became a great mentor and mate, was still serving a club-based suspension of five matches after getting a little too tipsy when back home at Christmas. King and Ottens, seasoned ruck and forward options, were both injured, while Nathan Ablett would not be available until round 4.

To say I enjoyed a dream debut would be an understatement. After a relatively even start, the Cats dominated the second quarter and went on to post a resounding 78-point win over the Blues. I managed to snare three goals, though a couple were cheapies as the margin blew out after half-time against an opponent destined to struggle through that season. So swiftly did we move the football that night, I suspect I could have not tried and still managed to kick a couple of goals, such was the space the forwards seemed to have.

Carlton coach Denis Pagan was a wily master in the dark arts of spinning the media, as many successful coaches tend to be. A dual premiership coach with North Melbourne, he knew when to drop a line that was capable of distracting fans from the bigger issues at hand, as he did after Carlton's big loss. 'Gee, he looks a likely type,' he said when reporters asked about me. 'I couldn't help but think he is an 18-year-old Tony Lockett, isn't he?' The comparison to the greatest goalkicker the game has seen only increased the publicity coming my way. TV and radio programs seized on the comment and so did leading print journalists.

I'm occasionally asked if footballers read stories about themselves, or hear things said about them in the media. Honestly, it is hard not to come across some of it, such is the popularity of footy in Victoria. It is more about how you handle the publicity and how you deal with any expectations that come with it, or filter through what is being said and accept only some of it.

I *absolutely* heard what Pagan said that night. The honest truth is that it gave me a lot of confidence, at least in the short term. After a tough pre-season, I felt like I belonged out there and when someone with the reputation of Pagan speaks, you tend to listen.

A week later, I was fortunate enough to play my first game at the MCG, which is something I'd long dreamed of, just as every kid to play footy has at some stage. We were pitted against the Demons and, if it is true that I enjoyed a bit of luck against Carlton when kicking three goals, against Melbourne I felt like I played really well.

In a 52-point triumph for the Cats, I was the leading goal kicker with four goals and, as a result, managed to snare a Rising Star Award nomination.

The acclaimed broadcaster Gerard Whateley, who was then working as a columnist for *The Geelong Advertiser*, seized on the theme of me making a promising start to my career. 'The best thing in the AFL right now is Tom Hawkins. He stands as a mountain of innocence, hope and joy. He dreams of becoming a great footballer. It's the mutual wish of every Geelong fan. It's this relationship that sport should be about.'

Things can get a little weird when hype takes hold. It was reported that The Cats Shop had to order in extra merchandise of the number 26 jumper, just a month into the season, to cope with demand.

My father–son selection also put me in the news. The AFL and rival clubs were taking note of the perceived advantage the Cats had been enjoying under father–son rules with some of the club's picks clearly bargains. The numbers tell the story: the Ablett brothers, Gary (pick 40) and Nathan (pick 48), Matthew Scarlett (pick 45) and me at 41, were all up and running early that season.

That year, the AFL introduced a bidding system designed to prevent such players from slipping so low in the draft, should their talent warrant a higher selection. The AFL noted: 'In 2007, given the increasing importance of the National Draft as a competitive balance measure, it was deemed that the father–son rule was delivering windfalls to clubs out of proportion to the best interests of the competition. The current bidding system was introduced to ensure Clubs paid something closer to "fair value" for players selected.'

The new bidding measure was dubbed 'The Hawkins Rule' by the media, adding to the spotlight I felt was on me.

Despite my strong start, Bomber stressed to me that the game was sure to get tougher as opposition coaches and defenders started to study my strengths and weaknesses. He had always been mindful of easing me through my first year. He said a maximum expectation would be that I would play 10 to 12 games for the season. After the win over Melbourne, he said: 'We need to manage him and rest him, and it will be the same with every other young boy that we've brought into the team. History shows they can't stand up to the whole season. We thought he was a little bit like a Tony Lockett–David Neitz sort of powerful, bounding, big, strong, heavy guy who can mark the ball. If he turns out half as good as Tony Lockett, he'll be a pretty good player.'

The Cats were winning, I was kicking goals and being compared to the greats of the game. Life, I thought, could not be much better. All of my dreams were coming true.

8

Footy lessons

IT WAS NOT long before life on the footy field became a hell of a lot harder. After a great fortnight to start my career, the reality of being key forward struck swiftly, as it has for many other young footballers starting off in attack.

The first loss of my career came in my third match against a rival soon to become very familiar – the Hawks. Shane Crawford, another Finley boy in his 271st game for Hawthorn, took out the three Brownlow votes, as the Hawks won by four points. Crawf is Finley's only Brownlow Medallist, but we do have a four-time premiership coach in Allan Jeans, who played in Finley's 1954 premiership team. The narrow margin equalled my input for the game – a miserable two kicks and two handballs.

This was the first time I went up against my great pal Xavier Ellis. Leading into the match we had exchanged plenty of banter, though it tended to be in group messages we shared with old school mates. Xavier, who is a very jovial guy, seemed to revel in it. I've always been a little more reserved closer to game day and tend to switch off from outside noise in the last 24 hours, focusing on what lies ahead. I prefer to avoid distractions before matches if possible. Unfortunately, that proved to be impossible leading into the first road trip of my career. Because I lived with Joel Selwood at the Jenners, it made sense to room with him on the road as well, but it was not long after we had gone to bed that I realised I had made a terrible mistake. Joel, who travelled with the team as an emergency, snored loudly and relentlessly, leaving me at my wits' end.

It was at least two in the morning before I managed to fall asleep and I am not sure I managed to grab too much sleep through the rest of the night. It was almost comical except I was not laughing; nothing I tried seemed to work. I tried counting sheep and even tried reading for a while, but nothing seemed to work. So much for avoiding distractions!

* * *

I was manned by Stephen Gilham and barely touched the football in the first half. At the break, Bomber clearly needed a target to unleash his frustration and I was the player in the firing line. A couple of weeks earlier, I had been called the next Tony Lockett and then, out of nowhere, I was getting one right between the eyes from the senior coach. At the time, it felt like a pretty savage attack and left me on the verge of tears. The spray was firmly directed at me, but I suspect the broader message was at some of my teammates who were also struggling. Throughout the opening weeks of the season, we were inconsistent; when we were good, we were very good, but when we were bad, we could not move the ball freely or quickly and this was one of those matches.

The verbal tirade was not the only thing Bomber aimed at me; at one stage, a boot was hurled in my direction, though I am not sure that it was launched with a view to hitting me.

Bomber was a coach who understood there would be periods in matches in which a player would struggle or be beaten by their opponent, but he hated it when that snowballed into a poor four-quarter team performance.

He and the other coaches would say: 'You can have an off day, but don't have a completely shit day.' Bomber's brutal message did not work, because my stinker continued after half-time. I reckon it is the worst game I have played and is one I remember so vividly given the circumstances that surrounded it. It is a memory I laugh about now – at least about Joel's snoring show – but my performance was another sharp reality check.

That was also the last time our players shared a room on a trip, as the club decided we could have our own room on trips if we paid half the bill. It turned out that sleeping in my own bed did not help, as my rough trot of form continued a week later when Kangaroos defender Shannon Watt stitched me up as North Melbourne upset us by 16 points at Kardinia Park. I scarcely got near it.

By then the spotlight was firmly on Geelong once again as the pressure was mounting. We were now in negative territory – two wins, three losses – and after the turmoil at the end of 2006, critics were wondering whether the Cats were contenders or pretenders.

The North Melbourne defeat turned out to be a turning point, this time led by the players. Paul Chapman was scathing in his critique of us in a post-match interview after the loss to North Melbourne. 'We're picking and choosing when we want to play and there's no excuses,' he said. 'I think, at the moment, we've probably got some passengers and we can't afford to carry them. We need 22 blokes who are going to live our values and die for the team. You can't just be happy playing, getting your money and having a good lifestyle or whatever it is. You've got to go out there and do everything you can to win, and that's what it is about.'

It was a searing assessment. But it was also an example of the honest feedback system we had adopted during that pre-season, aimed at making us a stronger side.

What Chappy said to the press was similar to the message the senior players passed on to the rest of the group as we gathered in the coach's room. AFL footy was still new to me but I could sense there was real frustration among the senior players after that loss to the Kangaroos, and there were a few hotheads among the group who were not afraid of challenging their teammates if something angered them.

At that stage we had won only 12 of our previous 28 games, dating back to that last-gasp loss to the Sydney Swans in the 2005 semi-final, and there was clearly a feeling that the changes instituted at the start of the season were not yet working. It was not just Chappy speaking as the emotion boiled over. But once he spoke, a few of the other senior players, including Matt Scarlett, spoke about their frustration at our failure to deliver on our potential. The general message was that we were too good to be delivering such inconsistent performances. It was clearly believed we could contend and win a premiership given the talent we had.

Whether the coaches had a role in orchestrating the feedback session is something I am not aware of, but Tom Harley was a great leader and excellent at acting as a conduit between the players and the coaching staff.

Cameron Ling, Jimmy Bartel and Joel Corey were others who were excellent at conveying what needed to be said – in a more measured way – but there are many different personalities in every club and our 2007 team was no different.

After the spray I received a week earlier, this felt like another daunting session for an 18-year-old, even though I understood it was part of the behavioural change that Leading Teams was trying to instil across the group.

We were determined not to be derailed from the goals we had set for the season – to be more consistent, being honest with each other, making the most of our talent, while fighting for a premiership.

The noise soon dissipated as Geelong went on a 15-match winning streak to cement the club as the clear premiership favourite. The streak started in stunning fashion when we defeated Richmond by 157 points at the Docklands, a truly remarkable game to be a part of. Stung by the loss to the Kangaroos, we opened the match with a 10 goal to one first term. We added another 10 in the second quarter, nine in the third and eased off with six in the final quarter, booting 35.12 (222), four of which came from my boot. Our score to three-quarter-time (29.9) was an AFL record and Richmond coach Terry Wallace described it as the worst day of his coaching career.

Despite a relatively bright start – 11 goals in my five games – had my older teammates in attack been fit enough at the start of the season, I'm certain I would have been out of the team after the opening month, but the patience from Geelong's selectors did not last. After another quiet performance against West Coast a week later, I was dropped for the first time in my career. I could understand why, given my youth and my inconsistent form.

Honestly, it was something of a relief. I was starting to feel overwhelmed by my inability to have a big impact on matches. I had gone from being a junior star who was bigger than my rivals to struggling to get a kick for quarters at a time. Nor did I have the skill set yet to work through the reasons for the dip in form.

I was frustrated. I could not find the answers but did not yet understand this was something I should be discussing with my coaches or my management group. As usual, Mum was my sounding board, because she was able to pick up on the cues that showed I was struggling. She knew me and she was able to simplify things. Her message was nothing out of the ordinary. She told me, 'Keep listening and keeping working hard and everything would turn out all right.' Mum knew not to overload me with too much information.

Part of me felt that playing in the reserves, I would not have the same level of pressure to perform, which would enable me to start enjoying my football again rather than feeling confused and frustrated. It might sound strange, but even though I was considered someone who would have been selected higher in the draft without the father–son opportunity, I never really felt the outside expectations. There had even been talk of me being the 'saviour' for Geelong, but that talk never added to the pressure I felt. I did not dominate in the VFL, but I was happy to be back playing at a level where I did not feel too uncomfortable.

* * *

During my first couple of seasons, bouncing in and out of the senior team became a regular theme. I would kick a bag of goals one week then struggle to get a touch or exert any influence the next. When it came to football craft, I was very much a rookie trying to find my way, and the senior defenders I was pitted against soon figured out how they could exploit my inexperience. I was aware there was some criticism in newspapers and on talkback radio. It is an interesting thing. When there are positive stories about you, they seem to be easy to find. It is the same when you are struggling – the negative headlines jump out at you. But social media was not prevalent at the time and I was never someone to listen to talkback radio, so the occasional critical article did not really bother me too much as I felt there was nothing in the criticism that could derail me.

The journalists writing those stories probably knew I was talented enough to make it as a player but also were increasingly aware of how underprepared I was to make a successful transition into our mature team. The bigger challenge was trying to figure out mentally how I was going to change my form, because I did not have the answer to that.

* * *

There were a couple of instances in particular which stand out as valuable lessons for me, with one from Brian Lake a glaring example of how much I needed to improve. The round 16 clash against the Western Bulldogs proved to be my final senior game of 2007 and was the last of a three-match streak in which I managed a solitary goal.

Lake, a dual All-Australian defender who later became a three-time premiership player with Hawthorn, gave me an absolute bath. He was a tremendous player and one whom I ended up enjoying a great rivalry against once I had matured. He was the first to really test the limits of my fitness by dashing down the ground with attacking flair, leaving me in his wake. I was being asked to do 200-metre sprints several times a quarter just to keep pace with the bloke who was supposed to be defending me. My aerobic capacity was just nowhere near the level required to maintain my performance when properly tested by such a player. The tactic of defenders running off me had started earlier in the season, but Lake took it to another level. I spent most of the game with my tongue hanging out, trying to regain my breath before being tested yet again.

The breathtaking speed that Geelong employed that year scarcely helped me either. I would be chasing my rival down the field when, if there was a turnover, the footy would be back in our attack in what seemed to be the blink of an eye. I was trying hard to follow the example set by Steve Johnson and Cam Mooney, who excelled as we surged in that streak of wins. They were well aware of what I was going through and were able to help me understand that while I needed to improve, what was happening was not surprising.

Johnson was a great supporter. For this book, he reflected on my early days in a positive way: 'We always knew he was going to be a very good player, but he copped a lot of criticism early on in his career, because he was very inconsistent. People did not really understand that he was such a young player. At times, he probably admits there was some self-doubt as well. He was big, but not that powerful early on. He was obviously pretty dominant in the juniors but given his lack of fitness, and with opponents working out that he did not know how to deal with body pressure, he probably got worked out pretty quickly early on. Defenders playing on young forwards will put time into them and know how to use their bodies. It is a learning curve, and there were things he needed to cut out. I mean, if you went to a bakery with him, he would order three sausage rolls and you would not even see the first one go down, along with a couple of donuts. He just did not know what he needed to do to be the best he could be at that time. It was always going to take Tom some time.'

This was the type of feedback also given by my teammates during sessions focused on professionalism as part of the Leading Teams program, though admittedly that feedback was not as specific as saying, 'Don't eat an extra sausage roll' or 'Stay away from the cinnamon donuts.'

I would love to say the penny dropped immediately, but I struggled to put into practice what was being said to me. Even in my second year, when I had moved in with Simon Hogan, eating to a more professional standard was something I struggled with. I'm not going to shift the blame, but at that stage, Simon was busting to put weight on and was having five to six meals a day to achieve that, and because we hung out all the time, I would find myself sneaking a treat in between lunch and dinner as well. It has never been a strong suit and even now I go through periods where I am tempted by food. I clearly had a lot to learn.

* * *

By the time I was dropped for the second time after that lesson from Lake, my form and confidence had fizzled. I felt burnt-out and exhausted, but Bomber did his best to shepherd me through this period by changing my responsibilities.

If an opponent ran off me, one of my teammates would try to help me if I was struggling to keep pace. I've played with a lot of small forwards and they are all so selfless and they work so hard. Travis Varcoe, Shannon Byrnes and Mathew Stokes were jets in the early stages of my career. I am not sure I have always reciprocated that support. I probably owed each of them more than a few hand-off goals.

The 2007 season really was the first time in my career when I felt properly challenged. As a junior, I would occasionally put in a poor match, but invariably I would bounce back the next week. But in my first season, it felt like I was playing poorly from one week to the next, without any sense of making real progress, and I had not yet developed the necessary tools to deal with the disappointment that comes with these periods.

Happily, there were plenty of people on hand to assist me through this development phase. Ken Hinkley, who was an assistant coach at the Cats at the time, has a ripping sense of humour and always had a joke or two that would help to lift my mood. As a view to improving my career, he was strong on trying to teach me how to become more involved by positioning myself in better spots and reading and understanding the tempo of a game. There was some craft work done in a one-on-one situation at training, but that was not done regularly as the coaches had an entire squad to look after.

The majority of the feedback from Ken was done in the editing room and he would identify when I was out of position and assist me with where I needed to be, either by adopting a different running pattern or by adjusting to what my teammates were doing.

Leigh Tudor, who was our VFL coach, was also a great help. When I got dropped, it was nice to work with Leigh, because he was more positive in his approach and, I suspect, was aware I was still a work in progress.

The advice I received from those at the club was that even if I was not playing well, it was important to do what I could on the training track to improve. They emphasised that I needed to train with intent every time I set foot on the ground. Each session was worthwhile and would be another step towards becoming the footballer both I and the club obviously hoped I would become.

There were plenty of role models – we had guys I would watch and wonder how the hell they had any energy left to play games, so great was their training intensity. James Kelly and Joel Corey, for example, were phenomenal in that regard. It became easier for me to piece things together on the training track when watching professionals like those two. Joel Selwood, as he did throughout his career, continued to show me the way.

* * *

Mindful of how well the team was performing as the season progressed, I started to focus on longer-term goals, believing it was unlikely I would be called upon in the finals. This approach did not please Ken, who gave me a serve in my end-of-season review because he felt I had conceded too early that I would not be part of the senior team. It was another lesson in a season where I received what seemed like a lifetime of schooling. It did not help that the review came when I was hungover after Mad Monday.

Bomber was in the review, but the feedback given to me by Ken is what stung the most. It was a pointed message aimed at ensuring I stewed over what was said with a view to arriving at pre-season training for 2008 with a sharper mindset. Ken may have joked around on the track, but he was not in a mood to joke that day and started his review with an expletive or two.

Perhaps because I was enjoying footy again in the reserves, I finished off the season training well, and the mood and atmosphere associated with Grand Final week lifted my spirits even more. Ken had noticed, as he made clear in his review. With venom in his voice, he effectively told me: 'How dare you train like that in Grand Final week and make us consider whether we are doing the right thing by not picking you for the Grand Final? What made you take so long to train like that?'

Despite his words, I was certain I was not in the mix to play in the Grand Final, because it would have meant they had to play three tall forwards and that was something that was never going to happen.

But I was starting to put into place what Ken Hinkley and Leigh Tudor were trying to teach me. The clear message was that I must continue to train like that into the next season.

That said, I felt really proud to be part of the Geelong VFL's premiership team, particularly because I had never played any finals footy. The older I get, the more I have appreciated what an honour it was to be part of that team under Leigh. At that level, I had been able to contribute more regularly and ended up kicking 16 goals in 11 games.

Because there were very few injuries in the senior team, Geelong's VFL team was extremely strong and we finished the season in second place behind Sandringham, with 14 wins from 18 home-and-away games.

We had a great side with players of the calibre of Tom Lonergan, who had returned to footy in June after he had been severely injured in a marking contest in round 21 the previous season, when backing into a pack, showing great courage; the accident resulted in him losing a kidney, placing his career at risk. Others in our impressive lineup included Charlie Gardiner, Henry Playfair, Kane Tenace, Sam Hunt, and future North Melbourne defender Scott Thompson. James Byrne was named the captain of the 2007 VFL Team of the Year, with Jason Davenport and Todd Grima also featuring in the representative side.

In the qualifying final at North Port Oval, we were far too good for Coburg, kicking 22.16 (148) to 17.15 (117) to win by 31 points. Coburg was then affiliated with Richmond and featured super talents including Jack Riewoldt and Jay Schulz. In the preliminary final, a fortnight later at the same ground, we again kicked a big score, winning 24.14 (148) to North Ballarat's 13.18 (96).

That set the stage for a rematch against Coburg at Princes Park two days after the AFL team had progressed to the Grand Final by defeating Collingwood in the preliminary final but the VFL decider proved rather one-sided, with Steven King returning to bolster the team.

The first half was pretty even, partly due to inaccuracy on our behalf, and we led by 14 points at the major break. Leigh Tudor swung the changes, with Lonergan switched from defence into attack, a decisive move.

Lonergan ended up kicking six goals in the second half, while I contributed two on the day as we went on to win 17.24 (126) to 7.10 (54). Not surprisingly, the Norm Goss Medal for best afield was awarded to Tom Lonergan.

After the match, Leigh told us to enjoy ourselves but also to remember that the AFL team was in the Grand Final and it was possible that a few of the VFL players were still in contention to be selected, should something go wrong during the week.

Even though I considered myself extremely unlikely, it was a message I followed, because we were training with the senior guys and I was sharing a house with Joel Selwood, who knew he was going to play in the Grand Final.

I went to a few of the functions but never had more than a beer or two and, even though I was never really a chance for selection, it was good to be able to enjoy the week on the edge of the senior team as they prepared for the big game.

* * *

This period proved a critical part of my development and is a time I look back at fondly, in part because it helped me to enjoy footy again. A couple of days after we claimed the VFL premiership, I told *The Geelong Advertiser*: 'This is beyond what I expected. I was hoping to maybe get a couple of games in the seniors and just be learning and developing in the VFL. But, as it turns out, I played a few more games than that and won a premiership in the VFL, so it's been a fairy tale start to my footy. I'm looking forward to getting out and running around and trying to get a little fitter because that is probably something that I lacked this year. I'm looking forward to the break and having a good pre-season. I can't wait.'

When someone introduces me as a triple-premiership player now, I am always happy to say, 'No. I have three AFL premierships and a VFL premiership.' It may not have been the most important premiership of my career, but I cherish that flag.

* * *

Meanwhile, the Cats' surge towards September continued and it was impossible not to be caught up in the excitement of what was unfolding. The longer the season went, the more I felt like I was a fan again, even though I was training and playing alongside players who would become club legends.

One of my earliest footy memories was Geelong's 1995 Grand Final against Carlton, which we lost by 61 points, and as we were preparing for that 2007 decider, I can remember thinking, 'Wow. What if the Cats win the flag?'

It was so special for Geelong to be in another Grand Final and at training sessions through that week, the grandstands were packed. The entire city was buzzing. The fans were locked out of the main training session that week but there were helicopters circling the ground, shooting footage for the television news. As we arrived for training, journalists and cameramen were waiting outside the club and every moment was filmed. Around the town, it was like a Cats' version of Christmas. It really was an unbelievable week to be part of the club.

Grand Final day turned out to be a dream as we thrashed Port Adelaide by 119 points in the most lopsided decider in the game's history. It was bedlam at Kardinia Park when the players arrived to meet the fans the following day. It was great to see those men I had admired and trained alongside celebrating, but also to witness the sheer joy on the faces of so many thousands of Geelong fans who had waited so long for this success. It had been a long time since 1963.

The flag was ours, but the lessons were not yet over for me that year, with my experiences on Mad Monday proving a sobering experience … once I had sobered up.

My first mistake that day was my choice of drinking partner. Steve Johnson was a hardened professional who knew a trick or two and was clearly a heavyweight compared to me.

He had rebounded from the difficult start to the season to cement himself as one of the game's premier forwards and he was world-class when it came to demolishing beers. To say that my attempt to match him beer for beer backfired is an understatement.

My memories of what unfolded that day are vague, which is scarcely surprising given the size of the celebrations. But I certainly needed assistance to return to my host family's home early in the afternoon. At the time, I was wearing only an apron, which was rather embarrassing. I have never minded getting around with my shirt off and never needed any encouragement to go bare-chested when I was young. Amid the exuberant celebrations, a host of us were wrestling and I am sure that what I was wearing would not have been too hard to rip off. I was in way too deep as I tried to keep pace with a very experienced crew and was extremely drunk by midway through the afternoon.

I sheepishly fronted up to apologise to both the publican and also to my host family for getting far too carried away with my performance on that Mad Monday. I've always been one to enjoy a good time and continue to do so now. But when you make mistakes, it is always important to learn from them.

9
A mate celebrates

IF KEN HINKLEY had hoped that the message he delivered in my end-of-season review would sink in, he would have noticed as soon as I arrived for pre-season training in 2008 that I was a slow learner. To my shame, I was once again overweight.

On exiting the club we had been issued with an off-season training program but my determination to make the most of the break while ensuring I would arrive back at the club in as good as shape as I left it lasted as long as my first Bintang on our footy trip to Bali. As you can imagine after Geelong had ended a 44-year premiership drought, everyone who headed away was determined to live life as largely as possible.

There was an extra incentive for me to enjoy a good break as I had missed out on the schoolies celebrations that mark the end of Year 12. While I was huffing and puffing on the training track in November 2006, my school mates were having a blast and I approached the Bali trip looking to make up for lost time.

My tale of woe will be a familiar for those who have over-indulged on an overseas trip. I left Australia weighing 105kg and returned a week later with another five kilograms added to my frame. Clearly my immaturity was showing.

I spent the rest of the break on the farm at Finley, which was a treat as a year earlier I had moved straight from the boarding halls of Melbourne Grammar to begin my new life in Geelong. As I came to learn, it was important to switch off from the routine of football to freshen the mind, body and soul, and life at home, seeing family and friends, was a great respite. But I did not work hard enough while there to retain my fitness.

Some say that things in footy are easier the second time around, but I'm not sure whoever came up with that thinking has ever completed an AFL pre-season. It really is a challenge to build fitness and harden the body again for the rigours of the game. I found it particularly difficult at that stage of my career.

I reckon I completed about 20 per cent of the off-season program I had been given and as a result showed up for the first pre-season session out of shape. That dubious distinction earned me a place in Geelong's 'fat group', which is where I spent some time each pre-season in my first five years at the club. Putting on weight comes too easily to me.

There were some faces in there with me each year and 2008 was no different. Paul Chapman made an appearance, so too Mathew Stokes, Cameron Mooney and Josh Hunt. Steve Johnson wore his appearance as a badge of honour.

Xavier Ellis told me at the time that if a player's skinfold measurement was over 45 at Hawthorn, you would end up in the Hawks' fat group. Geelong's was more lenient but if your skinfold assessment was above 60, you required extra fitness work. Ending up in the fat group was a form of detention. We would have to take part in extra cross-training sessions on Saturday mornings, and occasionally another midweek. Your time in the fat group lasted for as long as your skinfolds were above 60.

Being part of this 'elite' group should have had alarm bells ringing about the importance of maintaining my fitness, but leading into Christmas, I again had a stress reaction related to training, this time the navicular in my left foot, and needed to spend some time away from training for the second summer in succession. It was a different foot, but it raised my awareness of the potential issues I might face given my bulk, if I did not look after myself. The timing was fortunate, if there is such a thing associated with any injury, given the time of year, I was under no stress to rush back to training or miss games. With the wisdom of experience, and having watched other younger players coming through, I realise now how important it is for inexperienced key position players to be able to continue to play and develop at a consistent rate. Injuries in a season can really set back a younger player's development. At least in this case, I was able to resume pre-season training ahead of our first game.

* * *

There is a common view in our game that winning premierships can lead to hangovers. Party too hard after a premiership, or become too satisfied, and the team's performance can dip sharply the next year. Our club had celebrated that 2007 premiership in style, and even though some big names were sent to the fat group at the start of the pre-season, there was nothing to suggest the team was anything but determined to defend that flag. The club was still buzzing from winning the flag when we began pre-season training and the whole city felt alive with the memory of what had unfolded in September.

My goals heading into my second season were similar to those from 12 months earlier, though at least I had more of an idea about the challenge. My coaches had made it very clear to me that I needed to improve my fitness and also my strength, to further my education as to how to fill a key forward role and, most importantly, to find a way to become more consistent. Only then would I be able to command a starting role in attack every week.

But some changes to the club's list in the off-season opened the door for me to play more regularly at senior level. Nathan Ablett was always a reluctant, though highly talented, footballer. He was a quiet soul and someone who had grown up not necessarily wanting to become an AFL footballer. While his older brother, Gary, was able to cope with the fame associated with his surname, Nathan never seemed entirely comfortable in that role.

Because 2007 was my first season, I never really got to know Nathan, who was extremely shy. After playing in the premiership in 2007, he retired prematurely – still just 21 – and headed back to the local level, preferring a more laidback lifestyle, while he worked in the construction industry.

There was a lot of expectations placed on me when I arrived at Geelong, but while I was aware that while my dad was a high-quality defender, no-one has had the impact of Gary Ablett Snr.

I can only imagine the pressure Nathan faced as his son. After all, I was as guilty as the next Geelong fan when it came to worshipping Ablett Snr when I was a kid.

Early on, I actually told Gary Ablett Jnr how much I had adored watching his father and told him the story about once trying to send his dad a letter from the farm via a balloon. I was not over the top with it though; I did not want to come across as a fanboy with the men I was now playing and training with. Junior, to his credit, did not laugh at me, but he did have a little chuckle and told me it was a good story. It was not something I ever passed on to Nathan.

In his book *Bomber: The Whole Story* (Penguin Random House, 2017), Mark Thompson said that he believed Nathan Ablett could have been as good as Wayne Carey if he had continued. Thompson wrote that the celebrations after the 2007 premiership frightened Nathan off footy and Bomber felt that the club should have been more protective of him, given his background and his shyness. He did return to the club midway through 2008 but was injured and retired again. He returned to senior footy again in 2011, playing two games for the Gold Coast, then played for many junior clubs, until he finally gave it away in 2019, after a season with local club Modewarre. 'We made a mistake with Nathan after 2007 and it is a great sporting regret of mine,' Thompson wrote. 'It is a sporting tragedy, his story, and what a loss the game suffered … Imagine how good Geelong would (have been) with him and Tom Hawkins wandering around the forward line.'

The other big change saw our former captain Steven King making the shift from Geelong to St Kilda. He had been an outstanding performer for the Cats, winning the Carji Greeves Medal twice and also completing the rare double of winning a VFL and AFL flag in the same season. His exit opened the door for another father–son recruit Mark Blake (son of Rod, 176 games, 1971–1983), who had led the ruck for every game of 2007 before being left out of the Grand Final side, to assume the rucking role.

After playing nine games in my first season, and later playing in the VFL premiership, I wanted to make an immediate impact in the hope of cementing a senior spot. I started the season in the senior team and played well early on, but once again my inconsistency got the better of me. There were moments in games where I felt like everything was clicking and I could also sense I was making inroads on the training track.

But I would then go through periods when my form dipped. I would play one good quarter and then go missing in the next, which can be quite common in younger players, but it did not make it any less frustrating. It was the first time in my career where I began to wonder if I was cut out for a career in the AFL.

Hindsight is an interesting thing and in a newspaper column ahead of my 300th game, my old mentor Cam Mooney provided a good explanation as to why I found the transition to senior footy so difficult. 'He'd gone from monstering kids and dominating school footy to playing against key defenders (who were) the big, strong, gnarly gorillas of the AFL,' he wrote in *The Geelong Advertiser*. 'After a couple of promising games early on, teams paid him more attention, and he lost a bit of confidence. Thankfully, our team was flying that year and I had Nathan Ablett, Paul Chapman and Steve Johnson among others up forward for support, so the expectations on Tom were manageable. That changed, I reckon, in 2009. Tom was still only 20 or 21 and developing, but people were wanting more from him. Nathan was long gone and our team was chasing redemption after the disappointment of 2008.'

The scariest of those 'gorillas' was undoubtedly North Melbourne's Glenn Archer. He scared the living daylights out of me in that match where the Kangaroos had beaten us a year earlier, before the start of our magnificent winning streak. Archer, who was named the 'Shinboner of the Century', was working with Stride Sports Management and I went to his house to meet with him when we were seeking a manager, while I was still in school. He was the nicest guy off the field, but when we crossed paths about 12 months later, he had the 'wild eyes' thing going.

He whacked me in the back once and I realised immediately that he was incredibly strong. At one stage I tried to get around him in the forward pocket and it felt like I had been hit by a freight train. No-one in the under-18s checked you when you turned back towards goal. But those habits were ingrained in guys like Archer, hard-bodied defenders with years of experience – they were so tough to play on.

Champion West Coast full-back Darren Glass was another I played on a few times in the early years of my career and he was so strong. Any attempt to move him around was futile. It felt like he was anchored to the ground. But if you tried to find some space on the lead, he had the speed and reach to prevent you from getting anywhere near the footy. It was a tough initiation and there were times when I wondered whether I was ever going to match those guys.

This is where early mentors like Cam Mooney and Steve Johnson – and while he may not have realised it, also Matthew Scarlett – deserve praise. Although much of my learning was done in the video suite, one of the strengths of the coaching group was allowing me to learn aspects of the game from my senior teammates. Mooney and Johnson were great at showing me in training and during matches where I should be running, and how to position myself to handle the tactics of the gorillas. Mooney focused more on the technical side of the craft, namely when to lead, how I should be using my body and when to double-back on your rival.

Johnson always encouraged me to put pressure on my opponent. He would stress that as hard as you think you might be working in a match, or during a training session, you always had more left in you to allow you to outwork your opponent.

As for Scarlett, a six-time All-Australian, there was no better teammate to learn from. He never gave too much away, but as I have told him since, I learnt so much more about the craft of forward work just by having the chance to train on him and to see him pitted against the other forwards as well. These guys gave me a great education. They also showed me a competitive streak that still makes me wonder all these years later. In my first pre-season I was awestruck watching Steve Johnson and Paul Chapman having a dust-up at training, but I soon learned this was nothing unusual. Later on, Mathew Stokes and Mark Blake had to be broken up after a 'disagreement' and so too Johnson and Cameron Ling. What also struck me was that these 'moments' were soon forgotten. They would all shake hands and move on.

* * *

From an individual sense, the highlight of my year came early on when I kicked five goals in a match for the first time in my career. In the round 3 match at Kardinia Park, on a night we unfurled the premiership flag, we were pitted against Melbourne. The Demons had won just five games in 2007 and had lost their first two in the new season by a total of 199 points. Not surprisingly, the game was a sellout with only members able to attend. The atmosphere was absolutely electric.

I was manned by the tough Demons defender Nathan Carroll who played his footy with the typically physical, hard approach of a gorilla. But, as I noted after the game, I was fortunate to be the recipient of some exceptional work up the ground from my teammates as we posted a 30-point win. 'It is my first five-goal haul in the AFL, which is nice. The ball bounced my way a bit today, which was good. I'm happy with the game,' I told reporters. 'I'm still only 19 and I've still got more improving to do and there's a lot of areas of my game that I'd like to work on, like my second efforts and my fitness is still not up to it, but it is getting better.'

A year earlier, Paul Chapman had publicly lambasted a few teammates for playing too selfishly and worrying about their own careers. We responded in the most memorable fashion possible. After that good game against Melbourne, he warned fans it could still be a while before I produced the type of form consistently, which proved prophetic. 'It is going to take a little while for him. It's not just going to happen like it did today, but he deserved to kick five,' Chapman said.

A MATE CELEBRATES

A week later, we were up against St Kilda, who would emerge as a major rival the following season, and I had another good game, kicking three goals from 18 disposals. This prompted Bomber to say that I was looking 'more comfortable, more confident'. That is just how I felt at the time. But as with my promising early season form in my debut year, the good times did not last. By round 10, when we played against Carlton, my place in the team was under threat after I managed to win only three kicks for the day.

Bomber had my back publicly and would always defend his players if he felt they were under pressure; around the club, everyone else was supportive as well. 'I'm not answering (any questions) because you will write a negative story in *The Geelong Advertiser* and we don't want any negative stories this week,' he told the Addy reporter after my performance against Carlton.

Back at the club, I found him intimidating at times and there were periods where I was unsure where I sat in terms of planning, but I believed he always had faith that things would ultimately click for me and that I would make it as a player. He could be awkward in conversations; he could also be a hard arse. But when I look back now, I have no doubt he was incredibly good for me.

What made it harder for me to hold my spot was the great form of Tom Lonergan. No-one could be upset that he was able to make the most of his opportunity when he had fought back after the loss of his kidney in round 21, 2006. There was quite a celebration across the competition when he was able to return to senior football after almost two years. He showed great signs in attack, kicking 2.3 from seven kicks, clearly eclipsing my performance. The composure and competitiveness with which he played in attack throughout the rest of 2008 – kicking 34 goals in the next 15 games – effectively meant there was no position for me. That round 10 game was my last for the seniors in 2008. Once again, I headed back to the VFL and showed signs of my growing maturity by dominating games in attack. Midway through June, I kicked three goals in Bendigo. The next week I managed to boot seven at home against the Northern Bullants. But early in July, I started to feel pain in my foot once again, which turned out to be a stress reaction and caused me to miss several weeks. It was the third time the club had identified a stress-related problem with either my leg or my foot in under two years.

At that time, most medical issues were dealt with internally and Geelong had an experienced doctor in Chris Bradshaw. But Mum and Dad were adamant that we should canvas other opinions to make sure there was nothing more serious that was causing the problem. They advised me to arrange a formal meeting with the entire medical team at the club, along with Bomber. They sat in on the meeting because I was aware that they would be able to identify anything that might require further clarification and would also be able to ask questions to gain better information from the club. Would surgery or rest and rehab be the right path?

At the time, I spoke regularly with Matthew Egan, the All-Australian defender whose career was cruelly cut short by a foot injury suffered on the eve of the 2007 finals. His advice was to collect information from as many sources as possible before rushing into any decision. Eventually we chose not to have surgery and after a decent break, I was able to return for the last three rounds of the VFL season, finishing in style with 10 goals in my last two matches. I wore a moon boot at various times to ease the pressure on the hot spot; it provided support around the Achilles and was open at the front.

If Ken Hinkley's warning in the exit meeting a year earlier did not prompt an immediate response from me, the issues with my foot through 2008 did, particularly with Egan's early forced retirement as a clear reference point. His experience showed me that a career could end far more quickly than one might anticipate.

* * *

As great a highlight as playing in a VFL premiership and then watching my teammates claim a drought-breaking premiership was in 2007, the 2008 Grand Final encapsulated just how strange the 2008 season was for me.

This might seem sacrilegious to Geelong fans, but when I awoke on Grand Final day, a small part of me hoped at least one Hawthorn player would succeed. Before Geelong fans question my loyalty, I will stress that I was desperate for my Cats to defend their premiership. We had invested so much again in 2008 in trying to be back-to-back premiers for the first time since 1951-52 and believed we were clearly the best side throughout the season, with just one loss – an 86-point thrashing by Collingwood in round 9 proved to be a remarkable blip.

Xavier Ellis, my close mate from school, was beginning to make a name for himself with Hawthorn – he had missed just one game for the season and had settled well into the Hawks' strong midfield – and I wanted only the best for him, despite the fact he was playing for the opposition.

What unfolded that day is still hard to stomach. That we managed to have nine more scoring shots yet still be beaten by 26 points is a painful reminder about the importance of straight kicking. Of course, this was the game that changed the League rules on penalising deliberate behinds, after the Hawks forced 11 behinds in our score of 11.23. Still, we missed many shots. The events of that strange day I will never forget.

Geelong entered the Grand Final as the raging favourites and several of us still believe it is a premiership we should have claimed, with many of my teammates feeling burnt by what unfolded that day. We were definitely the better team in the opening half, with 18 scoring shots to 11, but our inaccuracy meant that instead of holding the upper hand, we trailed by three points at half-time.

The Hawks really came to life in the third term, with Cyril Rioli starring and Stuart Dew enjoying some remarkable flourishes when switched to attack, while our kicking woes in front of goal continued as we kicked away our chances.

Even though I was not playing, every time I see the scoreline of Geelong's 11.23 (89) to Hawthorn's 18.7 (115), it stings, softened a little by Xavier's good fortune. To his immense credit, Xavier produced an almighty performance on the day and was Hawthorn's leading possession winner with 28 disposals. I thought he was unlucky not to be named the Norm Smith Medallist, so significant was his influence. To watch him excel on football's biggest stage in just his second season was inspiring.

As Joel Selwood had done a year earlier, he set an example for me to follow. When I reflected on the match later that night, I remember thinking that if my two closest friends in footy were able to win premierships, maybe one day my time would come as well, if I could find that elusive consistency in my performance.

Understandably, my teammates were shattered in the aftermath of the loss. There is no greater gulf in emotion than the difference between winning and losing a Grand Final and even though I was on the sidelines of the team in my first two years, it was impossible not to feel as gutted as many of my teammates were clearly feeling.

But my happiness for Xavier negated that a little and afterwards, I contacted him to congratulate him. For a little while, I pondered whether it was worth tracking him down for a quick beer that night at the Hawthorn celebrations at Crown, where the Hawks were enjoying their victory. I decided it was better to allow him to party with his teammates. We could always grab a beer on another occasion.

That loss, and with me being out of the side, made me determined to cement my place in Geelong's side in 2009, because I was certain we would bounce back.

10

'Bomber'

IN THE EARLY stages of my career, some of the most awkward moments in my life came while sitting in an edit suite with Mark 'Bomber' Thompson as we reviewed passages of my play. As I watched the tape, trying to figure out exactly where I had gone wrong, the silence that followed would feel like it had lasted an hour. These periods without a word from the coach were excruciating.

I won't lie. There were times during the four years I played under Bomber when I would feel completely lost while sitting with him, trying to figure out what he wanted me to pick up from the session. You would spend half an hour watching an edited clip, as it was rewound again and again. Then Bomber would make his point, sometimes with just a single sentence or a question, 'Are you seeing what I'm seeing?' It could feel so awkward at times, particularly if he left you sitting there in silence. But eventually the reason for being there would click with me.

The one-on-one sessions with Bomber did not occur that frequently. After each match I would sit down with either Leigh Tudor or Ken Hinkley, depending on whether I had played in the VFL or the AFL, to assess my performance. The video technology has come a long way but at that stage, we could click on a folder bearing your name and watch every interaction you had in the game. Kicks, handballs, marks, tackles, spoils, smothers, you name it, all were covered. But there would also be more specific areas the coaches had identified to review, and they would tag you in those passages as well.

Those tags tended to be more the specialist reviews with Bomber. For example, the assistants might have identified a passage where I had made a mistake that caused an issue in our system more broadly, as opposed to mistiming a lead or dropping a mark. These edits were related to team outcomes rather than individual failings.

Bomber always wanted me to be a more imposing presence in attack and one instance stands out as a clear example of the type of incident that saw me booked in for a session with him. We were playing Essendon at the Docklands and a player was coming back with the flight of the ball at the Lockett end of the ground. I had the chance to make strong contact with him, and the ball. Instead he was able to take the mark untouched. Bomber had been pressing me to attack the ball and the body, which was something Cam Mooney was always good at. Instead it looked as though I had pulled out of the contest.

He rewound the incident a couple of times while we were together, and later also raised it in the main review meeting in front of my teammates as a discussion point. To be clear, it was not as though he singled players out in those reviews or thumped his fist and said, 'We don't do that at this club.' It was done more with an educational tone. He would ask, 'How would you approach this passage next time around?' I responded that I would create a contest at the very least, making contact with the opponent. As always, it took some time for the penny to drop and the individual edits became less frequent as I gained more experience.

* * *

I'm sure I'm not revealing anything new here when saying Bomber is not the most straightforward person I have ever met. He has a terrific sense of humour, but he can be quite unconventional at times and walks to a different beat of the drum – at least compared to me.

Indeed, he can be quite complex. It is well known he has endured some troubles after what was truly an incredible football career. When his issues were made public, they were difficult times for him, obviously, but also for the people who loved him. But one thing that I've always been sure of is that his heart was in the right place in every dealing or meeting that I had with him, and that continues to this day.

It is hard to overstate how remarkable Bomber's career in footy really was and it is something I hope is not forgotten when considering his broader legacy.

I was too young to remember him playing but his record with Essendon was superb. He captained the 'Baby Bombers' to the 1993 premiership, a game I am pretty sure I would have watched at home in Finley, even though I was only five years old at the time. He also played in two other premierships for Essendon in the 1980s – in the back-to-back flags of 1984-85, when he was a baby Bomber himself, playing just his 22nd game in the 1984 flag – during a 202-game career in what was an epic era for the Dons.

Bomber become Geelong's senior coach in 2000 after short stints as an assistant coach with Essendon under Kevin Sheedy and then at North Melbourne under Denis Pagan, when the Kangaroos claimed the 1999 premiership.

As a passionate Cats fan, I had a keen interest in Geelong's progress in Bomber's early years in charge and watched closely as he moulded a side capable of moments of brilliance. Some seasons were better than others. Geelong finished fifth in his first year, but the Cats were beaten by the Hawks in an elimination final. The next three years were tougher, but it was clear that some quality players were arriving at the Cattery. It always seemed possible that this list might become the basis of a team that could do something great.

But fortune did not initially fall the Cats' way. I can remember being absolutely gutted in 2005 when we made the finals before losing to eventual premiers Sydney by three points after Nick Davis kicked the last four goals of the match, as the Swans came from 23 points down to win by three points in the last minutes at the SCG.

Then there was 2006, a year when things looked rosy after a really promising start. The Cats won the NAB Cup and then the first two rounds of the regular season as Geelong fans started to dream that this might be the year our lengthy premiership drought ended. But it all fell apart in painful fashion, and when

Hawthorn thumped us by 61 points in round 22, Bomber's tenure at Geelong looked to be in peril.

Not too long after West Coast defeated Sydney to win that season's premiership, the club wrote to the members promising a searching review of the club. The review was scathing, blaming a dip in form after the promising start on poor physical preparation, a lack of leadership around the club and also on coaching mismanagement. Despite the savage critique, the administration led by Frank Costa and Brian Cook believed Bomber would be the man to take the club to the top, a decision that proved to be a masterstroke. Bomber vowed to deliver at the best-and-fairest dinner, stating: 'There's lots to look forward to, lots to change and we're going to embrace everything we need to get better.'

At a separate meeting with members, he told them they would see a 'different game plan' in 2007. How right he was, with a premiership coming 11 months later. Bomber backed players who would prove to be champions of the club, including superstar defender Matthew Scarlett, the 2007 Brownlow Medallist Jimmy Bartel, a more disciplined Steve Johnson, the emerging Gary Ablett Jnr and young gun Joel Selwood, to use their talent and play with freedom and they flourished as a result. They played exciting, rapid and free-flowing footy.

* * *

Despite those tense times in the edit suite, Bomber was a fierce defender of mine. I am certain there were periods where he gifted me games that I did not deserve in order to fast track my development. When I was struggling for form or had slipped out of the side due to the strength of the team or a dip in my form, he was on the front foot publicly with the press, defending me.

Although he could deliver the occasional clip in private, when speaking publicly about his players, I can't remember him ever being negative about any individual's performance.

He also developed tight relationships with some of the more mature players, which is not a surprise given the amount of time he spent at Geelong as their senior coach. There are several who arrived at Geelong as raw teenagers who later finished their careers as champions of the game and premiership players.

Under Bomber's coaching, I enjoyed some of the greatest highlights of my career and I'm forever grateful for the opportunity to have played under him. That does not mean that our relationship was particularly close, because I was not yet a core member of the team during his last four years at the club.

11
A premiership!

IF MY EXIT review at the end of 2007 hit me between the eyes, Bomber Thompson and his assistants were more inclined to offer me guidance leading into the 2009 season. I'd liken their approach to holding the hand of a child as you guide them across a road. The kid would probably be all right without the handholding, but some extra assurance is never a bad thing.

The emphasis was on me becoming a more well-rounded player than simply a forward who was capable of leading and marking. They wanted me to win more of the ball further afield and start to become a linking player, someone capable of marking the ball between half-forward and wing and then setting up a teammate in attack. This would be another step in my development as a footballer.

These conversations certainly encouraged me to consider how I could make a difference in matches. Rather than them being critical, they tended to focus on positive reinforcement. There had obviously been some frustration and even a lack of patience with my impact in my first two seasons, but I can genuinely say that such thinking did not bother me too much, though it may have worried those closest to me. Perspective is an interesting thing. It may have taken a while for me to understand what was needed to be more professional in my approach and to learn how to deal with adversity in games, be it against stronger older opponents or in quiet periods, but I was also mindful of my place in the squad.

I was still a young player in an exceptionally good side, with stars on every line, including in attack. There was no way, at that stage of my development, that I was able to match the output of Cam Mooney or Steve Johnson, Nathan Ablett, or Tom Lonergan – I did not have the strength, and, importantly, the experience. Perhaps I had my head in the sand, but I did not have an inflated opinion of my worth to the team. I was a developing forward. The pressure and expectation became more of a factor as I matured. My family did hear things from time to time – that is part and parcel of footy and family members will always hear some rough things from fans. But they always told me they believed I handled the criticism that came my way well.

* * *

After seeing out the previous season wearing a moon boot, there was initially an emphasis on making sure my foot had recovered properly before I ramped up my pre-season training. By the time the season began, I was feeling the fittest I had ever been and had confidence in my ability to play a more regular role. As the season progressed, I started to feel I was repaying the faith Geelong had shown when drafting me.

My consistency had improved from quarter to quarter and so too my overall game awareness. There was a slight uptick in the number of possessions I was getting and the marks I was grabbing compared to the previous season. I was also laying more tackles – in 2009 I averaged 2.3 per match compared to one a game in previous years – and I was also starting to be used occasionally in the ruck. Experience certainly helps.

Although I was never particularly dominant, I finally began to feel I was having an impact in games, and in critical moments, and more regularly. I was also kicking goals more frequently. As an example, I was able to gather 20 disposals and kick three goals against the Lions in round 5, and then a fortnight later, produce similar stats against Sydney.

Even when I was not firing or getting much of the ball, my ability to lay an extra tackle or provide an option that opened space to a teammate was improving. I was also more aware of how my teammates moved, and where they wanted me to kick.

Aside from our opening round win over Hawthorn, I was able to play every game for the season. That clash was an interesting game to miss, not least because of the emotions it stirred for those who had played in the Grand Final five months earlier. On the Sunday before the match, Hawthorn president Jeff Kennett made the statement that would haunt him for the next 11 clashes – all Geelong wins over the Hawks, a run that came to an end in the 2013 preliminary final. Kennett claimed, 'What they [Geelong] don't have, I think, is the quality of some of our players. They don't have the psychological drive we have. We've beaten Geelong when it matters.'

Talk about pouring fuel on the fire. We were already driven to right the wrongs from the previous year and did not need any extra motivation, but it did add to the fanfare surrounding our rivalry with Hawthorn, with that statement becoming known as 'Kennett's Curse', which has its own Wikipedia page!

The win over the Hawks was the first of 13 straight. The Cats were playing like a team hellbent on righting the disappointing end to 2008 and doing an excellent job of doing so. This was being driven by our super core, namely the senior players including Matthew Scarlett, Gary Ablett Jnr, Tom Harley, Jimmy Bartel, Steve Johnson, Cam Mooney and Paul Chapman. You could add Joel Selwood to that list as well, because he was already an established star – as his 45 games in his first two seasons clearly demonstrated. The Rising Star Award was well named.

By that stage it was increasingly clear who our chief rivals for the premiership were. The Hawks had fallen away, suffering what looked to be a classic premiership hangover. Rising sharply was St Kilda, with coach Ross Lyon harnessing a talented list of players who, similarly to the Cats, had demonstrated great promise in the early part of their careers and were coming off a preliminary final loss to the Hawks in 2008.

Heading into the round 14 clash, St Kilda was also unbeaten and given the two clubs were clearly the teams to beat, it shaped as a Grand Final preview. Games against key rivals were always built up and we were aware that Lyon was building a genuine flag contender. St Kilda's backline, headed by Sam Fisher and

Zac Dawson, was a really strong unit. The Saints played well together, and they were a tough side to score against.

It proved to be an incredible game at St Kilda's home ground at Docklands. The Saints had the upper hand early and led by 10 points at the last change, until we launched a big comeback in the final term to draw level after Mathew Stokes goaled in time on. It took Michael Gardiner, the talented former West Coast ruckman enjoying a career revival with St Kilda, to separate the two clubs as he took a great mark late in the piece to snare the match-winning goal.

It was my quietest match for the year – just five disposals, and one behind – which was concerning for me. It was a rare match in which I felt a little overwhelmed, dealing with the Saints' defensive pressure while trying to work out how I could have an impact. But the coaches made it clear they were prepared to honour the work I was putting in on the track and my good form throughout the first half of the season. Their message was not direct. Neither Bomber nor Ken Hinkley, the forwards coach, had ever guaranteed me a spot in the team. But it was rare that the message I received was overly negative, even after the St Kilda game. No more boots were thrown at me, for example!

The loss did not dent our confidence as we felt we had come close to beating the Saints on their favoured ground and Grand Finals are not played at Docklands. So bruising was the clash against St Kilda, we struggled to come up the following week against the Lions in Brisbane – we were forced to make seven changes for the match, with Gary Ablett Jnr, Matthew Scarlett, Cameron Ling, James Kelly, Andrew Mackie and Darren Milburn all missing the trip to the Gabba, a disappointing 43-point loss.

We were also defeated by Carlton in a surprise in round 19 and the Western Bulldogs a couple of weeks later at Docklands, but we soon righted the ship, winning our last four games, finishing with 18 wins, to sit second to St Kilda on the table heading into the finals.

After the last round against Fremantle, I was nominated for the Army Award, which came with a prize of a $10,000 travel voucher, for 'significant acts of bravery or selflessness to promote the cause of their team', also known as 'one-percenters'. These are the types of defensive acts coaches love to see, and so do the fans. This came after a vote by the fans, and I received 54 per cent of the votes cast, ahead of Port Adelaide's Jacob Surjan, with 26 per cent. The award's citation described a 'brilliant smother followed by a chase and a tackle', in the round 22 match against Fremantle. This was an example of the skills I was trying to add to my game, and the award was presented at the All-Australian awards on the Monday after we beat the Bulldogs in the qualifying final. The Army Award was discontinued after the 2009 season for reasons unknown – perhaps the Army did not get what it sought from the sponsorship – but I am proud to be on the honour roll with Essendon's Alwyn Davey (2007) and Richmond's Brett Deledio (2008). I believe that act helped me to cement a spot in the premiership team. I have always enjoyed the defensive side of the game and have loved using my bulk if I have the chance. Later in my career, statistics show I have often laid the most tackles per season in the Cats forward line.

In truth, though, that act against Freo may have been the result of me being desperate to hold my spot in the team, knowing that the finals were just around the corner and, despite the fact I had played every game from round 2, and had kicked eight goals in the last three games of the season, I was aware I remained a fringe player.

I was held goalless in the qualifying final, but the selectors still showed their faith in me, and I retained my spot for my first preliminary final. We were playing extremely well by that stage and proved far too good for Collingwood, and I managed to kick a couple of goals to seal my spot for the Grand Final, a great relief after watching from the sidelines in 2007 and 2008.

* * *

There is no more chaotic environment in footy than a Grand Final, particularly in a decider like 2009's against St Kilda. The lead changed six times after Max Rooke and Cam Mooney had kicked the opening two goals of the game. It was an absolute thriller, with so much at stake, particularly for the Saints, who carried the sentimental support of the general public given they had not won a flag since 1966.

The noise of the crowd at the MCG that day and the atmosphere and energy was unbelievable. It was something I will never forget. As I have been reminded many times, St Kilda fans will also never forget my first goal that day. It is the most polarising goal of my career. But it did have a good result! As well as restoring our lead, deep into the second quarter, it also led to today's video review.

As most observers know – and you can watch it on YouTube – that 'goal' was not a goal. From the moment it came from my foot, it was headed for the goal post. As the replay showed, there was a clear deflection as it clipped the post on the way through. It is a passage I can recall in great detail, from the moment I intercepted the kick from defence from St Kilda full-back Zac Dawson through to me looking towards the goal umpire to assess his reaction.

The score was level with about four minutes remaining in the first half, after goals from Shannon Byrnes and Gary Ablett Jnr, when Dawson marked the footy deep in defence. He then looked to switch play to the AFL Members side of the ground. It is a passage that perfectly encapsulates where I was in my development as a player. I did well to smother Dawson's clearing kick, an example of the message my coaches had been drumming into me, namely, to have an impact on the game when not in possession. But then I did what young forwards often do and panicked. In truth I had far longer to get rid of the footy than I realised, but I was keen to get the shot off as quickly possible.

In that instant, I felt embarrassed that I had missed from such close range. But when I glanced towards the goal umpire, I realised that from the angle he was positioned, it was unlikely he could have known whether or not it was a goal.

That's not the goal umpire's fault. He had no time to get into a position to judge the outcome of my shot – it all unfolded in a split-second, though for me, time seemed to stand still as soon as the footy clipped the post. I could sense the umpire was unsure, and I immediately put my hands up in triumph, and I turned away to celebrate with my teammates.

There is no doubt we were very lucky to get the goal. For all that, it is hard to argue that a goal scored with more than a

I was born and raised in Finley, NSW, a land of farmers and footballers. As a youngster I dreamed of being Gary Ablett Snr. Of course, I barracked for the Cats. Right from the rough-and-tumble of primary school through kick-to-kick at high school, I was pitted against kids who not only had a serious love and appreciation for footy but could really play. I was by no means a standout in those years and there were times when I got towelled up.

My Grade 1 report was a mix of compliments and forecasts: 'Thomas can be a very responsible student but at times is rather boisterous. He is very active and doesn't take kindly to correction. When he applies himself he works very well.'

St Joseph's School Finley

Pupil Report

Name: Thomas Hawkins   Yr: 1
June 1995

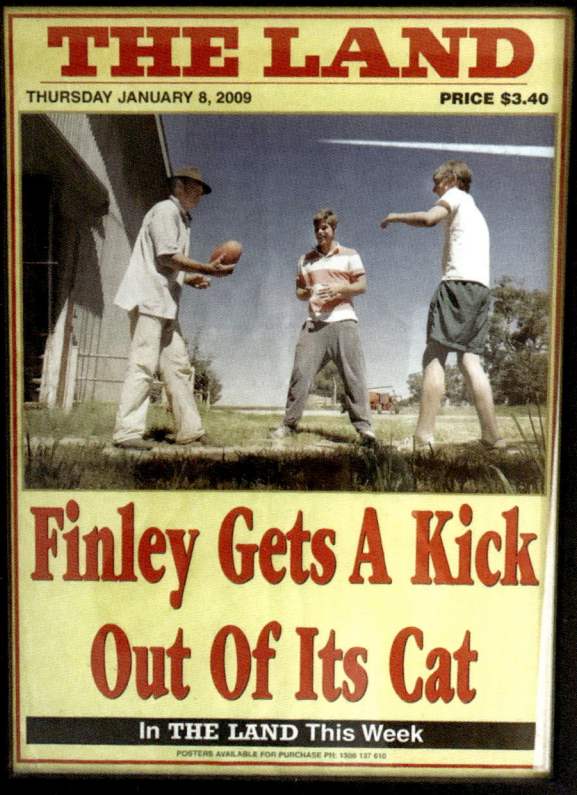

Springfield, the Hawkins family farm I grew up on, sits to the north of Finley, a town of 2500 people, about a 30-minute drive north of the Murray River. My family has lived and worked and played – and run footy – in this region for close on 100 years. It truly is Hawkins Country.

ABOVE: Pictured, as always with footy in hand with Dad. NEWSPIX

LEFT: *The Land*, a newspaper covering rural issues, profiled our family in 2009.

It was not until I headed off to boarding school at Melbourne Grammar in 2003 as a 14-year-old, that I began to realise that a career in footy might just be for me. I ended up being co-captain in Melbourne Grammar's First XVIII with Xavier Ellis, later to become a premiership player with Hawthorn.

ABOVE: In this photo of our 2006 First XVIII I am on the left of our coach — and my Japanese teacher Ben Hanisch — with Xavier on his right. MELBOURNE GRAMMAR SCHOOL

RIGHT: In action on the Melbourne Grammar oval against Caulfield Grammar. In my school years I often played in the ruck.

It was after a breakout series for Vic Metro in the 2006 AFL Under-18 Championships that I believed I might make it in the AFL. In that series I won the Larke Medal, as best and fairest in Division 1, and then made the All-Australian under-18 side. AFL PHOTOS

TOP: With teammates in Vic Metro guernseys.

LEFT: In action against Vic Country. AFL PHOTOS

ABOVE: Scott Selwood, Joel Selwood, myself and my dad, Jack Hawkins at the 2007 AFL Rising Star Presentation, when Joel Selwood won the Award. AFL PHOTOS

My first big highlight as a Cat was being offered the number 26 guernsey my father Jack had worn. It was a gesture I loved. My father played 182 games for Geelong in the 1970s and 80s. My mum, Jennie was also part of a Geelong footy family as a daughter of former Geelong ruckman Fred Le Deux. Fred played 18 games for the Cats between 1956 and 1958.

LEFT: Playing in a pre-season match against Richmond in March 2008. We had a 72 point win. AFL PHOTOS

RIGHT: Celebrating a goal with one of my mentors Cameron Mooney in round 3, 2008, that was a win over Melbourne. I kicked five goals and 'Moons' two.
AFL PHOTOS

Joel Selwood and I celebrate our win over St Kilda in the 2009 AFL Grand Final. My first Grand Final goal is one St Kilda fans will likely never forget. It is the most polarising goal of my career. I had missed from close range. But when I glanced towards the goal umpire, I realised that from the angle he was positioned, it was unlikely he could have known whether or not it was a goal. As well as restoring our lead, deep into the second quarter, it also led the AFL to institute the video review system. AFL PHOTOS

RIGHT: Celebrating after being awarded the AFL Army Award in 2009. The award was presented to a player for 'significant acts of bravery or selflessness to promote the cause of their team'. AFL PHOTOS

half still to play would change the result. There are thousands of moments in every game that have an impact. Admittedly the margin was only six points when the siren sounded before Rooke trickled through another after the siren, to cap off his great game, as the rest of us were celebrating madly.

Was I cheating with that boisterous celebration? Were the Saints robbed? The fact is the umpire is there to make the decision, not me.

When asked about it after our victory, I kept my answer pretty straight: 'I had a pretty good view of it. It went through. The six points were paid and that is all that matters,' I told reporters.

Was that a lie? In truth, I didn't give it much thought afterwards amid the chaotic celebrations in the rooms. I suspect it was a throwaway line, but nor do I shy away from what happened. It was a Grand Final and I was not going to stick my hand up to say anything more. There are no guarantees in football and after what happened in the previous year's Grand Final, we had a ruthless mentality. I certainly don't think of it as cheating.

There is no doubt the Saints received a bad call. Some St Kilda fans have still not let go of it. When we hosted the Saints in the opening game of 2024, I hit the post from a snap and the cheer squad gave me a Bronx cheer.

* * *

The other goal I kicked in that Grand Final is far more important to me given it came at a crucial time in the game, just after the bounce to start the last quarter. St Kilda had gone into three-quarter-time with a seven-point lead after being the better side throughout the third term.

There was a boundary throw-in on the 50-metre arc, and I positioned myself about 15 metres from the ruck contest, briefly having a look around to see if I was free. The footy spilled to the back of the contest and Paul Chapman, who had played a superb game, was able to gather it and find me open, inside scoring range. It was a perfect kick by Chappy, though I did fumble it above my head before clutching it firmly to my chest, with relief, as I fell to the turf. 'I don't know how Chappy saw me, or whether he kicked and hoped. But he kicked it to me, and it stuck. It was a pretty easy mark, but it slipped a bit,' I told *The Geelong Advertiser.*

I was left with a 40-metre kick for goal from a 45-degree angle. In usual circumstances, such a shot is scarcely a certainty, let alone in a Grand Final so tight that every goal felt like it was worth double. But I felt really calm despite the game situation. When I reflect on my reaction now, that calmness still surprises me given my relative inexperience. I felt no nerves at all.

I made good contact with the ball and, as it sailed straight through the middle, I jumped into the arms of Steve Johnson, thinking we were right back in the game. Geelong's next goal is a famous Grand Final moment, given the ingenuity and skill involved. It sits among the best team goals I have ever seen kicked, particularly given it effectively clinched us the premiership, and I still get a great thrill out of watching it.

It was a mix of classic big final moments, with some of Geelong's biggest names stepping up to deliver when it mattered the most. The scores were level. Johnson had the ball on the wing, saw Gary Ablett Jnr free in the middle of the ground. The pass was knocked clear by St Kilda's Justin Koschitske. In the next contest in the centre of the ground, Matthew Scarlett managed to toe poke the ball to Gary Ablett Jnr, who then kicked the footy long into attack. A huge pack formed, the ball spilled to Travis Varcoe, who handballed to Chappy to kick what proved to be the match-winner, even though there were still more than six minutes to play.

* * *

THE moments after the final siren were incredible, which is not surprising given the triumph came after such a tense, physical and hard-fought game. We were going wild across the MCG, our joy beyond belief, as the Saints either sank to their haunches or fell to the ground in devastation.

The commentators called it our redemption after the loss to Hawthorn the year before. I'm not so sure that was the case, as it was my first senior flag, but there is no doubt the entire club was driven throughout the 2009 season to prove we were a truly great team.

It was not as though we played badly in 2008 – we were the best team for all bar the Grand Final. But it was clear to me those who had played in that game did not want to waste another opportunity. There was a feeling that with the talent we had on the list, we should be trying to create a dynasty similar to the one created by the Lions when they won three flags in succession between 2001 and 2003. I've no doubt the senior players who had played in the 2008 Grand Final had fire in their bellies.

There had been shifts in personnel. Tom Lonergan, who had replaced me in the side a year earlier, was shifted from attack to defence but was ultimately overlooked in the latter stages of the season. Josh Hunt unfortunately ruptured an anterior cruciate ligament and underwent a knee reconstruction, which opened the door for David Wojcinski to take his spot. In the latter stages of the finals, Shannon Byrnes, with his dash and desperation, replaced Mathew Stokes, who was hampered with a groin issue.

It was an immense thrill to be part of a Geelong premiership team. I finished the Grand Final on the bench, which was not really a shock because you want your most experienced players on the ground when the match is on the line. But I spotted some good mates sitting near the fence as I was coming from the ground for the final time and later went up to them to give them a celebratory high five when the siren sounded.

It was just an awesome feeling on the MCG after the game. Bomber led the coaching staff down to the ground as I raced out onto the MCG to celebrate with my teammates.

Bob Davis, 'The Geelong Flyer' who was the club captain when my grandfather Fred was playing with the Cats, and coached the 1963 premiership team, had the honour of presenting the premiership cup. He was a legend at Geelong, Bobby, and his presence added another special layer to our triumph.

We all piled on to the stage for the traditional mayhem photographs, and then ran the lap of honour around the MCG; it was such an amazing experience to be a part of for a number of reasons. Celebrating it with my teammates, some of whom already counted among my closest mates, was awesome. But knowing that Emma and my family and some other great friends were among the Geelong fans going nuts in the stands made it an even greater experience to savour. It had taken me a couple of seasons, but I had finally achieved a childhood dream.

From a personal perspective, the Grand Final also provided some vindication for me as I was clearly aware of the criticism that had been directed my way during the season, as I told reporters afterwards. It was also a great reward for all of those hours spent practising my goalkicking back on the family farm and the work I had put in to refine my kicking action.

'I'd heard people and fans remind me of stuff (about my form),' I said after the match. 'It is what you dream of. I copped a bit of stick in the last couple of weeks, so it is such a great feeling.'

* * *

The clock ticks quickly after winning a Grand Final when you are a member of the premiership team, with the action as frenzied off the field as it was from the opening bounce.

The moment we made it back into the locker room, we locked arms and formed into a circle to belt out our theme song, beginning with the famous lines: 'We are Geelong, the greatest team of all. We are Geelong, we're always on the ball.' Never had I sang the song louder.

By that stage the rooms had filled up with teammates unfortunate not to have played on the day, as well as our coaches, support staff, family and friends. The party was kicking off. Journalists were hovering, seeking reaction, and a few players were discussing our triumph with the host broadcaster. That's always far easier when you win.

I spent most of the next hour or so celebrating with my family and high-fiving and hugging teammates while enjoying an ale or two. These are memories to treasure.

Then the official proceedings began. We were whisked off to Federation Square to be presented on the big stage to Geelong fans whose own premiership parties were well underway. After that, we headed to the club's official Grand Final function, at the Tennis Centre, which was another chance to spend time with family, a good thing, because the next few days were a blur.

The best part about winning a premiership is to be able to celebrate not only with the blokes you played alongside, but everyone who has helped you get there – family, friends, staff, and supporters. It always goes well into the night and the next day. Those are always the best times, particularly if you can remember them!

The celebrations after a premiership become a marathon and one of my fondest memories is being presented on the stage to our fans outside Kardinia Park the day after the premiership win.

The crowd was massive. It was brilliant to see so many people with massive smiles on their faces joining the celebrations. These are the gatherings that provide a broader sense of the connection that footy provides and it really is a special thing in our game.

The party continued on into Mad Monday and we all dressed up in special costumes. I know I didn't put too much thought into mine.

The costume theme became part of our post-season celebrations from the time Matt Scarlett arrived after the 2008

Grand Final loss dressed as Kevin Bartlett, complete with a Richmond jumper and his head shaved to mimic the Tiger legend's bald patch. A few other teammates got in on the act as well that year and it has grown larger every season.

Later in the week we were paraded through the City of Geelong on buses and the council honoured our premiership captain, Tom Harley, by making him mayor of Geelong for the day.

A favourite keepsake from that day is a photograph which ran in *The Geelong Advertiser*. It's me and Joel Selwood, both wearing sunglasses – for good reason, given we were at the tail end of a marathon party – holding aloft the premiership cup.

12

Changing agents

IF I BELIEVED life was going to become smoother after becoming a premiership player, 2010 proved again that the football world can be as unpredictable as the bounce of the ball. The biggest issue I faced involved my contract with the Flying Start agency, run by Ricky Nixon. This dilemma caused me no end of anxiety as I considered whether to tear it up and start again.

A 63-game player between 1983 and 1993 – with Carlton, St Kilda and finally Hawthorn – Nixon became one of the most formidable sports agents in the country. He signed some of the biggest names in the AFL and had a reputation for being absolutely ruthless when it came to protecting the rights of his clients.

With that in mind, it was impossible not to be flattered when Flying Start approached me while I was still in school, dreaming about a future in footy. I also spoke to a few prominent agents about my future, which clearly lay at Geelong given my ties to the club.

Xavier Ellis had been drafted by Hawthorn at pick three at the end of 2005 but preferred to complete his schooling the next year. He had already signed with Paul Connors' agency Connors Sports Management. At the same time, my sister Jane was going out with Jimmy Bartel, who was also managed by Connors. In the January before starting Year 12, I went to the Australian Open with Xavier and Paul and at that stage, I thought I was going to sign with the Connors group. But as always, Mum and Dad advised me to do my due diligence, and to see what else was out there.

As a result, I met with Ricky Nixon and Paul Yeomans, who was then his offsider. They both visited Finley that year and Mum and Dad were impressed by Nixon. Mum and Dad were heavily involved in the final decision, and we worked hard to identify what was important to me and what we expected from a manager. As Mum told the *Herald Sun* in 2009, 'When we chose his manager in a decision made by Jack, Tom and I, the money side of things was about fourth on our list of criteria,' she said.

Nixon always held the trump card, his stable having an all-star cast of forwards, an incredible selling point to a teenager. Among the players his company represented were Tony Lockett, Gary Ablett Snr, Jason Dunstall, Greg Williams, Glen Jakovich, Nick Riewoldt, Ben Cousins, Garry Lyon and Matthew Richardson, among many other high-profile players. I was excited Flying Start wanted to represent me and I ultimately had no hesitation in signing with them in September 2006, as I looked forward to my career at the Cats.

Although I had some meetings with Ricky after I had signed on, I tended to deal with his staff rather than directly with him, given he was busy running the agency. The early stages of my partnership with Flying Start were productive. They were able to secure great contracts and my impression was that Ricky always had the best interests of the player at heart, as opposed to himself or the club, and as a result he was formidable in his negotiations.

Things turned sour in 2009 when explosive stories about the difficulties he was experiencing in his personal life were starting to mount. In July of the 2009 season, he was issued with several charges over a crash with a tram in Swan Street, Richmond. Not too long after that, I had my 21st birthday back home at Springfield. The barn where I had practised my goalkicking was the ideal venue for the celebration. Ricky was unable to drive at the time as a result of the accident and a staff member brought him up for the party. I enjoy a good time as much as anyone, so passing judgement is hard. But he was clearly under the weather by the time he got to the party, which added to the concerns I and others had for his welfare.

We all have to make choices. People make mistakes. Ultimately, Ricky made a few bad ones, which tainted his reputation and forced him out of footy.

After discussions with Emma and my parents, talks which had started before the birthday party, I decided that, no matter the cost, I needed to break my contract with Flying Start in order to protect my reputation. Deciding to sever ties was one thing, but telling Ricky that I was leaving, and that his behaviour was a key reason for me walking out midway through what was our second agreement, was daunting. He could be such an intimidating figure.

Joel Selwood scarcely settled my nerves when relaying the details of a phone call his brother Troy, who was playing with Brisbane, had with Ricky when he severed their relationship shortly before I made my decision to move. Joel said Ricky 'absolutely obliterated' his brother during the call, which I will admit absolutely terrified me.

Rarely have I felt so nervous as I did in the hours before I was due to meet Ricky in his office in the Docklands. Mindful of Troy Selwood's experience, I also felt that I needed someone with experience to assist me when it came to informing Ricky that our relationship was over. Dad accompanied me to the meeting.

To Ricky's credit, the meeting was amicable. I explained the discomfort I was feeling and my reasons for seeking a fresh start elsewhere. It was not about money. In fact, the switch cost me a decent amount of cash. The meeting occurred in the pre-season, which meant that I owed Flying Start their commission – $30,000 for the final two years of the three-season deal I had signed with Geelong at the end of 2008. We asked for a discount given the unusual circumstances and Ricky agreed, with the final payout to terminate the contract reduced to $25,000. For a young player, that was a reasonable percentage of my wage, but I felt strongly that leaving was the right thing to do. I was soon proven right, although, as it turned out, if I had waited a few more months, I would have been able to walk away for nothing.

I want to stress that I always felt well looked after during my years with Flying Start and I still have really good relationships with some of the people who were working there at the time.

When we have bumped into each other on occasion in the years since I left the agency, our dealings have always been respectful.

The next step for me was to find a new agent. That was far easier, with Joel Selwood proving himself to be a more than handy friend once again. He was signed to Stride Sports and was managed by Tom Petroro. I had met Tom a few times as a result of my friendship with Joel. Tom had started his career with Flying Start before being one of the founders of Stride in 2005. He had also presented his credentials to me in 2006 but had lost out to Flying Start. This time, after Joel's strong recommendation, he happily took me on, and he has looked after my footy contracts and commercial negotiations ever since.

13

Bouncing around

On top of the anxiety that surrounded the sacking of Flying Start, I never really felt settled throughout the 2010 season as Bomber moved me all over the place – from a key forward position to the ruck, then to the bench, and then back around again. I guess he and the line coaches were trying to identify where I was best suited.

It was the beginning of a period of change for the club. After captaining Geelong to two premierships, Tom Harley retired at the end of 2009. Via the Leading Teams process, which involved lots of discussion and feedback, it was decided Cameron Ling would be the best fit to replace Tom and take the Cats forward – a perfect fit. There was also a significant change in the coaching structure in the off-season, with Ken Hinkley heading to the Gold Coast to take up a senior assistant position. Brenton Sanderson, the 2001 Carji Greeves Medallist, had worked under Bomber since 2007 and assumed control of the forward line.

I trained as a forward through the pre-season and started the year in attack. I managed to kick six goals in the first four weeks, with the best a bag of three in our loss to Fremantle. Things soon changed. Brad Ottens was starting to have some issues with his body. He had injured a hand in a boating incident shortly after Christmas, then had a stress reaction in his foot, and the decision was made to rest him for two months, from round 5. The coaches told me that in Ottens' absence, there was an opportunity for me to play both forward and ruck. I suspected it was also their way to continue my development. Despite me playing all but one game in 2009, I was still considered a fringe player. My attitude was that if there was an opportunity to explore something that might add to my game, it was worth considering. It was also not uncommon at Geelong for players to be asked to fill different roles. Tom Lonergan was a classic example, having replaced me in attack midway through 2008 only to be swung into defence, where he blossomed after Harley's retirement. As you get older, you appreciate the importance of role-playing and understand that not every player gets to play where they want to, either because there are better options, or because the coaches have decided that a player's skills might serve better elsewhere.

I had also improved my aerobic fitness enough to think that I would be able to handle the extra work in the ruck and the coaches were also aware of the high-jumping ability I had shown at school. But it was a punt. I was also mindful that if it did not work, it was possible someone else might come into the side who would add something I did not have to the forward line.

Through this period, I spent more time with Brendan McCartney, which is interesting as I had trodden warily around him in the early part of my career. In those early years I felt some negativity from him towards me. It was not so much what he said, more what I perceived. If my skinfolds were too high, or I was too heavy, it felt to me like he was rolling his eyes.

He had the reputation of being a great development coach but, in my inexperience, I felt he was a proper hard arse. On reflection, that feeling was likely due to my immaturity. Similar to my early relationship with Bomber, I did not yet have the confidence to seek Brendan out and ask him if there was an issue or to explain my concerns. Confidence to ask these questions was a tool I developed as I grew older.

I've since learnt that my old forward line mentor Cam Mooney took it upon himself to arrange a meeting with Bomber and the rest of the assistants, including McCartney. He urged them to consider that things would eventually click with me.

In an interview for this book, Moons says that the difficulties I experienced in trying to find my place in the footy world were similar to those he went through in his early playing years. As a 19-year-old he played in North Melbourne's 1999 premiership but spent much of that Grand Final on the bench and did not touch the footy. At the end of that season, he found himself part of a trade that saw former Geelong skipper Leigh Colbert joining North Melbourne. Cam subsequently played in our 2007 and 2009 premierships, seasons in which he was the club's leading goalkicker.

Being aware of my doubts and sensing that the coaching staff may not know of my concerns, he marched into Bomber's office midway through the year. 'It is something Macca (McCartney) and I still laugh about whenever we see each other,' Mooney said. 'Tom was frustrating everybody. He had the talent and the size, but his work rate wasn't quite there yet. But the thing that I had in common with Hawk was that he was like me, but he was 10 times more talented. He was a kid from the country who didn't really know what professionalism was, who didn't quite get what it took to be an AFL player at a young age.

'It took me until I was about 24 to mature and then to finally start to get it. I told them that this kid is going to be 23 or 24 by the time that he gets it – he was then just 21 – so just get off his back and let me look after him. I guess from there we formed a relationship – a big brother–little brother type of thing, if you want to call it that.'

Those were the types of things that made Cam such a good mentor, but also an example of why Geelong has become such a strong club, because the senior players felt comfortable challenging the coaches if they believed there was any shortfall.

When I reflect on that season, I have no doubt it was critical in terms of honing a skill set that allowed me to become a more complete footballer who would excel for Geelong for a long time, and Bomber and Brendan's roles were critical. Hats off to them, I say.

I'm not ashamed, however, to concede that I felt absolutely terrified on the field at times as I contested the ruck, in support of Mark Blake, against some of the biggest and strongest men in footy.

The change in my role was also partly due to a change in our game style, because of the wear-and-tear Ottens was showing, but also because Mooney and James Podsiadly had become a powerful combination in attack and were now the preferred option as key position targets. Podsiadly, who had joined the club at the start of 2010 as a mature-age recruit – he was then 28 – had dominated at VFL level. He quickly showed the higher level was no issue when he kicked five goals against Port Adelaide in round 4. Podsiadly's career story is one of the best in footy, because he showed so much resilience after being overlooked for so long. He had played for Essendon reserves, Williamstown, Collingwood as a rookie, Werribee, and Geelong reserves, before being drafted by the Cats as a rookie with pick 58.

The left-footer became a high-quality forward for Geelong and later Adelaide between 2010 and 2015. At the Cats, Podsiadly kicked 169 goals in 83 games and claimed the club's goalkicking award in 2011, with 53 goals, a mighty feat in a premiership year. I managed only 27 that year!

As a result of the shift in my role, I roamed further afield more frequently, which took me back to my junior days at Finley and Melbourne Grammar. But there is a world of difference between the rucking role I used to play as a kid compared to the hybrid forward-ruck job I assumed during the 2010 season.

Although I had played 43 games in my first three seasons, I was still relatively immature, and it felt as though I was not playing well enough to make it as a forward, yet I was certainly not tall enough or athletic enough to prosper as a full-time ruckman. But the hybrid model has been used by teams at different stages during my time in footy and even though it was clear to me that I was far from a critical cog in the team, I was determined to make as good a fist as possible, filling whatever role was asked of me.

In the 18 games I played in 2010, I notched 96 hitouts and kicked 21 goals. From a physical sense, it proved to be one of the toughest years that I have endured. It was brutal. There was a scare, though, when I felt pain in my right foot after the round 4 match against Melbourne, after I had kicked four goals for the second time in three weeks while also rucking.

A scan revealed a hotspot in the foot and there was initially a fear it could develop into a stress fracture, so once again we consulted with specialists and I also sought Matthew Egan's opinion. Bomber told the media that the club had allowed me to decide how I was going to treat the injury. After various consultations it was decided that rest was the best approach. Bomber said, 'We didn't really know which way to go at the start, but they decided through all the specialists and Tom making the decision with his friends and family that he is going to play in one or two weeks. All we did was lay the cards on the table and let him make the decision from hopefully the best advice we could possibly give him. We don't know if it is a new injury or an old injury or if it has been there for two weeks or for 10 weeks. Once we identified there was a problem, we had to deal with it, and we've done that, and Tom has made a decision based on the best information.'

After a period of rest, and after considering the advice that Matthew Egan, Dr Chris Bradshaw and Mum and Dad had provided, we decided to push on and return to footy in the latter stages of the season, once the hot spot in my foot had settled. My first game back was against Sydney in round 18 and I played the final seven games for the year through to our preliminary final loss to Collingwood, a match in which I recorded 12 hitouts; my second highest for the year.

* * *

During my stint as Mark Blake's second string, Bomber had told me that although I was not the same size as the ruckmen I was going up against, my role was to move around the ground and try to tire them out. But given the athleticism and endurance of players like West Coast's Dean Cox, that proved far easier said than done.

I have always respected ruckmen, having flirted with the prospect in my youth that I might well become one during a growth spurt, while also mindful that my grandfather Fred le Deux had played in the ruck for the Cats. But going up against stars of the competition including Cox, Aaron Sandilands and Darren Jolly gave me a greater understanding as to how good they were. They did not just have great skills, but also toughness and influence. You need great courage as well, and I still marvel at the bravery needed to master the position. We have all heard the tongue-in-cheek jokes about ruckmen not being the smartest people but let me tell you what I learnt as a part-time ruck. It is so bloody hard to do, particularly if you are undersized. They are no duffers.

Jolly, a premiership ruckman with Sydney and Collingwood, was not the greatest runner I came up against, but he was tough and very, very smart with his ruck work and body positioning. But nothing compared to rucking against Fremantle's Sandilands, a man mountain who ended his career as a four-time All-Australian during an era of outstanding ruckmen.

The times I had to ruck against Sandilands were the most frightening experiences of my career, particularly as I never really rated myself as being brave. I felt completely powerless trying to match it with big 'Sandy'. The tactic adopted by most ruckmen was to leap into the Fremantle star, which must have been so hard on his body. I am amazed he managed to play 271 games over 17 seasons, given the amount of physical punishment he must have endured.

Every generation of football has had elite ruckmen. But I do feel fortunate to have had that brief experience rucking against some of the all-time great champions of the game. This includes Cox, a six-time All-Australian who I consider to be one of the best footballers I have seen. Not only was he outstanding in the ruck, but his skills and mobility around the ground were something to behold. He could run like a thoroughbred, possessing the speed and agility to break through lines despite standing 203cm. He was a smart player as well and it has not surprised me that he has gone on to enjoy a long career as a senior assistant coach with the Eagles and then the Sydney Swans.

Playing in the ruck that year and against those champions taught me a lot about controlling my body and also how to position myself in marking contests to turn them to my advantage. As my body matured and my experience grew, I relished the opportunity to take rucking contests in the forward line, feeling I might be able to get one over the specialists from time to time.

The clearest demonstration of this came in the 2022 Grand Final against Sydney when, amid a frenetic opening where neither team was able to land an initial blow, I was able to use my nous to twice out-position Swans ruckman Tom Hickey at boundary throw-ins, grab the footy and snap our first two goals.

My strength as a ruckman in attack also proved an advantage as our primary ruckman did not have to run forward into attack for ball-ups or boundary throw-ins. This has allowed them to position themselves a kick behind play and, hopefully, remain a little fresher than their rivals, while also ensuring our forward line was not too top-heavy at a stoppage, which also helped us to apply pressure to try to keep the footy inside the 50-metre arc. It also worked in general marking contests.

In the second half of my career, I was also regarded as one of the best forwards in one-on-one marking contests because of my ability to out-position my direct opponent. Towards the tail end of my career, that experience really helped me as I taught Geelong's younger forwards how to use their bodies in contests, skills initially learnt from Mooney but also through that extended period in the ruck.

* * *

Geelong had learnt the hard way in 2008, 2010, and again in 2012, that defending premierships is far from an easy task. We were the hunted side following our flag in 2009, and our opponents seemed to lift against us most weeks that season, determined to take a leading scalp. Of course, every player and every team tries their best every week, but there is an extra incentive in knocking off a top team.

Geelong was that target in the years we fell short. As in most of those years, I felt we were right in the mix for the premiership in 2010, after we finished second with 17 wins. With some luck in the qualifying final against St Kilda, we might have made it to the Grand Final. A win in the qualifying final means a week off to prepare for the cutthroat preliminary final. It makes a difference. The Saints were able to edge us by four points, with an inaccurate last quarter when we kicked 1.7, damaging our hopes.

We rebounded in dominant fashion against Fremantle in a semi-final with a 69-point win, set up by an eight goal to one opening term. But the shoe was on the other foot in the preliminary final a week later, with the Magpies putting us to the sword in the opening term, kicking seven goals to one to put an end to our premiership defence. This was not really a surprise, for Collingwood, the minor premiers, always seemed to be the team to beat throughout 2010. And so it was; after a drawn Grand Final, the Magpies were dominant in the replay, winning by 56 points. For the Saints, the drought continued.

* * *

If the changes at the start of the season were significant, they were nothing compared to the upheaval at the end. The great Gary Ablett Jr decided to head to Queensland to captain the Gold Coast Suns in their inaugural season. An even greater shock occurred when Mark Thompson resigned, stating he was fatigued with the coaching business, only to join his old club Essendon as a senior assistant to James Hird a few weeks later.

The decision by Gary was far from a surprise, given there had been considerable conjecture through the season that he would be the first mega-signing for the new club. He was the best footballer in the game at that stage and the money he was offered was life-changing.

Some of his teammates, whose privacy I will respect, were disappointed that he was leaving, as they felt Geelong was still more than capable of contending for premierships and it is indisputable that he would have strengthened us further in 2011, not that it turned out to be an issue in the end.

Even though I had now played at Geelong for four years, I still considered myself to be on the fringes and had no discussions with Bomber or Gary about their decisions before or after they left. It was not that I did not like or admire them, more that they were senior personnel and I was still very much a junior. My relationship with Gary strengthened significantly when he returned to Geelong to finish his wonderful career and we became friends, which delighted me. Gary is a great person. I have always admired how respectful he is, with anyone, given his public profile. Bomber and I also got to know each other better once he was out of football, at premierships reunions and other gatherings where the Geelong people get together to celebrate milestones.

14

Overcoming doubts

Although the resignation of Bomber Thompson shocked almost everyone at the club, the surprises did not end there as the Cats looked towards the future. In the weeks after Bomber's exit, it seemed to me that the next coach of Geelong would be Brenton Sanderson, who had been an assistant coach at the club since 2007. Because he had played with some of the older guys at the club before his retirement in 2005 after a 209-game career – 199 of them with Geelong after brief stints with Adelaide and Collingwood – he had a strong relationship with our senior players. He was also very good with me as the assistant coach I was most involved with in the months leading up to Bomber's resignation. It seemed to me he was a natural fit for the job given his strong communication skills.

It seemed from media reporting that his appointment was almost a foregone conclusion. When Chris Scott was mentioned as a potential candidate, I did not think too much about it before he was appointed as our new coach on October 18, 2010. Sanderson did remain as an assistant for another season at Geelong before being appointed coach of the Adelaide Crows. He took the Crows to a preliminary final in 2012 and his record of 39 wins from 69 games – a 57.6 per cent win rate – in three seasons stands up. But he was sacked in 2014, despite the Crows winning 11 games finishing only one game outside the eight. He still has the second-highest winning strike rate as a Crows coach, and my experience showed he was someone capable of improving players.

That said, I was immediately impressed with Chris, particularly the way he handled himself coming into a new club in the senior role at such a young age – he was just 34 when he was appointed, after three years as an assistant to Mark Harvey at Fremantle. Ironically his last task in that role was in Freo's 69-point loss to Geelong in the 2010 second semi-final.

As a keen footy follower, I was aware of the great career he had at Brisbane, where he was the 1994 AFL Rising Star winner, best and fairest in 1998 and was a member of the 2001 and 2002 premiership-winning teams, but I did not know much about him as a person.

I did wonder how he would connect to some of the older Cats because Sanderson had not just been a teammate of theirs, they were also good mates. I also wondered whether that might cause some problems for Chris, with Sanderson seeming to have been preferred for the role.

In a shared press conference before my 350th game – against Hawthorn on Easter Monday in 2024 – Chris touched on that as something he had been nervous about as well. 'The club took a chance on me as a young 34-year-old and I remember being a little intimidated by the quality of the squad and the senior players the Cats had,' he said. 'But I was also so enthused by some of the younger guys coming through and I guess I could relate to Tom, a little bit, when I first got to Geelong. He was clearly a highly talented player who had not quite cracked it ... but there was a sense, for me, that we had a lot to look forward to. I was always going to learn from the senior players, but I was more hoping that there was a group of young players coming through I could learn from.'

What struck me about Chris in those early days was the way he was able to sit back, listen to what the group was saying and assess that information. I have since heard him say that he was aware he had great resources in the players he inherited and that, while he had his own theories on coaching, he was prepared to work with the group and give ground if required. It never felt like it was his way or the highway.

When he first arrived, he told me he was looking forward to working with me, given both my youth but also the talent and versatility that I had shown in my four seasons. He asked me where I thought my career was at, where I thought it was headed and how I envisaged my future with the Cats. I told him that while there were still areas I needed to work on, I felt I was improving every season and that I still believed I was capable of being a better player.

It felt to me in those early meetings he was trying to get as much information as possible from the players to devise a strategy that would work for him and the club in the short term, while thinking further afield as well.

Unfortunately for me, despite the early optimism and encouragement he offered me, the initial change of coach did not bring about a surge in form and for a period it felt like I was going backwards.

As Geelong was flying to Perth to tackle the Eagles midway through the winter of 2011, I was sitting in a real estate office in Queenscliff, preparing for a career after footy, riddled with anxiety. I suspected my days at Geelong were numbered.

Even by the middling standards of those first four years, which included the premiership in 2009 and a decent enough follow-up in 2010, my form was average at best in 2011. In the first four months of the season, I bounced in and out of the senior side three times. In my first nine games of the year, which fell between round 1 and round 14, I managed a paltry five goals, well under half of my career average to that point.

Meanwhile, the Cats were flourishing under Chris – we were unbeaten in those 14 rounds – and with my great supporter, Mark Thompson, no longer there, I had genuine concerns for my future. An AFL player's career averages about 30 games, or less than three seasons, and I had already seen some talented footballers cut by the Cats during my time there.

I had played 61 senior games to the end of the 2010 season, which included the flag that meant so much to me, but now it seemed like I was going backwards, and fast. Even in the VFL I was struggling to get a kick, let alone take a mark or boot a bag of goals, and my lack of form seriously dented my confidence and muddled my thinking. Finding a new career path, or at least having something to fall back on should I be moved on, was very much at the forefront of my mind by the middle of the year.

Courtesy of a contact provided by my former agent Ricky Nixon, I was able to spend a couple of days a week doing work experience with the Fletchers Real Estate team at Queenscliff. I also completed a real estate course at Gordon TAFE, something I really enjoyed. Some of the other guys at the club were investing in the stock market, but that was a field I did not understand nor have any interest in. Real estate, on the other hand, was something I felt I could succeed at, having been used to buying and selling livestock and produce from a young age.

As a young footballer, the importance of buying your own home was drummed into me and my teammates. It is the great Australian dream, after all. But it was also a way to ensure that the money we were earning was not wasted on the good life.

Having grown up on the land, I always enjoyed getting out and about and felt a real estate role would not tie me to a desk. I've also always loved meeting and helping people, and the thought of assisting someone to buy their dream home appealed to me. I still retain a strong interest in real estate – just as a hobby – but it may well be an area I pursue more in the future if I have some free time. Only a couple of years ago I had the chance to do some more work experience with Anthony Stevens, the former North Melbourne captain who now works in real estate in the Geelong region.

* * *

With the benefit of hindsight, these steps were probably over the top but were indicative of my uncertainty and mental state at the time. Even if Geelong had decided I was unlikely to improve,

I *had* kicked 55 goals and played 42 matches in the previous two seasons, and with my youth and experience, the Cats would have been able to find another club interested in my services in exchange for a draft pick, at the very least. But at that stage of 2011, when I was out of form and confused about the future, it was hard to think clearly about such possible options.

As my concerns mounted, I should have sought help from someone like Ron Watt, who had put me through my paces on the training track when I first arrived at the club and had become someone I got on well with.

In the early part of my career, if I was struggling with something Bomber wanted me to do, or I had issues with Brendan McCartney, I would ask Ron for advice and he helped me develop strategies to cope with those moments. We often discussed my development and he helped me put the pieces together when it came to taking steps forward in my career, but also to learn more about myself. Mum and Dad always told me that they were only a phone call away, but Ron was seeing me every day at the club and as the club's player development manager, he became an important influence.

Ron was a fun-loving guy. But he was also honest. If I needed to do more work, he would tell me. I always found him great to deal with and it has been good to see him succeed away from Geelong, having spent time with the AFL Coaches Association and later coaching the Gordon Football Club to premierships in the Central Highlands League, among other coaching roles.

Instead of seeking such advice from such a proven ally, I internalised my fears. Around the club I became a little introverted. It was a behaviour that I can track back to my childhood; when I was at school and struggling in the classroom, I adopted a similar approach. I would keep to myself and try to work things out alone instead of seeking help, which is not the best idea. Mum, though, understood something was up, even though I was not saying too much. A mother's intuition? She had that with me. Both my parents were very positive people. They liked to work hard and enjoy the company of family and friends and were always up for a chat and a laugh over a drink. Over the course of the season, I gradually opened up to Mum about my fears and, not surprisingly, it always seemed she would have the right answer. Dad, too, was a big help.

We talked about my confusion and lack of confidence about the direction my life was heading when Mum offered some words that provided a clearer perspective. She advised me to consider what my friends in Finley and Melbourne Grammar were doing, and to remember that not all of them had their lives figured out either. She reminded me it was natural for younger people to feel uncertain and believe they had the weight of the world on their shoulders as they tried to figure out where they were heading. And that this thinking happened in all walks of life, not just in a footy club. Mum also told me it was important not to rush myself and that things would work themselves out. I have always been someone who takes time when considering things – that is another habit that hasn't changed from childhood – but I needed someone who knew me well to straighten up my thinking and Mum proved to be that person.

She encouraged me to meet with Ron Watt and tell him what was going on and to his great credit, he was able to point me in the right direction and get me going again. I also travelled to

Melbourne to meet with Tom Petroro, but we never discussed the potential of looking elsewhere. It was still early in our relationship but I'm glad we had the chance to chat about this important stage of my career. In an interview for this book, Tom said, 'We were just building our relationship, so I was nervous as to how we would work through it. He was told he was going to be dropped but Tom was honest with how he was going, and, at that moment, I knew he'd learn from it and get back in the side. Throughout his career, Tom has always been a bit harsh on himself, but it has probably helped him get some great outcomes.'

As in 2010, part of the solution was to try to lessen my focus on footy and my future as I struggled to reclaim a spot in the senior side. My old housemate Simon Hogan was studying and following his lead I enrolled in a short course in business management. He also said to get out on the golf course and get back to the hobbies I had always enjoyed doing.

The message from the coaching staff was similar – to simplify things. At different stages, I would meet with Brenton Sanderson, who again stressed the importance of contributing small acts in the game, because there were still periods in matches where I was not involved enough in the action. He said it was not about hunting more of the footy to the detriment of the team's system, it was about laying tackles if I was going through a dry spell or to lead repeatedly to present an alternative to either Cam Mooney or James Podsiadly. That, he said, would ensure I remained mentally in tune with the game. In the second half of my career, as my game sense grew, it became easier to vary the way I played. If the game was not suiting me, or the footy was not coming my way, I would roam further afield to try to find the footy a little more. There are ways you can manipulate where you are on the ground as a forward, just to take one or two more marks, and to give your opponent something to think about. 'Sando' helped me stop over-thinking my game. The simple approach was beneficial.

From that point on, I never really looked back.

* * *

The most selfish moment of my footy life occurred midway through that year and it is arguably the critical play that helped me reboot my career. But I still shake my head at how desperate and out of character my actions were that day.

Playing in a VFL match against the Box Hill Hawks in June, I did something so against what I stand for that I would drop myself straight away if I did it again. Put simply, I became goal hungry. Rather than kicking goals if they were there or handing off opportunities to teammates in a better position, I was desperate to kick a bag and prove I was a viable option for the seniors. I became selfish, something that should never be part of any team sport. The most glaring example of this selfishness robbed my teammate Steve Motlop, who was also fighting for a senior spot, of a fine moment.

Motlop was sprinting towards the 50-metre arc at full pace and unloaded with a great kick that was clearly going through for a goal. I was in the process of shepherding my opponent away when, at the last moment, I pushed off him and marked the ball on the goal line. We still joke about that moment – Steve told me recently it was not the only time I did that to him – but it was a clear sign of my desperation. It is the age-old story in football. Hitting the scoreboard counts, and in a season where everything seemed to be going awry for me, every goal counted. But this moment had a lasting impact on my career. I thought long and hard about it and vowed never to let my needs get in the way of my teammates. It was from then on, that selflessness on the field became my thing, something I can now reflect on with pride. To be second on the all-time list of goal-assists, at least since records began – behind only the great Eddie Betts – is something I treasure.

My form in the VFL was not outstanding – in three matches I managed six goals – but when Brad Ottens was suspended in July, the match committee turned to me to fill the breach. The coaching hierarchy never verbalised just how important it was for me to be ready should another chance arise in the senior team. They didn't need to. I understood that if I did not seize a chance when it came, it was likely another would not arise heading into September, given clubs like to field a settled, well-drilled team in the finals. The themes were the same as the ones that Sando had outlined. Play your role. Provide a target. Have an impact on the contest where possible and, if not near the footy, try to do something that would help the team out.

Perhaps it was desperation, but after a period of flux, I struck the richest vein of form in my career to that point after returning to the side for the round 17 clash against Brisbane at the Gabba. It was an important stretch for the club, because after winning our first 13 games, we lost a couple of tight matches in succession, to Essendon and West Coast.

James Podsiadly was dominant against the Lions that day, booting eight goals but I also enjoyed a good game in a support role, kicking 3.3. The pattern of my career had been to play a good game and then put in a quiet one but this time my form held as my confidence began to rise, perhaps helped by the fact we were pitted against lower-performing rivals through this period. In the next three games against Richmond, Melbourne, and the Gold Coast, I was able to kick another 10 goals.

We completely dominated the Tigers in the first half, booting 11 goals to one, before easing off a little on the way to a convincing 62-point win. It was great to be back in the senior team and I was able to win plenty of the footy and kicked four goals from 15 disposals. Admittedly, I almost stuffed one up right on half-time, when Mathew Stokes chipped the ball to me while I was next to the goal square and I spilled the mark. As Alex Rance lunged for me, I managed to stop it from going through for a behind, but then slipped before regaining my feet to snap the goal. That was the confidence boost I needed, because I would have dwelt on that moment if I had squandered the opportunity to kick such an easy goal. It was also important that I stood up as James Podsiadly, who had kicked three goals, was crunched earlier in the second quarter and subsequently missed the next match against Melbourne. I was able to start the second half with another goal and added another couple in a boost to my confidence.

The match against Melbourne went into the record books, and also led to the end of Dean Bailey's coaching reign, after four years and 83 games. The Demons were at their lowest point and we had regained our bounce and were determined to ensure we made the most of every opportunity. From the opening bounce we put Melbourne to the sword in a match that was, without any doubt, the most one-sided game I have played in.

In the opening term we kicked 8.3 to three behinds. But that was nothing compared to our dominance in the second term – at half-time we led by 20 goals to one. We added another 17 goals in the second half to kick a record score against the Demons – 37.11 (233) to 7.5 (47).

The 186-point margin was the second-highest in history, and the club's biggest win, and was a combination of the Cats being right at the top of our game and the Demons at their lowest. Maybe not their lowest, as they hold the 'record' as the game's biggest defeat – 190 points against Fitzroy in 1979! The scoreboard was just one reflection of our dominance, but we had control everywhere, gathering 510 disposals for the match to Melbourne's 282. The ball was whizzing from player to player and the delivery into the forward line was a dream, which helps explain our accuracy. It was rare when we had to take a shot from a difficult position.

Joel Selwood had 43 disposals, the equal most of his career. Steve Johnson kicked seven goals. Cam Mooney and I kicked five goals each.

It is never ideal to see any coach get sacked, no matter their success rate, but the nature of football means that you tend to focus on your own club rather than worrying too much about the fortunes of others and I must admit that although I knew the Demons were struggling, I was too focused on my own form and trying to stay in the team to concern myself with what was happening elsewhere.

There was another element at play that day as well. As my senior teammates had drummed into me through the period where Geelong became the hunted given our success, when the opportunity arises to cash in, enjoy 'the feast'. We rarely missed the chance to do so and that day was indicative of how ruthless we could be.

Our run continued the next week when we hosted the Gold Coast Suns in their first visit to Geelong. There was great hype surrounding the game as it was to be the first time Gary Ablett Jnr was to return to Kardinia Park as an opposition player but unfortunately he had a hamstring injury and was not able to play. While there was great chatter publicly about whether he would play, for us it was just another match and his possible return was not something we dwelt on.

But such was the anticipation, Gary issued an apology to Geelong fans, stating he had been injured against the Saints the week before and would not be playing. Gold Coast's coach Guy McKenna made it clear: 'I'd prefer him to miss a week rather than a month. There's just been a bit of bleeding into his hamstring. It's a shame. He's disappointed, of course. He would love to have gone down there and faced his old mob.'

It was almost as one-sided as our clash against Melbourne, as we destroyed the Suns by 150 points to post our 29th straight win at our home ground. We also set a couple of new records, handing the Suns what is still their heaviest defeat, in the process becoming the first VFL/AFL club to win at least 17 games in a season for five years in succession. We also set a new record for entries inside the forward 50-metre arc and while I only kicked a couple of goals, Steve Johnson added another six while James Podsiadly booted five on his return.

The game that is among the most important in my career came against the reigning premiers Collingwood in the final game of the regular season. The Magpies had lost only once for the season – we had beaten them by three points in round 8 at the MCG – and they came into the match off a run of 14 straight victories. The Magpies were favourites to go back-to-back, but it was clear that Geelong – we had 18 wins before that round – were their chief rivals for the flag.

Coaches occasionally hold an ace up their sleeve heading into September but in front of a crowd of more than 85,000 at the MCG, we ran rampant to sew up second position on the ladder and boost our confidence heading into the finals. Daniel Menzel was the star in attack, with five goals in the 96-point drubbing. I was again able to snare a couple of goals as well, but importantly there were some moments in the game when I felt I was having a real impact, including a strong mark running back with the flight of the ball, resulting in a goal.

My form left the match committee with a selection dilemma heading into the finals, which is so often the case at that time of the season. My old mentor Cam 'Moons' Mooney was a true finals warrior and felt fit and ready to go after serving a week's suspension from round 21, in what would be his last season. He was not recalled after that and he approached Chris Scott to find out where he stood and was told that the match committee had decided he would be missing, and that my form was strong enough to retain my spot.

When penning a tribute ahead of my 300th game a decade later for *The Geelong Advertiser*, Moons outlined his feelings on the club's decision: 'I was dirty at the time, but deep down I knew I was cooked, and Scotty's instincts were right,' he wrote. 'Hawk transformed himself that finals series from an unsure kid into a man mountain. His confidence blossomed, as did his maturity and consistency. In my mind, he has been in the best three key forwards in the AFL every season since.'

It is interesting to note those comments, because my recollection differs slightly on the period leading up to the Grand Final. While the message may have been passed on to Moons, the coaches never told me directly that I would be playing and that he would not be. That might have been a ploy to ensure I was desperate and focused through this period. Which I absolutely was.

In an interview for this book, Cam said he has since come to the view that it was one of the best decisions Chris Scott made in his coaching career. 'Going into that finals series, I was on my last legs, but Hawk still hadn't established a permanent spot in the forward line. It is funny that this kid I had tried to nurture and help along the way was the one who took my spot. But I was thrilled. I am sure Geelong would not have won the premiership if I had played. Jimmy Bartel won the Norm Smith, but Hawk was the difference and there is no way in the world I would have been able to do what Hawk did that day. Chris Scott has made some big decisions in his coaching career, but I think that might have been his biggest and his best, to have Tom in the team that day.'

Moons furthered his reputation as an outstanding teammate and consummate professional throughout that September. In my first years at the club, he had acted as a teacher and confidence booster for me. Even when I was still learning the caper, he would be in my ear before a match, encouraging me and telling me that I was 'the man' to change the upcoming match. His encouragement continued through that finals series, even though he was clearly disappointed to be on the sidelines. His message began to sink in as I started to deliver that September. I kicked a couple of goals in the qualifying final win over our arch rivals Hawthorn and then another couple more against West Coast in the preliminary final.

Heading into the Grand Final, I was aware my role might expand after Steve Johnson had dislocated his kneecap in the preliminary final, an injury which would require an operation after the season. His absence would have been a real blow because he was so important to our forward structure but also someone capable of going into the midfield for a burst to give us a lift if required. Given the extent of the injury, I doubted he would be able to play and still can't quite believe it that he did.

Had it been someone else, I doubt they would have played, but right from the start of the week Steve was optimistic about playing and, as skillful as he was in so many different facets of the game, I believe his biggest strength was his mental toughness. There was clearly an element of risk. Under Bomber, players under an injury cloud were asked to be honest as to whether they believed they would be capable of performing to their best under adversity.

The example of Mathew Stokes, who believed he had let his team down in the 2008 Grand Final when carrying an injury and then had selflessly withdrawn from the 2009 Grand Final with a groin problem, was fresh in our minds. Steve was adamant he would be able to perform, though he did require a painkilling injection. Despite the injury, he played an outstanding match for us, kicking four goals from 14 possessions. Would we have won without him? Perhaps. But the challenge would have certainly been much harder.

Ahead of that Grand Final, Moons was again in my face, telling me that I was 'the man' and in the match I lived up to that, playing an absolute ripper.

My strong block of form leading into the Grand Final meant I was starting to feel more certain of the role I was to play, having kicked 19 goals in the previous eight games, including two in both our finals. It was not just the goals that were giving me affirmation – I was laying tackles inside the forward 50-metre arc and offering an option to guys down the field with what we call a 'release mark'. I'd find a position from the forward flank to the wing to help the transition from defence to attack. For all that, I was not over-confident, mindful that footy has a habit of knocking you down a notch if you get too far ahead of yourself.

I lined up on Ben Reid, a Wangaratta boy, and someone I had played a lot of junior footy against. I had also played a few senior games on him in the early stages of my career. Ben was an accomplished player who had played in Collingwood's premiership a year earlier, when he was named an All-Australian. He was clearly a challenging opponent. My confidence was boosted after hearing that he had been having injury issues through the finals and I did not feel overawed being opposed to him in the Grand Final.

We had an early setback just before half-time when James Podsiadly dislocated his shoulder after crashing to the ground in a big pack about 18 minutes into the term. At first I was not sure how significant the injury was but quickly saw he was in a bad state. His shoulder was still out of its socket and the doctors were initially not able to get it back into place. Such was the severity of the injury, 'Pods' was stretchered off the field, with Mitch Duncan substituted in his place. It was a huge moment in the game and as we were walking off the ground at half-time, my brain was working overtime. Pods, who had kicked 52 goals that season, usually took the best opposition and he was also the man who crashed and bashed packs. He had become the senior forward at the club, the player who was relied on to have an impact when we needed a lift. With his history and background in footy, it was rather shattering to see such an injury happen in a Grand Final.

Moons came to me during the half-time break and reinforced a version of what he had always stressed to me. He told me, 'You are the reason we are going to win this Grand Final. We need you to have an impact. You are the man. This is the time to stamp your authority on the game.'

Confidence is a funny thing. I was still not quite convinced I deserved to be there, but my belief was building and the longer the game went, the more I had an impact. I ended up taking nine marks, which was a match high, had 19 disposals and was able to hit the scoreboard when it mattered the most. I finished with 3.3, an output that could have been even better as I also put another couple of shots out of bounds on the full.

I had another opportunity with 16 minutes left in the last term after marking not far from goal. As I was walking back to take my kick, Steve Johnson came up to offer some advice. At that stage our lead was only nine points and, feeling a little nervous, I asked him if he wanted to take the kick. With the Collingwood defenders distracted, he made a little space for himself and I handballed it to him, and he was able to snap a critical goal, with the Stevie-J curve kick. Was my decision to hand off a case of the yips? Perhaps. I was certainly nervous. But if you wanted someone to kick a critical goal, there was none better than Steve Johnson.

He has told me since that had I chosen to kick the goal myself, he believes I would have won the Norm Smith Medal. I'm not sure about that, but I suspect I might have drawn a couple more votes if I had kicked a fourth goal. For me, Joel Selwood was best afield, having kicked a couple of goals in his 28 touches as we ran away from Collingwood in the final quarter, booting five unanswered goals to win by 38 points. The Norm Smith judges disagreed. Jimmy Bartel, who produced a midfield masterclass, kicking three goals from 26 disposals, polled 12 votes with Joel next on nine. I gained five points, with SEN's Matt Granland giving me the final three-point vote that Jimmy had missed! Joel always performed with courage and skill and was clearly a critical cog in the team from his first moments at the club. But finally, I believed I was as well, and that felt bloody great.

For me, my form at the end of the season was a remarkable turnaround, given I was contemplating life after football just a few months earlier, wondering whether I was set to become another football castoff. This Grand Final felt more special to me than 2009 because even though I kicked a couple of goals in that match, 2011 was the game when I felt I had demonstrated my full potential for the first time. Perhaps my decision to seek out other possibilities in the middle of the season was critical to my starting to deliver on that potential. It had given me something to think about aside from football. Winning the premiership was a massive triumph and so too was being a pivotal player in the Grand Final. But falling back in love with footy again was the best thing of all. Perhaps I had a career in the game after all.

15

Great moments

Having such a big impact in the 2011 Grand Final meant a lot to me and provided a massive confidence boost heading into the next season, as I took up the role as our leading key position player in attack following the retirement of Cameron Mooney. But it was not only my deeds in the Grand Final that boosted my confidence. My form in the two months leading into that match had also been consistent and I no longer felt like I was a fringe player. I believed I now truly belonged.

There was a clarity in my thinking – everything I had worked on with my coaches through the previous seasons was starting to click and there was proof of this in matches. It was not only the goals I kicked. To that stage of my career, I had been cast as a leading forward, though I felt my contesting work was reasonable for a player of my age and experience. I wanted to become a proper contesting forward, believing this would add another facet to my game and make me harder to defend against.

I went to work during that pre-season with Matt Scarlett, then towards the tail end of his career but still such a phenomenal player. In his last few seasons, he really helped me with my craft and I always looked to man up with him during training sessions. He would beat me in these contested situations far more than I was able to edge him. But those moments when I did get the better of him were becoming more frequent, bolstering my self-belief.

While I was shouldering more responsibility, it was nothing compared to the burden assumed by Joel Selwood, who was given the honour of replacing Cameron Ling as captain after he had retired after the premiership. I was certain Joel would captain the club at some stage, but I thought he was too young then, at 23, even with his obvious maturity, to take on such a significant role. My doubts were not through any lack of faith in Joel's leadership qualities; rather, I was the same age as him and knew there was absolutely no way that I would have been able to handle the role, but, with great support from his teammates and senior off-field mentors at the club, he thrived in the role. It was unbelievable.

* * *

Our premiership defence started slowly. We were edged by Fremantle by four points in Perth in an amazing game of footy. The Dockers jumped us early, kicking the first five goals of the match, but we were able to draw level midway through the second term after finally settling into a rhythm. In the end, Fremantle champion Matt Pavlich kicked a ripper off the ground to secure their win shortly before the final siren. For me, four goals was a reasonable start to the season.

The following week we went up against our great rivals Hawthorn and managed to win another thriller by two points, a heart-thumping start to our bid for back-to-back premierships. After round 8, with a win-loss at four-four, it was clear to all that we were going to have to improve significantly.

Despite the team's struggle for consistency, my good form continued, and I booted 21 goals in those eight matches, including six goals against the Lions in round 5.

After losing to Collingwood by two goals in round 8, after we had drawn level in time-on, we were able to turn our form around, winning seven of our next nine leading into our return clash with Hawthorn. This was another amazing game, which is not surprising given so many of our clashes against the Hawks were absolute classics. But of all those clashes, this was the most memorable for me. We started like a rocket, kicking nine goals in the opening term to take a 45-point lead into quarter-time but the Hawks gradually reeled us in, but they were still 19 points behind at the last change.

They kicked the first two goals of the last quarter before James Podsiadly gave us a 13-point margin. That last quarter was one for the game's highlight reels, especially for Geelong fans, and for me. After Pods' goal, I added another to restore our three-quarter-time lead before the Hawks kicked four unanswered goals, taking the lead for the first time in the match. When I scored another goal deep in time-on, their margin was reduced to four points.

It was then for my moment in the sun. With less than a minute left on the clock, the ball was situated deep in their attack and our chances of pulling off another win appeared doomed. It looked as though our eight-game winning streak against the Hawks – and the Kennett Curse – was about to come to an end.

The passage that unfolded next is something I remember vividly and fondly. Hawk forward Paul Puopolo kicked the footy from mid-air on the goal line in a bid to boot the sealer, but the ball instead fell into the arms of Andrew Mackie on the last line of defence. He was able to boot it to Mitch Duncan, who turned quickly and hit a leading Steve Johnson on the chest on the half-back flank. Johnson spotted Joel Selwood, who one minute earlier had been crunched in a contest, in the centre, and he was able to hold a mark despite pressure from Brad Sewell. He played on as I led from the half-forward flank back towards the middle of the ground and he found me with a well-weighted pass just outside the 50-metre arc. There were just 20 seconds left in the match.

I'd enjoyed a ripper of a night already, having kicked five goals to that stage, but I was a long way out and immediately looked around for options, with Tom Lonergan rushing up to me, telling me to pass it to Jimmy Bartel, who had found some space in the forward pocket.

But I also felt confident with the challenge ahead and thought that I had the distance in my kicking leg. I joke now that I was about 80 metres out but in truth, I was about 55 metres from goal and was full of confidence and belief after the night I had enjoyed.

The siren sounded as I was running in to launch the kick but did not prove a distraction. In such moments, you are only focused on the task ahead. I struck the ball as sweetly as I ever have, and I knew after the footy had travelled about 20 metres that it was going to be a goal. I was ecstatic as I watched it sail straight through the middle, having fulfilled another boyhood dream of kicking a match-winner after the siren on the MCG.

I had practised that moment a thousand times in the backyard when growing up, imagining that Geelong were five points down in a match and I needed to kick the winning goal. I could not quite believe that it actually panned out the same way as it did in my childhood dreams.

To manage it against our greatest rival made the moment even sweeter. I was mobbed by my teammates as I jumped into the air to celebrate, with Steve Johnson giving me a boost as the pack of my teammates formed around me. It was a moment to savour.

In the second half of the season we dropped only three more matches, but our surge in form came too late for us to book a top-four spot and we suffered a frustrating loss to Fremantle in the elimination final, in part due to some poor kicking in front of goal. I was disappointed at being held goalless for only the second time in 2012, with the two behinds I kicked scarcely the way I wanted to finish what had been my best year to date, the first time I had broken the 50-goal barrier, finishing with 62 goals.

* * *

The action on the field ended earlier than we all had hoped, but the remainder of September proved rewarding from an individual sense, though I would swap this for team success every day.

The first highlight came on 17 September when I was named in the All-Australian team for the first time, at full-forward. This was a thrill for me with good reason. Given the stunning success of the Cats in my first five seasons at the club, it was understandable that several of my teammates had been named All-Australians each year.

The 2007 team featured a staggering nine Cats, with Mark Bomber Thompson the coach. The next season seven of the 10 Cats named in the 40-man provisional squad made the cut. In 2009 we had five All-Australians. A further six were named in 2010, while in 2011, it was three.

When you break that down, it is a stunning performance. Over a five-year period, more than one quarter of the All-Australian teams had come from the mighty Cats, a remarkable salute to our squad, so to be able to join Darren Milburn, Joel Selwood, Matthew Egan, Gary Ablett Jnr, Jimmy Bartel, Joel Corey, Cameron Ling, Corey Enright, Paul Chapman, Harry Taylor, Matthew Scarlett, Tom Harley, James Kelly, Steve Johnson and Cameron Mooney, was really cool.

To consider some of those who were named in 2012 and others who missed out made it even more special, because I was the only Cat from Selwood, Enright, Lonergan and Taylor from the initial squad of 40 players who made it through to the final team. They were all teammates I had the highest respect for.

The calibre of forwards I was named alongside is also remarkable, with the great Buddy Franklin stationed at centre half-forward and his fellow Hawk Cyril Rioli to one side of him and Patrick Dangerfield, who was then at Adelaide and yet to join the Cats, on the other flank.

Alongside me in the forward pocket was Dean Cox who, as I described earlier, is one of the best players I have ever seen, while sharking the pair of us was St Kilda's Stephen Milne, a highly talented small forward who knew where the goals were. It was an almighty attack and one that would have given every defender in the competition a nightmare, even those players who were named as 2012 All-Australian defenders!

* * *

Even though I was now an All-Australian and had finished equal-second in the Coleman Medal behind Richmond's Jack Riewoldt, who had kicked 65 goals, I received a bigger surprise at our best-and-fairest dinner.

I arrived at the Carji Greeves Medal count thinking that, for the first time in my career, I might feature on the leaderboard for a decent period of the count. That says something about my impact in the years beforehand, as I am pretty sure the leaderboard runs down to 20th in terms of the players in contention and I had never been in that number before. To finish somewhere in the top five would have been a brilliant result, but I was certain Joel Selwood would win his second medal to go with his 2010 success.

To see my name in contention late in the night and finally be honoured with the Carji Greeves Medal was truly a great moment. It was a close thing: I polled 1394 votes, beating Joel (1388) and Corey Enright (2009 and 2011 winner, on 1380). That's a lot of votes. In 2012 the system was convoluted, with the five coaches rating each player out of 20, so the maximum for a player in any round is 100 points. There was a catch too – only a player's best 19 games were counted. I played 22 games that season, so perhaps the two games I was goalless were discarded!

Perhaps Joel was unlucky: in the Brownlow, he polled 14 votes to my 10.

Dealing with individual accolades in a team game is never an easy thing. Some handle it better than others and for most of your career, you tend to downplay personal achievements. But this was a real thrill, not just for me but also for my family given our extensive history at the club. My father was absolutely thrilled. According to club historian Bob Gartland, Dad finished in the top 10 in the Carji Greeves Medal five times, with top-five finishes in 1976 and 1978. Aside from my win in 2012, I managed a further six top-five finishes in the Carji after that and was in the top 10 ten times, clear evidence of my consistency in the second half of my career.

* * *

Often you will hear a player say that an individual award is something they will reflect on once their career is over and there is truth in that, because the importance of improving from one week to the next is something that is drilled into players from the start of their careers. There is no time to rest on your laurels and little benefit in thinking you can ease off on the training track from one match to the next.

One bonus of winning the Carji Greeves Medal is that it allowed me to engage in cheeky banter around the club. It really was such a special night for me in a season when I reached the 100-game mark and took out Geelong's goalkicking award for the first time. Having felt so much uncertainty about my career just a year earlier, it was nice to see the hard work and sacrifices

I had made were worth it and that my career was finally coming together. To be able to celebrate alongside my family, who have such a rich history with Geelong and provided so much support for me, made the night even more memorable.

There is a tradition each Carji Greeves Medal night of recognising former winners if they are in the room and that is something I have really enjoyed in the years since my 2012 triumph. I love spending time around the club and with my former teammates, so I'm looking forward to getting to as many of those nights as possible in the future. It really will be one to put in the diary each year.

* * *

The off-season was also one to remember as Emma and I headed off overseas to enjoy a longer break than usual. Winning the best and fairest was something to celebrate, but it was important to be able to take some time away from the game with my future wife. We chose New York and Mexico to take a break. I'm a country boy at heart but New York is one of the great cities in the world and being able to enjoy those experiences with Emma is something I just loved.

But after the best season of my career, I was ready to get back into it when we returned home. As I told Geelong's yearbook: 'It sounds silly, but you just need to get back into a routine. Holidays are great, but routines are what you need.' Had I known what was to come over the next 12 months, Emma and I would have spent far longer in the Big Apple.

16

Old man's back

THAT A SEASON from hell would unfold in 2013 is not something I was expecting when I arrived at Falls Creek with my teammates for a testing pre-season camp late in 2012. Fresh from the holiday abroad and full of confidence after winning the Carji Greeves Medal, I felt ready to conquer Mt Everest. The Victorian Alps are far from Mt Everest but a training camp at altitude is challenging as we set about rebounding from the disappointing elimination final loss to Fremantle.

Perhaps more than challenging! My thighs were screaming with pain on a 30-kilometre ride bike ride from Mt Beauty to the top of Falls Creek, a rise of 1100 metres, although my later comments to the Geelong website might have been a little over the top: 'It's bloody tough and mentally challenging. But it's one of those things that you finish and think, "How good is that?" You get so much out of it,' I said. 'We'll all be telling stories about it throughout the year because you know nothing is going to be as hard as having to ride from the bottom of Mt Beauty up to Falls Creek.'

It turned out that I could not have been more wrong with that prediction. There is a saying about golf that just when you think you have mastered it, the game has a way of biting you back. Footy is the same. Within months of earning an All-Australian guernsey and winning Geelong's best and fairest, I was struggling to walk some mornings, suffering from chronic back pain. Despite a strong start to the year – 25 goals in my first eight games – the knives were soon out. My critics – some Geelong fans and many in the media – were quick to note that my form had dipped in the space of just a few months. Despite the goals I kicked, they were right.

For the best part of 12 months I dealt with the serious pain, caused by an instability in my back muscles and I have no doubt that had the pain lingered for much longer, it would have brought an end to my career, such was the impact it was having on my quality of life. When the pain was at its worst, I was going through a tube of *Deep Heat* a day. Anyone who has ever suffered from a bad back will know just how debilitating it can be. The pain can make even the most mundane of exercises a real mental battle. It can also take a toll on your emotional wellbeing.

Geelong's physiotherapists put the problem down to the fact that there was a significant disparity in the strength of the muscles connecting with each other in my lower back and, as a result, they were not working together. Once that diagnosis was made, an extended break from playing would have allowed my back to realign but given the uncertainty surrounding the issue, it was decided that managing the condition while playing on was the best option. Every month or so, I would have an epidural cortisone injection into the space around the spinal cord and I also took a lot of anti-inflammatory tablets that year, under the guidance of our medical staff.

The injury affected everything – from my form, which really suffered when the pain was at its worst, to my mood. I was unable to get out for a round of golf to free my mind or make regular trips to Melbourne to visit Emma and other friends without readying myself for the discomfort of sitting in the car for an hour or more both ways.

Every day I would take a powerful painkiller to ease the symptoms and at night I would be back and forward to the microwave, warming up wheat and rice packs in the hope the heat might provide some comfort. Broken periods of sleep did not help my mental health or my mood.

It really was a hellish year.

I can trace the cause of my back complaint to the bad habits I picked up while working on the farm in Finley during my youth and also whenever I ducked back there to give Dad a hand. Picking up things the wrong way was the issue. When you are working on the farm, you are often bending over to grab various heavy objects and then tossing them into the back of a ute. From hay bales to pieces of machinery needed a tune-up, I would use my heft to throw things into the truck without giving much thought to the consequences.

The size of my legs and glutes might have fooled some people into thinking I could lift heavy weights, particularly while doing squats in the gym. I had the size, but I certainly did not have a great core strength or power, and, in truth, I was among the worst at squats at the Cats in both technique and the weights I could lift.

With the benefit of hindsight, I realised that there were warning signs of the problem to come in each of the pre-seasons I had completed. As the training load and intensity increased in the middle part of each pre-season, my back would always stiffen up and I would feel some pain. But in 2013, this was something different altogether.

* * *

The failure of the injury to correct itself through the pre-season, as it tended to do when I was younger, or into the season despite the ongoing medical intervention, was extremely frustrating. I felt I was coming into the peak of my powers and ready to take another step forward for the club, but instead I needed help just to tie my shoelaces.

It really was an eye-opening experience. Until that stage, the only serious problem I had dealt with was the navicular injury that forced me to miss the latter stages of the 2008 season. That period on the sidelines was enough to alert me to the fact I did not handle injuries all that well. Not being able to train or play is something that has always bothered me. This was another level of frustration, because even acts as simple as getting in and out of the car could be excruciating.

Another irritating factor was that on some days I felt reasonable, and it would seem I was finally on top of the problem, but on other occasions I would have preferred to stay in bed. The uncertainty of not knowing how I would feel from one day to the next made the issue more complex, as it was almost impossible to plan anything with surety.

From a playing perspective, the club and I tried to mask the extent of the problem throughout the season, even though it was evident in my form and my movement that something was wrong. There were a couple of moments, for example, where I was unable to bend over when trying to pick up the footy, which drew the derision of those in the grandstands.

To manage the issue, I scarcely did any work on the training track from one week to the next, which caused another problem as my aerobic capabilities dipped and my weight started to edge back towards the 113kg I was carrying when I first arrived at Geelong as a teenager. You'd never know these days as the AFL has banned the publication of player's weight. I'm not sure whether the weights released by the clubs were ever accurate anyway – in the AFL's official guide to season 2007 my weight was listed at 105kgs; if only!

* * *

In the round 8 clash against Collingwood, I managed to boot four goals, and a week later against Port Adelaide, I kicked a season-high six goals, but the longer the season went, the more I began to struggle. I still had my moments, and some days were better than others, and against the Saints in round 18, I managed to kick five goals. I was all but shot by that stage. The last few months were a misery, and the reaction of the fans made my mood even worse.

I can still hear the Bronx cheers from the crowd when I

managed a solitary goal from five kicks in the return match against Port Adelaide in round 20 at Kardinia Park, a strong win by us, although we gave away a 63-point lead in the third quarter to get home by 25 points. I have always believed in the adage that if you take your spot on the field, you are fair game and open to criticism, no matter the circumstances.

There was one moment in particular which prompted some Geelong fans to unload on me. The ground was a bit of a bog and as the footy was coming towards me, it skidded and hit my shins. It certainly did not look great as I failed to bend over, and it was one of those instances when the fans lost patience with me. Their reaction prompted a stinging defence from Chris Scott after the match, when speaking to *Fox Footy*. 'I heard some of our supporters almost come out with the Bronx cheers,' he said. 'It's embarrassing. It is embarrassing for all of Geelong. We've got some pretty ugly supporters if that is the case. They've been well looked after for a long time, and we expect better.'

After the match, it was decided that the best strategy was to go public with the issues I was dealing with. An interview was arranged with my former captain Cameron 'Lingy' Ling, on Channel Seven. In our chat I explained I had been battling a bulging disc for some time and why I had trouble bending down to pick up the footy in the Port Adelaide game: 'I just wasn't expecting it to come in so quickly. It skidded in and bounced into my shins, and it did not look good. I looked like an old man.' I told Lingy I was really thankful that Chris had been so strong in his defence of me given the pain I was dealing with. 'I've known throughout my career that I've had the support of my coach and my footy club and my teammates, but I can see why the crowd is frustrated. I'm sure I can be very frustrating at times for supporters,' I said.

The Bronx cheers were deflating because I was putting in so much work and was trying my hardest. It added insult to the injury and to my frustration. I felt like I was on a hiding to nothing – I could have stepped aside and missed three months trying to get my back right, but instead I was doing all that I could to perform.

During that press conference, Chris made what I believed to be another salient point. Despite the difficulties I was dealing with, he noted I had still been able to kick 45 goals to that stage. 'Tom is a handful forward,' he said. 'He's a handful for even the best opposition. We're comfortable with what Tom is giving us but no-one in our team's got a golden ticket. Tom would like to be playing better, but I don't think he was disgraceful by any stretch.'

This was the message that Chris and the rest of the coaching staff had relayed to me when my back was at its worst. Clearly, I was not as influential around the ground as I had been a season earlier but being able to take on a leading defender each week and still managing to kick goals was a benefit to the club.

The Cats enjoyed another great season, dropping just four games to earn a home qualifying final, but I was far from confident in my body or ability to perform, and it was apparent to me early in the week leading into what was a unique final on our home ground against Fremantle that I would need a miracle to take my place.

My back had deteriorated, and it was likely I would be more of a hindrance than a help if I played and although I did my level best to try to ease the pain and the tightness, ultimately, I fell short. But so too did the Cats, unfortunately, in a loss that effectively derailed another premiership campaign.

I was able to return for the second semi-final against Port Adelaide, and at least contributed in our victory with a couple of goals, but we came up short against Hawthorn when beaten in another thriller by five points in the preliminary final, after we had led by 20 points at three-quarter-time. That match ended an 11-game winning streak against the Hawks, dating back to the 2008 Grand Final. They went on to win the premiership, the first of a three-peat.

For all the trouble I went through in a bid to get on the ground that year, which included dozens of hours spent with Geelong's physiotherapists, my season appeared reasonable from a statistical sense, as I topped the club's goalkicking for the second time, finishing with 49 goals. I have often wondered whether Geelong might have snared a fourth premiership in seven years if I had been fully fit. There is no answer to that question.

* * *

Rectifying the problem leading into the 2014 season was a clear priority, for obvious reasons. The club appointed a new head of sports science and sports medicine, Peter Stanton, who specialised in spinal issues. He had extensive experience, working with outstanding athletes, having spent a decade at the Australian Institute of Sport, a role which saw him work with national teams at Olympics, World Championships and Commonwealth Games. Importantly, he understood the demands on footy players, having worked with the Brisbane Lions between 1999 and 2006. Along with Geelong's strength and conditioning staff, Peter developed a plan that would allow me to rebuild my back so it could withstand the rigours of footy. The early stages of that program involved really simple twisting movements done at a low intensity and low speed which made me feel like I was a little kid some days, given their simplicity. It took a long time to build up strength again through my lower back and I was not 100 per cent fit throughout the 2014 season, but it was an improvement on 2013.

When I look at photographs from that period, I was clearly carrying additional weight. I had crept back to about 110kg due to the restrictions in my training, in particular running and cardiovascular exercises. As a result, I played far closer to goal than I had in previous seasons and, despite these restrictions, I enjoyed a good season, kicking 68 goals, which is still the highest in my career.

The period a few years earlier when I was playing as a hybrid forward and ruckman really helped me in marking contests at a time when I was not able to cover as much ground, but the biggest plus was being pain free again. Everything in life felt better.

* * *

We enjoyed another strong home-and-away finishing third, on percentage, behind Sydney and Hawthorn – all of us with 17 wins. We began the finals believing we were a strong chance to win the premiership if we were able to produce our best footy. We had enjoyed some good wins during the year, including a triumph over Hawthorn in round 5 by 19 points, a match that was my best for the year given the calibre of the opposition, even though the five goals I kicked that night was short of the seven I booted at the tail end of the season, against Brisbane in round 23.

Unfortunately, our best form deserted us and we were knocked out. The Hawks overpowered us by six goals in the qualifying final at the MCG and although I managed to kick five goals a week later, the Kangaroos were able to edge us out by a goal in the semi-final. Losing in straight sets is the worst way to end a season – short of a Grand Final loss.

For a side that had experienced so much September success in the first seven years of my career, to exit without really firing a shot in that campaign was more than disappointing.

17

Missing my greatest supporter

WHENEVER THERE IS a clear night at our home just outside Geelong, I'll take our kids outside after dinner and try to find the biggest and brightest star in the evening sky. I'll point to it and tell them that star is their Grandma Jennie looking down at them from the heavens with a lot of love.

Mum, who died of oesophageal cancer in April 2015, did not live to see my marriage to Emma or the birth of our children. She missed out on another Geelong premiership and so many great celebrations among our family and our friends.

It is an idea I picked up from Erin Johnson, the wife of Steve Johnson, after she lost her dad a couple of years before Mum died and wanted to make sure that her children knew all about who he was and what he meant to their family. My mum was a guiding light in my life, and in this way she can continue to shine her star onto my kids. These moments with the kids are special, but it is also a good chance to keep alive Mum's legacy.

She grew up in Barwon Heads and went to school at Geelong College before meeting Dad at a local dance while he was playing with the Cats. Mum was then working as a dental nurse and after they married and moved to Finley to begin a life together on the farm, she continued that career. She absolutely loved the Finley community and devoted so much time to helping out at the local schools, the Finley Football Club and any other organisations that required a hand or a form of leadership.

Mum was part of the fabric of the region and was determined to make things better for those living in the community. She gave a lot more than what she was ever given, such was her community spirit.

She served as a Berriguin councillor between 2004 and 2008 and was also a former president of the Deniliquin National Party branch. She was instrumental in setting up the Murray Hut CWA in Finley, where she served as the president and also the treasurer. She was also a Nuffield Scholar, an honour received from one of the nation's leading agricultural bodies whose aim is to bring positive change to agriculture through the development of its future leaders, and was awarded a Centenary Medal from the Australian Government for her services to regional communities.

Mum was also at the forefront of driving change at Springfield, with a particular focus on the important issue of climate change. In 2013 she told the Climate Champion Series, 'It's only when we get involved that we learn more and understand the importance of what drives us for a better and more sustainable future. Whether those conditions are climate or economic, we need to be flexible enough to be able to change and adapt to them. In the past, we just made farming decisions that were based on weather rather than climate. Our future farming leaders ... will be farmers adapting and understanding the changing climate alongside the "experts". I am inspired by everyone who is committed to developing sustainable practices today that protect our tomorrows.'

Mum was a very generous woman in so many ways. She tried to make time for everyone, and she had the most infectious laugh, the type that would ignite the room around her. There are plenty of days when I really miss hearing that laugh.

She never forgot her roots and continued to serve the school that she attended long after both her education and also those of my sisters were completed, as a member of The Geelong College Council from 2007 until her death. A scholarship at Geelong College recognising leadership in young, rural-based women and enhancing co-education, diversity and excellence in girls' education, is named in her honour. 'Jennie put quite a lot of work into the girls' boarding side of Geelong College and that led ... to the idea,' Dad told the *Deniliquin Pastoral Times* after her death. 'Geelong College has had a good presence in the Riverina, and we wanted to highlight that as well as continue Jennie's passion of inspiring young women in leadership roles.'

As the parents of two daughters, this is something that Emma and I are passionate about as well. But when I speak to my kids about Mum, I want to make them laugh as much as possible so that they enjoy their time learning about their grandmother, because I think that is the most appropriate tribute to someone who loved the lighter side of life.

One thing she absolutely insisted on was that her name be spelt as Jennie. She was never Jenny with a 'Y' and she hated it when a letter or email arrived with her name spelt like that.

I can see a lot of Mum in me and also in her granddaughter, Arabella, with our taste for chocolate a massive weakness we inherited from her. That led to a nickname for me that Mum loved and one that I still get today – 'Tim Tam Tommy'. Devouring these chocolate-coated biscuits the night before games was my guilty pleasure, a habit that started when we were playing in Adelaide in 2013. Some teammates and I went for a walk the night before a game against Port Adelaide and I was feeling hungry and bought some Tim Tams. My teammates ribbed me, but the next day I went out and kicked six goals, my high for the year.

Josh Walker, who was in his second season with Geelong and who gave me the nickname, asked me a few days later how many biscuits I had eaten and I told him it matched the number goals I kicked! Josh later moved on to play with Brisbane and North Melbourne and whenever we were due to play, I'd text him the night before games with a number – it might be five, six or even 10. 'Be ready for me to kick a bag against you tomorrow, Josh.'

* * *

Mum was never one to complain about feeling unwell and would find a way to soldier through whatever it was that was bothering her. Getting on with the job was the habit of her lifetime, an ethic she passed on to all of us. I'm far from tough, but even a simple thing like taking a Panadol for a headache was not something we ever did when growing up. You just kept on pushing through.

But in the latter stages of 2014 it became clear to the family that Mum was unwell. She was getting really bad recurring headaches and was struggling to show her usual zest for life. As a result, she decided that she should see her doctor while in Geelong on a visit to see her parents. True to form, she had not told any of her kids that she was going through a rough patch, though Dad was obviously aware that something was wrong. Because I was living in Geelong, Mum asked me to come along for an appointment after she had undergone a series of tests and scans. That is when we were told the bad news.

I don't think I will ever forget the awful moment when the doctor told Mum that the scans showed she had a tumour growing on her oesophagus. She became really distressed and it was not too long before I became really upset as well. I'd been lucky up until that stage and I did not have much experience with people being sick and it was such a shock that I immediately feared the worst for Mum and our family.

It was decided that she would stay with her parents at Barwon Heads, her 'happy place', as she underwent bouts of chemotherapy nearby. Her approach to the illness was to try to do the best that she could in fighting the cancer. It is strange when I look back at it now, particularly as Mum was so unwell, but I was relieved and proud to be able to spend time with her and offer support when she was receiving treatment, as much as I wish I had never had to do so.

Although she was knocked around by the chemotherapy, the initial results were positive and it was decided that she could stop the treatment for a period early in 2015 and head back to Springfield, which boosted our hopes. But it was not long before those awful headaches came back and when she returned to Geelong for further testing, it was discovered the cancer had spread beyond the original tumour.

She was admitted to St John of God Hospital in Geelong and Dad came down from the farm as we all hoped for the best. Not surprisingly, footy became a more distant concern for me, though I still fulfilled my obligations from a training and playing perspective.

Even though Mum had been unwell for a few months, that moment in April, when the specialist told us that she would not be getting better, struck me like a bolt from the blue. We were advised to start getting the family together for a farewell as Mum might have less than a week to live. This was such a shock because, to me anyway, Mum still looked okay.

One thing that stood out to me throughout this entire traumatic period was that Dad was just unbelievable in the leadership and empathy he displayed for all of his kids, immediately turning his mind to helping everyone in the family.

We contacted my siblings to let them know the news. The call that I made to my brother Charlie, who was in his first year at Bond University on the Gold Coast, is probably the toughest I have ever had to make, given he was so young and so far away.

Given our extensive family history with Geelong, the Cats reacted with love and dignity while providing as much support as possible. Most at the club had been aware for a few months that Mum was not well and right at the start of Mum's sickness, Chris urged me to let him know if I ever needed anything. Several others were the same. Once we knew Mum would not receover, I met Chris in the car park, in front of the club, and I broke down sobbing as I told him that Mum would not recover. Football may be a business, but clubs are very much a family and when someone is going through a testing time, the whole club will rally around them.

I was a late withdrawal from the round 3 clash against the Gold Coast as Mum died on the weekend, just five days after the specialist had spoken to me and Dad. A small consolation is that while it was a traumatic period, all our family members were able to get to Geelong to spend time with Mum during her last few days.

I am so relieved that as a family, we all had the chance to tell her how much we loved her.

* * *

The Cat who dug the deepest to help me through this time will scarcely surprise you. From the time it became clear that Mum was seriously ill, and through those difficult days, months and years after her death, Joel Selwood was a constant source of support. It might have been a text message to check how I was going each day. Or a brief phone call. At training and in matches, he would do his best to assist me, knowing that I was struggling to hold myself together as I dealt with the loss of Mum.

Joel was the first person off the Geelong bus in Finley on the day of Mum's funeral and I was so grateful to know that so many of my teammates were there to pay tribute to a wonderful woman. It is testament to Joel's care that he did not realise just how helpful he was to me and my family through this period as I came to terms with our loss.

In fact, he has since told me that he really wished he could have done more. 'It was a really tough time. We all knew Jennie was sick, but I felt too young to understand that, "Holy shit, she is going to pass away",' Joel said. 'I really don't think I did a great job through that time as a mate. The whole thing really didn't sit well with me. So, I think I tell a different story about that time to Tom. I'm like, "I could have been so much better." He had Emma there. And I would go around him at times to check in with Emma to ask, "Hey, is he all right?" I'm not sure that we gave him enough love at the time. Not that he needed a lot of love in his life, because he has always been a giver. He loves giving more than receiving so when he did receive it, you know, he probably remembered it a bit more. But I felt weird about it.' It was not until much later that Joel told me this, but I think when people reflect on significant moments in their lives or those they are close to, it is not uncommon to believe that they could have done more.

I was a closed book at the time because I still wanted people to be normal around me, rather than treating me differently. It never felt to me like Joel, or any of my friends or teammates, could have done any more. Joel's support was more than enough and something I greatly appreciated.

* * *

Even though I kept playing footy and produced some good form at different stages over the next couple of seasons, I really struggled through what was an extended grieving period.

I occasionally wonder whether I should have taken some time off and if that would have made a difference to my ability to cope. I did feel dirty with the world for a while and I'm certain that in everyday dealings, I became more impatient and snappy with people. Before I played my 350th game, in 2024, I was interviewed by Glenn McFarlane, for the *Herald* Sun. I told him about that time: 'It was certainly a frustrating period in my life. There was no coincidence. I wasn't enjoying my footy as much. I am more a lover than a fighter, but I think it was a period when I was a little frustrated.'

That was so true. I really did feel more negative about life, which was an attitude that is completely at odds with my usual approach, and I was particularly concerned that everyone else had forgotten how wonderful a person Mum was, while I was feeling anxious that my memory of her would fade as well. I wondered how I would go moving forward with my life without her guidance, given how much she had understood and helped me.

At one stage midway through the season, I even asked the footy manager if I would have been able to get a transfer back to Finley to play for the local Cats to enable me to spend some time at home.

It wasn't quite a throwaway line, but it was certainly a spur-of-the-moment question, in part to gauge whether there was any room for me to have time away. Had I pursued it more earnestly, I am certain the Cats would have granted me time away from the club to mourn, but I doubt that would have extended to playing elsewhere.

It was another sign of my confusion and frustration, but in hindsight I have no doubt that spending time with my teammates, and at the club, helped me to recover, even though it was a lengthy process.

Time, it is said, heals all wounds but I'm not convinced that's the case when it comes to the loss of your loved ones. There was no sudden moment for me when I flicked the switch. But gradually I worked through that intense sadness and learnt to appreciate all the good parts of my life again.

I would have loved Mum to have been at our wedding, to have met our kids, and to have watched them growing up. It is not to be, but I feel so lucky to have had her as my mum. Even now I get a little upset when I have a big milestone match because I know Mum would have loved being there to celebrate it.

18

A magnificent leader

I HAD BEEN AT Geelong for almost a fortnight, trying to keep pace in the pre-season, when the 2006 AFL National draft night took place, on November 25.

Although I knew I would be selected as a father–son recruit, I was keen to find out which players would join me at the Cats. I could not believe it when Geelong called out Joel Selwood's name with pick 7 after Carlton had picked Glenelg's Bryce Gibbs as the year's top draftee. My initial reaction to Joel's selection was: 'How good is this? I actually know who he is, and he seems like a really good guy', although I would have been hard-pressed to say a good word about him based on our first meeting on the footy field.

In 2005, when I was playing for the Sandringham Dragons in the TAC Cup, we travelled to Bendigo for a game and it was not too long before Joel made himself known on the field.

I was well aware of his reputation heading into that game, not least because his older brothers, Adam, an Eagle, and Troy, a Lion, were already playing in the AFL. Joel's younger brother, Scott, was also a quality player, as he proved when winning a best and fairest with West Coast before joining us at Geelong between 2016 and 2019.

When I was boarding at Melbourne Grammar, Xavier Ellis was always talking Joel up as a likely top draftee in my age group. They had travelled together in an Australian Institute of Sport side and got on well, and Joel had earned a reputation of being an absolute gun. But there were concerns among recruiters about the health of his knees after he experienced some injury concerns as a teenager.

There must have been something about being back in the bush for me, but I enjoyed a really good day in that game in Bendigo, kicking a bag of goals.

Joel was simply outstanding for the opposition and I have no doubt he was best afield in a losing side. But it was not just his footy skills that stood out to me that day. His ability with the lip when delivering sledges was just as strong and he seemed to have an insatiable appetite for it.

Don't get me wrong. I have enjoyed engaging in a bit of banter with opponents during my career, particularly when the timing was right. Although I was never an A-grader when it came to sledging, I have received some rippers on occasion and most of the time, they made me chuckle.

But Joel was absolutely relentless that day, although not much of what he had to say is printable. Every time I was running in to kick for goal that day, he called me every name under the sun. It seemed like he took a particular delight in sledging me, perhaps because he knew how close I was with Xavier.

On the bus back to Melbourne that night, I can remember shaking my head, unnerved by how competitive he had been. He later told me, 'It was just how I played as a kid' and it was indicative of the fierce competitor in him. The following year, Joel dropped by the boarding house at Melbourne Grammar on a couple of occasions when in town to catch up with Xavier.

It was not long before I realised that what I had witnessed in that under-18 match was simply a case of white-line fever. Away from the field and with no footy to be won, Joel was far more relaxed.

When asked about his memories of that day at Golden Square, he said that I stood out as a man mountain among boys. 'Tom was massive. He probably weighed close to the most he has ever weighed. He came down and I think kicked six or seven for the day. We had no answers. There were four or five schoolkids who had compulsory school footy, and when they went back to their under-18 teams, like Tom did that day, they would change the competition.'

* * *

From the day Joel arrived at Geelong, the local paper earmarked him as a future captain of the club. There is always a lot of hype surrounding young players, particularly those who are selected in the first round, but the predictions about Joel were spot on. In almost every measure imaginable, he was a ready-made senior footballer.

The sheer desperation that he had to win every single contest during his career is something that made him one of the best players in the competition. He was ruthless in the way he attacked the ball and every contest. I'd be hard-pressed to imagine someone who put their head over the footy more consistently over such a long period. That led to some brutal knocks, scrapes and injuries. There was a time when it seemed as though he was getting assisted off the ground every second week, finishing matches wearing more bandages around his head than an Egyptian mummy.

His passion for Geelong has been immense since the day he was drafted. He joined the Cats determined to have an impact on the club and to ensure his time at Kardinia Park was a success. To say that he delivered on that is an understatement. But he also has great compassion and will find a way to assist someone if they are seen to be struggling. When I have needed him most, he provided wonderful support. Those attributes, to me, are as much a sign of strong leadership as his performances on the field.

* * *

From his opening game, it was clear Geelong had a bona fide star in the making. Joel made his debut a week before me in the opening game of the 2007 season against the Western Bulldogs. He was never one to burst away from a pack like Chris Judd or Patrick Dangerfield, but his skills and decision-making, combined with his prodigious hunger to win the footy and the bravery of his play, made him the complete package. The high level of his skill is something which has been overshadowed by his leadership and his courage, but his skills were as good as anyone. His ability to place passes to perfection, or to spot a gap in order to bring a teammate into the play, were exceptional. He also proved remarkably durable.

While my form faded after a promising start in our opening season, Joel just got better and better. There have been few more brilliant starts to a career than his debut season and he was a dominant winner of the Ron Evans Medal as the AFL's Rising Star. Most importantly, he also finished the year a premiership player.

* * *

There are a couple of treasured memories involving Joel that really stand out in my mind. The 2009 premiership, clearly, is one. And so, too, our final game together in the 2022 Grand Final, as the emotion of our embrace after his great goal late in the game showed in spades.

Having watched Joel and then Xavier Ellis enjoy the ultimate success in footy in successive seasons, it was my turn to join the party in the 2009 season. To be able to celebrate the flag alongside Joel, and to know that I contributed to what proved to be a thrilling Grand Final triumph over St Kilda, is a cherished memory.

The decider a couple of years later against Collingwood is another memory I treasure. We both played particularly well in that Grand Final, which made it an even more satisfying success. There is a photograph from after that match that I love, with Joel and me celebrating with Travis Varcoe, a fantastic teammate who later joined the Pies.

Joel was already established as a proper leader by that stage, and I was starting to make my mark. In the seasons that followed, we had the type of relationship where, at pivotal moments in matches, we would give each other a nod as if to acknowledge: 'It is time to go here. Time to make a stand.' More often than not, we could deliver.

I'd like to think that over the 11 seasons of his captaincy, I was as supportive to him around the club as possible as he dealt with the demands of captaincy. It might have been something as simple as taking on an additional press conference or passing on a word of encouragement to a young player just making his way at the club. The amount of extra responsibility captains take on is significant. They have to handle so many different facets, from sponsors to player welfare to being the front men for the club, in good times and in periods of difficulty. That is all beyond worrying about their own form, let alone the demands of life outside of footy.

Our friendship and support for each other extended beyond the boundary line. We have shared so many important moments in our life. We have been groomsmen in each other's weddings, celebrated the next generation of our families together and been there to act as a sounding board whenever needed. Long may that continue.

It is hard to imagine anyone has handled the role as club captain as well as Joel did at Geelong, let alone across the broader competition. The day that he broke the AFL record for captaincy sits as one of the proudest days I have had the privilege of being a part of at Geelong. Carlton legend Steve Kernahan, whose leadership record of 226 games Joel broke when we defeated Collingwood at the MCG in round 23, 2022, was full of praise for my mate. He told *The Age*: 'I took it off Dick Reynolds, and he said some lovely things about me. I can say nothing but great things about Joel Selwood. He is a warrior. I have always loved the way he played. I couldn't think of a better, more apt, bloke to have it. And he is still getting it done. Good luck to him to have the record. He is the most deserving bloke to have it.'

I couldn't agree more. When it comes to legends at Geelong, I can't imagine anyone will ever carry more goodwill than my mate Joel.

19

Committed to the Cats

2015 COULDN'T HAVE started worse, but in July, I signed the longest contract of my life, a five-year deal which effectively confirmed I would be a Cat for the entirety of my career. Even with the emotional turmoil I was experiencing, and that I was eligible to move as a free agent, I was now confident in my sense of worth to the team and what I could do to help the club in the future. I had just turned 27 and had played 160 games.

To make that commitment was something I considered carefully. Was I doing the right thing? Could I cope with a contract that would place me among the elite players in the competition in terms of its worth? There was much to weigh up. Such a signing was a leap of faith for the Cats as well, but one I believe was justified given I had continued to improve.

The Cats always balanced the salary cap astutely under footy manager (now CEO) Steve Hocking and were very mindful of the risks associated with signing players for too long or for too much money. Pressure comes from signing a big contract like that. But having worked through the back issue that had plagued me in 2013, I was confident in my body and believed my best was still to come. Hocking also believed I was worthy of the deal and I felt more than ready to assume a more senior role around the club.

As my agent Tom Petroro said, 'We never considered exploring free agency at this time as Tom had always been loyal to the Cats. He did take some time to make a decision as he wanted to make the right call but there was never any consideration about going somewhere else.'

A year that had started so poorly finished on a high when Emma and I got engaged in Fiji at the end of year and we were married just before the season started in 2016 at Oak Hill House on the Bellarine Peninsula, outside Ocean Grove. It is the best day of my life, though the births of our three kids in the years since have run a very close second.

When I headed down to Geelong to begin my career at the Cats at the end of Year 12 in 2006, Emma followed her own dreams after finishing school. She went to Monash University to study a communications degree, with a major in criminology, and landed a great job after graduating with ACP Magazines, later acquired by Bauer Media.

She loved living and working in Melbourne and I'm not sure she was thrilled with the prospect of living in Geelong initially. She did not have the same family connections and familiarity with the town that I did and she also had a great career and plenty of friends in Melbourne.

Not long after the horror year in 2013 when I really struggled with my back, we decided it was time to live together and Emma moved down to Geelong. Emma sacrificed so much in order for us to be together, although we both know it would have been difficult for me to move elsewhere given the importance of both my footy club and the town of Geelong to me.

As Emma explained to the *Herald Sun* shortly after I played my 300th game, she understood more and more as our relationship grew just how deeply connected I was to the Cats: 'When he got to 300 games … we haven't really reflected on it, but it means so much to him and his family,' she said. 'Tom brings so much joy to his family and his friends and it has been such a treat to be on this ride the whole way through. We are so proud.'

It would not be accurate to say Emma sacrificed her whole career after leaving Melbourne, because what she has done in her professional life since moving to Geelong astounds me. The clothing line she runs with her close friend Penny Hunt is brilliant and she also consults with and represents a number of brands that are important to her. Her creativity and adaptability, her entrepreneurial skills and thirst for work are among Emma's many admirable traits.

* * *

The decision to commit to the Cats for five years was vindicated as that period corresponded with the best form of my career and coincided with feeling comfortable and fulfilled in my personal life. There is no doubt our marriage, the birth of Arabella a year later, the arrival of Primrose in 2019 and Henry in the premiership season of 2022, all had a positive impact on my footy career, which really flourished during this period.

I feel like the births of my kids made me more purposeful. All of a sudden, I was carrying extra responsibilities and it was important to me to ensure that I used my time wisely.

When you don't have kids, you don't have to worry about changing nappies, or finding babysitters, or making sure the house and the car are clean. But when you become a parent, even the most mundane things can be important, and being organised to ensure you maximise your time during the day is part of that.

At this time, I was a decade into my career, and I remember pondering how I would be assessed as a player.

Then I felt as though the external assessment of my career would have been something like: 'Tom Hawkins? He was a good player, but he could never quite put it all together for a long enough period to be considered a champion.'

I really wanted to have a period in my career where things went smoothly after seasons interrupted by either a debilitating injury or the difficulties I experienced when grieving after Mum's death.

I had Mum in mind when we bought a farm outside Geelong during 2015. I had lived in Geelong since my first season with the Cats, and Mum had always thought I would be better outside the town, effectively living the life I had so enjoyed at Springfield. As always, she was right. I loved moving back to the land. It brought back so many memories of me going back home and helping Dad, and I could now be doing the same with our kids as I had as a kid, tying in the younger me with the current day product, as a farmer. It's a great release, and it may have been a motivator for others – Jeremy Cameron has done something similar, Rhys Stanley is building a house outside Geelong, and Sam De Koning has moved out of Torquay. I am sure it made a difference for me. Perhaps it's no coincidence that my form since the move out of town has been some of the best of my career.

* * *

Chris Dennis arrived at the start of 2016 as our new strength and conditioning coach and he had a big impact on my performance. Having dealt with the back issues through 2013 and 2014, and then struggling with the death of my mother in 2015, it was a period where I was heavy and was not able to cover the ground as well as I wanted to, and certainly not as well as I had in 2012. Now past my mid-20s, I was acutely aware of the constraints of age and injury. I believed being lighter might extend my time in the game. It was a balancing act because I did not want to lose my strength, given how important it was when it came to contested marking.

To maximise my cardiovascular fitness while maintaining the strength to be able to be a threat in the air, we adapted my workload in the gym. I was still lifting weights, but there was less heavy lifting with a greater load on explosiveness and movement. I was lifting things quicker. Specifically, I wanted to add some pace in those important first 10 metres, and also be light enough to move further afield to provide a linking role as well.

As I explained to the Geelong website during the pre-season, the AFL's decision leading into 2016 – to reduce interchange rotations – was also a factor in my thinking: 'I think as the game continues to evolve and clubs try different ways of playing. and particularly as a power forward, I've had to adapt over the years. This year I've tried to fine down and, with the interchange bench going to 90 rotations, it probably means I spend more time on the ground and less time on the bench. The ability for me to be able to cover more ground, and more often is really important. My mobility to be able to get off the mark quicker is something I have worked on a lot more with Chris Dennis over the pre-season. And then my repeat efforts, my agility and speed over zero to twenty, thirty metres has really improved.'

Chris was great to work with through the five years we had together. He understood me and was great at motivating me, but also when to acknowledge when you did things well during matches, particularly highlighting improvement in areas we had been working on.

There is no doubt it had an impact – I kicked 55.31 in 2016, up from 46.20 the previous season. I also enjoyed an uptick in the number of marks (126 from 93), disposals (288 from 196) and tackles (61 from 43).

* * *

The added responsibilities in my life, both at home and with Geelong, proved important in enabling me to take another big step forward in my career and from the birth of Arabella onwards, that consistency I was after came to the fore. There is no coincidence that this happened when I was feeling really comfortable in life.

20
Champions come and go

FAREWELLING A FRIEND is never easy and because of my lengthy career in footy, I saw many of my closest mates depart the game. It is one of the few certainties about any footy career. At some stage, you will play your final match and for most players, the end comes too quickly with only a small percentage having the luxury of calling time on their career when it suits them. I'm among the fortunate ones in that regard but I am certain a few of my teammates finished before their time, which can be a difficult thing.

Of all the farewells, there are a couple that truly stand out to me as memorable. The embrace I shared with Joel Selwood on the MCG in the moments after our 2022 premiership stands as a defining image of our friendship, even if I did not know at the time that it would be Joel's last game. The other involves our farewell to Steve Johnson, James Kelly and Mat Stokes, all who left Geelong at the end of our testing 2015 season, though Steve subsequently went on to play for two more seasons with GWS, and 'Kel' and 'Stokesy' joined Essendon as top-up players after the Bombers were torn apart by the supplements saga.

Steve, who won the Norm Smith Medal in 2007 and was a three-time All-Australian, is a huge personality and was a teammate I really connected with from day one. In my first pre-season, his career was under a cloud after an off-season misdemeanour in his hometown of Wangaratta. It led the club to impose a five-game ban on him. It proved the turning point of his career, when he returned in round 6, he was so driven and passionate about team success. It is remarkable that he missed the opening five rounds that year yet still managed to kick 49 goals that season.

To carve out the career that he did – he kicked 516 goals in 294 games over 16 seasons – is incredible, given he had to manage ankle problems associated with some tomfoolery that went wrong when jumping the fence at a Torquay pub, along with knee issues and the usual niggles from getting older. His footy smarts allowed him to overcome all those issues.

I loved the way he played footy. His highlight reel features those remarkable moments when he would kick miraculous goals. When Steve was sizzling, he was magical to watch. He was remarkably competitive on the field, but he was also a particularly selfless player who was always looking for opportunities to bring his teammates into the game. Unfortunately, those moments don't make highlight reels – they should.

Watching the way he covered the ground, found space and worked over defenders are traits that helped me develop as a forward. I tried to mirror Steve's craft as much as possible through my career.

The connection he brought to the club was just as strong off the field. He had terrific social skills, which is part of the reason why he has become a sought-after coach since his retirement. In the locker room, he always displayed a great sense of humour, which is a talent that helps to bring together players all across the team. We had great times on the golf course or out on the bay, fishing.

The round 23 clash against Adelaide in 2015, his last game for the Cats, was a curiosity for me as it was the first time in my career where we headed into the last round of the season knowing we were not going to be playing in the finals.

Our form in the month before that match against the Crows ultimately cost us a chance to play in the finals. The Hawks, who won a third premiership in succession that year, crunched us in round 20 and we then drew with the Saints before being badly beaten by Collingwood.

That month pretty summarised our season. We had been such a successful side from 2007 onwards that when the wins were not coming as easily or as regularly, it came as quite a shock. All of a sudden, we were all being challenged in a new way almost every week. Our rivals had improved and we were in a period of transition. It really was a disappointing season. Mediocrity was new to me and while I had grown as a player, I struggled with the fact that we were no longer a League leader.

Our season started on a low note when we were trounced by Hawthorn by 62 points on Easter Monday. A week later we were rolled at home by Fremantle by 44 points and from then on, we were always behind the pace in our bid to keep our finals streak going. Every time it looked as though we were about to find some momentum, we would slip a cog. We had been nearly unbeatable at home for so long, but the Kangaroos beat us in Geelong by 16 points a fortnight after that loss to the Dockers, and it does not take long for an aura of invincibility surrounding a club to erode when losses start to mount.

With the season over, we were able to send off Steve and a couple of other favourite teammates in style with a 39-point win over the Crows. 715 games went out the door, Steve having played 253, James Kelly 273 and Mathew Stokes 189.

Steve could have enjoyed a spectacular farewell match but ended up booting 2.6 for the day, a more than handy performance for a player who had been told his time at the Cats was up. This was a really tricky time for Steve. As was later to be proven he, along with Kelly and Stokes, had much more to give. Steve proved that when he headed to the Giants and kicked another 64 goals from 40 matches in two seasons to finish off a truly brilliant career.

Kelly, an All-Australian in 2011, came out of retirement in 2016 to help Essendon after 34 players had been suspended after the supplements scandal as a top-up player and ended up playing another 40 games of really good footy. He later returned to Geelong as a gun assistant coach. Stokes also went to Essendon as a top-up, playing 11 matches for the Bombers in 2016.

After the final siren sounded and we did our farewells to the fans on the ground, we headed into the locker rooms to sit down for a proper debrief. There were about four Eskys filled to the brim and the room was full of players and coaches, administrative staff and others with close ties to the Cats.

Normally we would be looking ahead to the first weekend of the finals and wondering whether we might be able to play well enough to secure another premiership. Even though our season was done, there was much to celebrate in the contribution the departing trio had made to Geelong. Clearly, we would have loved another crack at the premiership, but there was a relief for me that the season was at an end after such a complex and draining year. I finally had the chance to take some time for myself and spend more of it with my loved ones.

This was an unusual moment in my career, as none of the three wanted to retire, also the case with our 2009 Norm Smith Medallist Paul Chapman, who spent the last two years of his career at the Bombers after leaving the Cats to extend his career in 2013. Other stars of the club who left during my time included Tom Harley (2009), Cam Mooney (2011), Matthew Scarlett (2012), Joel Corey (2013), Jimmy Bartel and Corey Enright (2016) and Andrew Mackie and Tom Lonergan (2017). We were rapt that Gary Ablett Jnr came back to the club for an encore to enable a proper farewell to a true legend of the club.

I would have loved to see them play forever, or at least for as long as they were able to contribute at a high level. When a player has given so much to a club, it is easy to believe they should be allowed the chance to say goodbye on their own terms. But that is not the reality.

There is a balance footy clubs must strive for, which is why some players are asked to finish earlier than what they might have hoped. Successful clubs try to avoid a scenario where a group of champions retire in one hit, with good reason. That can really hurt a team and you can't always find replacements in the reserves.

Each retirement proves a blow in its own way. Champions leave holes that are hard to fill. The coaches are there to guide how a club plays and, if they do that job correctly, how it fares on the field. But good clubs also rely on senior players to set standards on and off the field.

We were fortunate throughout my career to have many champions doing just that, which minimised the impact of their departures. Their ability to educate younger players and to steer them through difficult periods has helped the club remain in premiership contention for so long.

21

Regrets

I HAVE NEVER CONSIDERED myself a dirty player and if that were a widespread belief, I would find that really uncomfortable. But there are certainly some instances in my career that I feel embarrassed by, and time has not healed the feelings of regret when I reflect on those moments.

The frustration I was feeling after the death of Mum and my struggle to cope with my swirling emotions had a negative effect on my behaviour on the field. An undisciplined period when I found myself getting suspended started about that time, though it is important to note that there is no excuse for overstepping the mark. For a time, it became an unwanted, unnecessary and ultimately bad habit and in the latter stages of my career, I had to make a conscious effort to channel my aggression towards winning the footy and putting my energy into helping the team.

As a key forward, I consider my position no different from a midfielder. You have a rival who is playing tightly and is determined to stop you. The less effective you are, the better the opposition team's chances of winning. It might be as simple as blocking your path to the footy or the full-back doing everything within the rules to make your life difficult. That can be frustrating and there were occasions when the angst this caused bubbled over, to my regret.

The biggest embarrassment of my career occurred when I touched senior umpire Dean Margetts during the round 7 match against the GWS Giants in 2018. We were in control at the time, leading by 22 points late in the first half, when the footy was kicked in my direction, only for Giants defender Nick Haynes to intercept it. I was late to the contest and my attempt to spoil him was crude at best, with my left fist making contact to the back of his head and my left knee corking his backside.

As Haynes' teammates Phil Davis and Ryan Griffen remonstrated with me, Margetts came towards me to say he was going to pay a 50-metre penalty for the late contact I had with Haynes. I reached out with my left hand and made contact with his hand, and his response was captured clearly on the microphone umpires wear during matches: 'There's no need for that. Hey! Don't touch me either,' Margetts said.

My old captain Cameron Ling, who was providing special comments on the match for the Seven Network, knew immediately that I was in trouble. 'That is unacceptable. You cannot touch the umpire,' he said.

It was all over in a split second and I ended up enjoying a pretty good match against a side that went on to play off in their first-ever Grand Final later that season. The Cats won by 61 points and I grabbed eight marks and kicked four goals, which is as many as the Giants managed for the match.

Understandably, the headlines were not about us returning to the eight in what was a congested ladder at that stage of the season, it was about me going to the tribunal. I was asked about the incident immediately after the match and explained that it was accidental and occurred in the heat of the moment, and I had already apologised to Margetts.

As with any incident that requires a tribunal appearance, it prompted great debate among the footy talk shows over the next few days, with some arguing that it warranted a hefty suspension while others pointed to it as a spur-of-the-moment accident. As always, Chris Scott was in my corner, noting the umpire did not feel the need to pay an additional 50-metre penalty at the time the incident occurred. 'If he had a problem with it, he would have paid another 50. So, I think that part is pretty clear, isn't it? Common sense should take over at some point,' he said.

I always found the time between being reported and appearing in front of a tribunal a strange experience. Nothing changes in terms of your week-to-week activities. You go through recovery with your teammates and try to get as much rest as possible over the next couple of days before resuming training. But what is different is the giant cloud hanging over your head: whether or not you will be able to play. It can mess with your head.

Meetings are held with the footy manager as to how to handle the hearing, with consideration given to entering a plea, attending the tribunal in person and the merits of actually giving evidence in your own defence. If a club or player feels particularly aggrieved with the outcome, they can appeal a suspension, which means the whole scenario drags on.

In this case, with the game on a Friday night, I had been referred to the tribunal the next day and had to wait until Tuesday night for the hearing. It proved to be a jarring few days.

Before the hearing, there was a meeting between Geelong's lawyer Ben Ihle and the AFL's representative Jeff Gleeson – both silks – where the offer of a one-match ban was discussed. I had already decided I would plead guilty and agreed that one match was an acceptable penalty, even though it meant I would miss a big match against Collingwood.

A difficult part about a tribunal hearing is walking out of the room after the penalty is handed down and facing the media. But it did give me an opportunity to discuss publicly just how upset I felt about the incident and the furore it caused. 'I feel embarrassed by what happened. My intention is to respect umpires and their importance in the game,' I told reporters. 'If I could take it back, I would. But that is football. It is a high-pressure game and you are asked to make decisions in a split-second and I've made a couple of bad decisions through frustration. This has been a tough week. You are getting labelled as someone I don't necessarily see myself as. Whether you are not thinking, or it is a bad error of judgement, because football is so publicised, it gets heightened and it makes you out to be, not worse than what you are, because that is not right, but a bigger event than maybe it was. It wasn't malicious. But you have to move your mindset, otherwise you can get left behind contemplating what might have been.'

On reflecting on it now, I am not as sure it is the blight on my career that I thought it might prove to be and feel the good that I did throughout my career has far overshadowed the occasional transgression. But my embarrassment stems from knowing better and understanding the importance of the involvement of umpires and being mindful they deserve the utmost respect from players, coaches and fans.

* * *

Another transgression that still upsets me is the incident in which I struck West Coast Eagles defender Will Schofield in the jaw during a semi-final in 2019.

The match was in the balance midway through the third term, with the Eagles holding a five-point lead, when I clipped him with my right arm as we were running together. In those instances, when you are jostling with each other, it is not uncommon for a player to swing their arm across a rival's chest in a bid to find some space and break away. That was my intention, but I clearly got it wrong and struck him far too high. It is risky behaviour to swing your arm, particularly when your opponent's head is at risk. I was immediately apologetic and can remember standing over him as he was lying on the ground at the MCG.

Among the things that bothered me about the incident is that Will, who grew up in Geelong, and I get on really well. This was a guy I liked and respected and had known for quite a while. It is something that we have spoken about since and I think we are both comfortable where it sits now, even though I still feel awful about it.

I've appeared on his podcast and I have also spoken at length to him for a really informative article he wrote for *Code Sports* about the difficulties of losing a parent while playing footy. For

Will, it was his dad, John, whom I had met. He died when Will was just 23 and making his way as an Eagle. My mum died when I was a couple of years older than Will was when he lost his dad. It is another unfortunate thing that we had in common and something we bonded over.

But we also had lots of other connections, including some mutual friends, and I felt I had seriously let them down as well with my actions in that game. I mean, I knew his mum, Jan, as well and could not imagine what she must have been feeling as her son lay prone on the MCG turf. It was something I really struggled to handle at the time and in the days and weeks that followed.

The price that I ultimately paid for the strike was high for both me and the club. We went through the tribunal process again, but this time it was deep in September and the stakes were critical, given we were in the race for the premiership.

Ultimately, the one-match ban forced me out of the side beaten by Richmond by 19 points in the preliminary final. We were right in the game for much of the night, having led at half-time and trailed by only four points at three-quarter-time. I sat alongside Mitch Duncan in the coach's box that night and I was blown away by the quality of footy we produced in the first half against a champion team.

But being on the sidelines for such an important match – as the team's spearhead and a senior player – was very disappointing; there is no doubt I let my teammates and the club down.

I'm well aware there are instances when senior coaches have put the blame firmly on players who are suspended for big matches. A famous one is the spray North Melbourne's dual premiership coach Denis Pagan delivered to champions Glenn Archer and Wayne Schwass, after North lost the 1997 preliminary final, telling them they 'fucking cost us'. They had both been suspended after North's first final.

Chris Scott was never like that. He would never hang a player out to dry publicly and was always very supportive of his players and that, to my mind, is one of his greatest strengths.

But sharing the same box as him as we were trying to make our way into another Grand Final rammed home the consequences of my action a week earlier. I knew it had put pressure on the coaching department, because they had to shuffle our attack in a bid to kick a winning score. For all that, I am not convinced that's why we lost the game. Richmond was then a champion team and they turned it around that night, as they so often did through that period.

Others might argue the toss. Maybe I would have had enough of an impact to make a difference. It is something I will never know and missing that game under those circumstances is something that I still regret. When you let your teammates down, boy, you really do feel terrible about it.

* * *

Revenge can be a powerful motivation. When it comes to dishing it out on the footy field, you have to be prepared to accept a few blows as well.

As a key forward, it is common to be whacked around the head or jumped into – all in the name of defence – though there is no doubt the game has become cleaner.

There is one instance when a player I had whacked was able to get his revenge, though admittedly there is a humorous side to it. In my 200th game, in round 11, 2017, we were playing against the Adelaide Crows at Kardinia Park when I gave Matt Crouch a love tap to his chin. It was another pretty stupid act, but we were scuffling with each other and I was trying to shake him off. He was not hurt, and he jumped up and jogged straight back into the action. But it occurred at a time when there was an AFL crackdown on jumper punches to try to reduce the number of occasions when players would grab a rival's guernsey and effectively punch them with it during a scuffle.

Once again, I was on the front foot immediately after the game as I tried to explain the incident. 'It was a bit of a funny one … on a night when there was a bit of push and shove, I felt like I got him in the chest,' I told ABC Radio after the game. 'I know there's obviously been a lot of talk about jumper punches, but in no way did I intend to hit him high after it had been pretty well talked about through the week. I suppose it is out of my hands now, but I feel like I didn't get him high, but we'll wait and see what happens.'

Not for the first time, the tribunal did not agree with my account and suspended me for the following week's match against West Coast. I still think I was a little stiff there. Crouch ultimately got his revenge. We were in Adelaide the following year and while celebrating my 30th birthday, we went to a pub in town for a beer. I knew Crows champion 'Tex' Walker pretty well and always found him to be good company, so I flicked him a few text messages inviting him along. He happened to be great mates with the Crouch brothers, who also joined us. As the festivities took hold, we took the chance to replicate the incident and it would be fair to say he got one back on me that night. Good on him for doing so.

* * *

My overall tribunal record stands at 11 citations, all of which I was found guilty, with suspensions of six matches and fines totalling $9,500. It is a physical game. Very few players are perfect and sometimes it is difficult to avoid contact. Admittedly, though, seven of the 11 times I was cited were for striking, but in four of those, a fine was imposed, suggesting there was not a lot in those incidents.

My biggest suspension was for two weeks for striking Sydney defender Dane Rampe in round 20, 2017, yet that is probably the only penalty I would really question. I thought that the penalty for a jumper punch in this instance was severe, given it was basically a tummy tap.

It was a frustrating game for us, and the entire team was criticised for a lack of discipline in a shock 46-point loss to the Swans on our home turf. I managed to kick three goals, although I was obviously a little agitated, as former Saint and Kangaroo Nick Dal Santo noted when assessing the incident for Fox Sports: 'I just get the sense that he wants to hurt someone, then he remembers that he is not allowed to do what he wants to do, and he gives him a little one,' Dal Santo said. I paid the price for not being smart enough once again at a time when the AFL was cracking down on jumper punches.

I had not learnt my lesson and was disappointed in myself, which I noted when writing a column for *The Athlete's Voice* about jumper punches during the finals series. I also noted that mid-season rule changes or crackdowns were hard for players to adjust to. 'I was embarrassed after the second time, so I'd be really embarrassed if there was a third,' I wrote. 'I don't want to say that I'm really confident it won't happen again, because footy is a funny game, but I'll be doing all that I can to ensure it doesn't. It's a bad look and I understand the AFL taking it out of our game, but it becomes hard for players, and a little bit frustrating, when rules get changed during a season. I know you've got to be adaptable and change with them, but these are split-second decisions.'

22

Copping a right whack

We enjoyed another strong home-and-away season in 2017, managing to clinch the double chance after winning 16 games, after starting the year with a five-match winning streak, to share top spot with Richmond and Adelaide, a run in which I managed to kick 18 goals.

Surprisingly we then dropped three in succession against Collingwood, Gold Coast and Essendon before rediscovering our form heading into the bye to sit firmly in the top four.

After missing the round 13 clash against West Coast due to a one-match ban for that jumper punch to Matt Crouch, I was less potent in attack and managed to kick only 21 goals in the last 11 games to take my season tally to 51. In part that was due to a shift in my role. Throughout the second half of the season, I was roaming further afield, with the Cats keen to use my ability to set up teammates through my kicking. A statistical analysis at the time published in the *Herald Sun* showed that the number of times I was involved in 'score assists' more than doubled in the last month of the season.

An illustration of this occurred in our final round 44-point win over the GWS Giants, who finished fourth that season, when I was able to kick a couple of goals from my 20 touches. In that match Wylie Buzza played deeper in attack, Sam Menegola spent time at centre half-forward and Daniel Menzel proved a dangerous forward floating in and out of the 50-metre arc.

In theory, having more avenues to goal made us less predictable and harder to shut down. Unfortunately, it did not work in September, and it was incredibly disappointing that we were trounced by the eventual Grand Finalists, Richmond and Adelaide, in the qualifying and preliminary finals.

We had managed to defeat Richmond by 14 points at home midway through August – one of two matches I missed while suspended for striking Dane Rampe – but the Tigers were far too good for us when they thrashed us by 51 points in the qualifying final. We rebounded a week later to defeat the Swans by almost 10 goals, a good win given they had beaten us easily at Geelong only a month earlier. In the preliminary final in Adelaide, we were on the back foot early and never recovered.

The Tigers ended a premiership drought dating back to 1980 thrashing the Crows in the Grand Final. At that stage, I was still reeling from the most scathing exit review of my career.

* * *

The usual process with an exit review is to undergo a medical and physical assessment, chat with your strength and conditioning staff to devise a program for the off-season and then meet with your coaches for their feedback.

I was aware parts of my second half of the season had not been great, with the suspensions a problem, and I had managed to kick just one goal per match in the finals.

But I was not expecting any great drama until I walked into the meeting room and saw the entire coaching staff, along with the footy manager, Steve Hocking, list manager, Stephen Wells, and chief executive, Brian Cook. It was highly unusual and I immediately felt uneasy. The thrust of the meeting was that while I was in the top 10 best-paid players in the competition – a claim I believed was not correct, by the way – I was a long way from being the footballer deserving of the money I was on. I was pissed off at the assertion. Was I right to feel that way? At the time, I believed so. To my surprise, it was Stephen Wells who led the charge and to this day, some of his comments sit uncomfortably with me. What annoyed me was that before that meeting, there had been no mention of any of this and my form on the field had been decent.

Wells was not alone with his criticism. Steve Hocking had a crack at me. So too did Brian Cook. Chris Scott made clear his disappointment in the way I had performed. Their message was clear: something needed to change my performance and my attitude.

Although I felt like I had played reasonably, there *were* parts of the assessment I agreed with.

My mood really had suffered during the period I was mourning the loss of Mum. Looking back, I was grumpier around the club than I had ever been before during my career. Footy had become too consuming for me and I was not enjoying it. It got to the extent where I was not enjoying training like I usually did, and perhaps that was evident to my coaches. I would be sitting in pre-game meetings and pondering, 'Why am I even playing?'. The excitement had waned. The issue was that I did not relay this to the club at the time.

But I had claimed the club goalkicking award once again and had managed to boot more than 150 goals over the past three seasons. My motivation had dipped but I was not going that badly.

The meeting was unnerving. As I walked to my car afterwards, I wondered whether I was a chance to be traded midway through my five-year contract. I immediately called my agent Tom Petroro and told him I had been 'absolutely crucified' for 15 to 20 minutes during the review and that I felt they might want to trade me. His response was: 'No. That won't be the case. But I can follow it up if you would like.' Tom said that if there were any concerns, we would be able to work through it.

When I got home, I told Emma about the meeting and her advice was to consider whether I was happy and if Geelong was where I wanted to be. As rocked as I felt, there was no question of that. I still loved playing for the Cats.

* * *

Thankfully, there were no concerns in the long term, the club and Tom assured me that the meeting was simply a rocket fired. When pre-season began, although I felt a little dirty about what had been said, it proved a moment where the penny dropped again. It was a reminder that life moves quickly and that, having been with Geelong for 11 years, I should be making the most of my time. On reflection, with the help of a psychologist, I was starting to cope with my emotions better as I moved through the grieving process. It also might have been that review, but it was more likely nature taking its course.

Either way, through the pre-season of 2018 I felt my enjoyment for training return and had clarity in what I needed to do to improve, which is where my work with Chris Dennis came to the fore. I worked really hard on my footwork in heavy traffic – namely trying to find space to provide an option, or to get a quick kick away from a contest. It is an aspect of the game I feel became one of my biggest strengths outside of reading the game and contested marking. So instead of focusing on a burst of speed of 10 to 20 metres, as in 2016, in 2019 we tried to enhance my ability to snare a split-second over a couple of metres – we called it working within a phone box. I started to appreciate how even the smallest improvements could have an impact on my game.

But anyone who looked at the start of the 2018 season might have felt that I had spat the dummy, because I managed to kick only six goals leading into our clash with the Giants in round 7. The strange thing was that although the scoreboard suggested otherwise, I was winning enough of the footy, having taken 31 marks to that stage, and it felt like my luck would soon turn. I then had a decent game against the Giants, kicking four goals, but that was the match in which that incident involving umpire Dean Margetts occurred.

On my return from that week 'off', I was determined to make a statement, feeling as though I owed it to both the club and myself; fortunately I struck form straight away against the Bombers and ended up kicking 50 goals in the last 15 games to finish with 60 for the season. That was the type of footy a top 10-paid player would produce. It was a good rebound.

The coaches noted that I had performed well through the season, though there was no reference to that exit review of a season earlier. I finished fourth in the Carji Greeves Medal, only five votes behind Mark Blicavs, who claimed the honour for the second time.

My form was also recognised externally as I was short-listed for the All-Australian team, though I missed making the final team, and was nominated for the AFL Players Association Most Valuable Player Award.

I was happy with the way I finished the season, but we were a middling side that year. Against the lower-placed teams we proved too good, with the lead into the finals a case in point. We thumped 14th-placed Fremantle by 133 points and then the 17th-placed Gold Coast by 102 points in the last two rounds, but we limped into the eight with 13 wins, a game clear of North Melbourne, Essendon, Port Adelaide and Adelaide, all with 12 victories.

Those last two games were massive wins, but they were also quite soft matches and the lack of a competitive outing heading into the finals cost us in September, as we were not match tough. We had beaten Melbourne twice during the season in tight matches but in the elimination final, the Demons were able to get the better of us with a 29-point victory to end what proved to be another disappointing season.

* * *

My good form continued in 2019 in the second-last season of my five-year contract, and clearly Arabella and Primrose were proving lucky charms. I managed to kick 56 goals, which was good enough to earn a spot in the All-Australian side for the second time.

Did I feel any extra motivation given it was the end of a lengthy contract? I know there is a common perception that some players deliver their best footy late in their contracts and then tail off once they have received an extension and perhaps this is true – for some. But I never felt that way. I felt my performances were generally strong through this period and the prospect of a contract extension was never extra motivation.

We enjoyed another strong home-and-away season, winning 16 matches to claim the minor premiership, but unfortunately the year again finished on a negative note.

We had started the season well with a seven-point win over Collingwood at the MCG, a match in which I managed to kick the 500th goal of my career, snapping accurately from 45 metres out on the run.

But anyone who can remember my celebration – namely, pretending to rock a baby – after I kicked a goal earlier that night would have realised that I had something more important on my mind because a couple of days earlier Primrose, aka 'Mimi' was born.

Emma, who raised awareness of the severe form of morning sickness called hyperemesis gravidarum she had suffered during her pregnancy, announced Primrose's arrival via social media. She wrote we were 'so blessed to have a second daughter to love unconditionally'.

Mimi was exceptionally unwell with bronchiolitis over the Easter weekend leading into a clash against Hawthorn and it was certainly a stressful time. Emma had taken Mimi, then just two months old, to Deniliquin for a few days and while there, she started to deteriorate. Emma initially took her into the local hospital, and she was advised to keep monitoring her. After taking her back to Emma's parents', Mimi continued to go downhill and the decision was made to take her by ambulance to Shepparton, to stay overnight on Wednesday leading into the weekend.

I jumped in the car early on Thursday morning to head to Shepparton, and later that day the decision was made to fly her to the Royal Children's Hospital. As the plane flew to Essendon Airport, we jumped in the car to drive to Melbourne, which was a stressful drive as we were really concerned about Mimi's condition and were extremely sleep deprived.

My aunt Lisa, Mum's sister, is a nurse at the Children's and she was able to meet Mimi when she arrived at the hospital, and to reassure us that our little girl was going to receive the best treatment. It was our first experience of dealing with a sick child and she spent time incubated there. She was not out of the woods and her condition was stable for a couple of days before she started to improve, leading into the weekend.

I spoke with Chris Scott as to whether I should play but once we received news that Mimi was improving, I decided to try to give my best, and managed a goal in our 23-point win over the Hawks. Chris explained my circumstances afterwards: 'He missed some training, so again, I'm not sure whether I should say this, but his young girl was ill, and he had to spend a lot of time away from the club. He did not sleep as well as he normally would.' Chris was only half-right. Losing sleep was only part of it. Our baby was in hospital! I have never felt so stressed. And Emma too, obviously. We are so grateful to the medicos at the Royal Children's. Happily, Mimi came through it unscathed, but the memory of it still has me wobbly.

* * *

I soon found the consistency I was craving, contributing to the scoreboard regularly while also involving my teammates as well. As an illustration, there was a five-game period leading into the bye after round 12 where I managed four goals in each match to take my tally to 35 at the halfway mark.

My form in the second half was not as strong – only 21 goals – particularly leading into what proved to be a disappointing finals series, individually and for the team.

It was a year in which I took the third-most marks across the competition inside the forward 50-metre arc, seventh in terms of goal assists per game and sixth, with 56 goals in the Coleman Medal, won by Jeremy Cameron (67 goals), the eighth straight year he led the goalkicking at GWS Giants.

But I must have put my boots on the wrong way in the qualifying final against Collingwood, with just four behinds in a low-scoring match which we lost by 10 points.

We bounced back against West Coast, the reigning premiers, the next week in a semi-final. I kicked four goals in our 20-point win, but it proved a bittersweet experience. As detailed earlier, my year ended on a sour note when I was suspended for striking

Will Schofield, which forced me out of the side that lost to Richmond in the preliminary final.

There was a high point in the post-season when, during the Carji Greeves Award night, I received the Community Champion Award from AFLW player Kate Darby, who said she 'personally had seen the positive effect he has on everyone around him'.

It was an important award and, as I said that night, while our goal every year is to win the premiership, it was also critical to assist others wherever possible. The privilege that we have as footballers to try to boost members of the public going through tough times is not something we take lightly. 'I was always told that no matter how tough you feel your life is, there is always someone who is facing challenges tougher than yours,' I said. 'To be honest, I have had to remind myself of that a few times in the past few weeks. Myself, my teammates and my coaches, and you the supporters, are still hurting that we did not get to the Grand Final. However, if our work in the community can teach us something, it is perspective and how fortunate we are. We all try to give back when we can and we all try to encourage each other to be better on and off the field, even when sometimes we fall short.'

It really was a season where the highs were life-changing and the lows particularly deflating.

Surely 2020, the last season of the five-year contract I had signed, would prove a smoother ride. Little did I know.

23

A season like no other

It was March 9, 2020, and the address from our coach, Chris Scott was the sternest I had heard him deliver before a match and it is one that I wish he had never needed to give. We were sitting in the change rooms in Colac as we prepared for a pre-season clash against Essendon. The mood of the coach was sobering. He had warned a few teammates who were joking around to smarten up. 'You all need to take this very seriously,' he said. 'It will have a huge impact across the whole world.' As we are all aware, Chris was absolutely spot on with his dire predictions about the impact COVID-19 would have on the world.

Senior players like Joel Selwood, Mitch Duncan and me were old enough to remember the scare when illnesses like SARS and Swine Flu flared in the early 2000s. But it was also made clear to us that the COVID-19 pandemic was going to have a far greater impact than had those viruses.

By March 2020, the whole world was on alert and the AFL had already introduced measures aimed at minimising the impact of this deadly virus on the competition. We were told to limit our contact with the crowd in Colac, even though it was extremely unlikely there would be cases in a regional town of that size at that time. It went against everything I loved about playing matches in the country. Mixing with the crowd and signing autographs for kids is part and parcel of those experiences and I think most players enjoy those matches as much as the fans. That warning was but a small pointer that our lives were about to be turned upside down.

The Bombers edged us in that encounter, winning by four points, but there was even less concern than usual about the result of a pre-season match as we nervously eyed the future.

* * *

I admit I was worried when news broke about the outbreak of COVID on the cruise ship *Ruby Princess*, which had docked in Sydney. Our opening match of the season was against the GWS Giants in Sydney and now we were to fly into a city that could well become a hotspot for the virus after passengers had been allowed to disembark from the ship. The crisis that would engulf the world had really hit home for me and it felt like we were to be on alert in every aspect of our lives.

There were clear signs at both Melbourne and Sydney Airports that things were slowing down, which was disconcerting, to put it mildly. For instance, there were far fewer flights listed than normal on the departure boards and nowhere near as

ABOVE: Holding the cup after our victory in the 2011 AFL Grand Final, after defeating Collingwood by 38 points. Winning the premiership was a massive triumph and so too was being a pivotal player in the Grand Final. It was also Chris Scott's first premiership as a coach, in his first season at Geelong. AFL PHOTOS

BELOW: Relaxing with a beer in the clubrooms after round 23, 2015: (L–R) Tom Lonergan, Andrew Mackie, Steve Johnson, me, Joel Selwood and Jimmy Bartel.

ABOVE: Mum, Dad, Jane, me, Edwina and Charlie on the family farm in 2015.
BELOW: Mum and me napping on the couch at Springfield.

ABOVE: Wearing a black armband, and paying tribute to Mum on 26 April 2015. AFL PHOTOS

ABOVE RIGHT: Nothing prepared me for just how strange it was to play matches inside empty stadiums. Although restrictions were not as tight in Queensland during COVID, only 3378 fans could attend the round 12, 2020 match against Port Adelaide Power on the Gold Coast. AFL PHOTOS

RIGHT: After the disruptive COVID year of 2020 winning the Coleman Medal, as the game's leading goalkicker with 42 goals, was a satisfying achievement.

When I played my 300th game against Port Adelaide in 2021 Granddad Fred joked that at least I had made a reasonable contribution to the 'family business'. 'With my 18 games, Jack's 182 and you up to 300, that gives us 500 between us,' he said. AFL PHOTOS

I was very proud to be a part of the 2022 All-Australian team, my fifth selection. It was a great surprise when I was announced captain in a side that also featured club leaders the calibre of Max Gawn, Patrick Cripps and Touk Miller. It was nice to have the (c) next to my name for once.
BACK ROW L-R: Isaac Heeney (Sydney Swans), Mark Blicavs (Geelong), Sam Taylor (GWS Giants), Max Gawn (Melbourne), Charlie Curnow (Carlton), Andrew Brayshaw (Fremantle), Tom Stewart (Geelong).
MIDDLE ROW L-R: Jack Sinclair (St Kilda), Callum Mills (Sydney Swans), Jeremy Cameron (Geelong), Brayden Maynard (Collingwood), Steven May (Melbourne), Christian Petracca (Melbourne), Clayton Oliver (Melbourne), Lachie Neale (Brisbane).
FRONT ROW L-R: Touk Miller (Gold Coast Suns), Adam Saad (Carlton), Patrick Cripps (Carlton, vice-captain), me, Connor Rozee (Port Adelaide), Shai Bolton (Richmond) and Tyson Stengle (Geelong). AFL PHOTOS

Winning the Grand Final in 2022 was a thrilling end to the year except that my best friend, captain and teammate, Joel Selwood, hung up his boots. The 2009, 2011 and 2022 Grand Finals stand out as treasured memories playing with Joel. We have shared so many important moments in our life. AFL PHOTOS

I've been fortunate not to suffer any serious injuries but the end of 2022 saw me wearing a moon boot as I recovered from surgery on my foot. I managed to make it to the Melbourne Cup on crutches in my boot! It worked out well and I was really excited about being able to move properly again in 2023. GETTY IMAGES

BELOW: One of the many milestones in my career was celebrating my 350th game in round 3, 2024 against Hawthorn at the MCG. Carrying me from the ground after our big win were Jeremy Cameron (on my right) and Mitch Duncan. AFL PHOTOS

Chris Scott has been my coach since replacing Mark Thompson in 2011. We have forged a great relationship over the years, and I was grateful when he joined me at a press conference to reflect on my career after passing Joel Selwood's Geelong games-record of 355 games in May 2024. AFL PHOTOS

BELOW: Geelong's group of 300-game players (L-R) Jimmy Bartel, Joel Selwood and Ian Nankervis joined me before I equalled Joel Selwood's club games-record. Unable to attend were Corey Enright and John 'Sam' Newman. AFL PHOTOS

LEFT: Marrying Emma was the best day of my life, though the births of our three kids in the years since have run a very close second. We are pictured at the 2023 Brownlow Medal. AFL PHOTOS

BELOW: Family is the most important thing to us and having our children, (L-R) Arabella, Henry and Primrose with us to celebrate my milestones has been a great joy. Wouldn't it be amazing to see them all playing for the Cats, continuing our family tradition! AFL PHOTOS

many people were around. Strict regulations had not yet been introduced for the general public, but the AFL had tightened some protocols.

It is not uncommon for bugs to take hold in a club environment and run through a team and no-one wanted that with COVID, given the terrible news we were hearing out of Europe and the United States. Amid the uncertainty, our start to the season was not great either as we were beaten by the Giants by 32 points at the Sydney Showground. But it did not take long for the disappointment of the loss to pass. Within 24 hours, the footy world had changed.

* * *

It was chilling to watch AFL chief executive Gillon McLachlan the next day as he announced the season would be paused because of the pandemic. His message was alarming. To hear him say that the pandemic posed the greatest threat footy had faced in 100 years was particularly dire, but it was the tone with which he spoke that really shocked me.

Even though I understood the coronavirus was a real concern, I never envisaged that we would have to spend a couple of months at home. Our approach was to try to make the most out of what was clearly a bad situation for everyone.

Emma and I were lucky we had plenty of space to roam about on the farm. It might sound strange but there was a part of the initial lockdown that I treasured because it allowed us to spend far more time than we usually would with each other and our girls.

Like everyone else, we moved any social interaction with friends to Zoom calls and enjoyed the occasional drinks catch-up online, while the club arranged Zoom trivia nights for the players to ensure that we remained as connected as a group as we could.

* * *

Among the major challenges that occurred that year was that every player in the competition had their pay cut in half for that season. Do not get me wrong. I am well aware we were very fortunate compared to a lot of others. Some of the stories were devastating to hear and the AFL was not immune – the shutdown caused carnage across the competition, with many club and AFL employees having their jobs cut.

The nature of any sport means that senior players, or those who were better performing, will be paid more than players at the start of their careers, but in this case, everyone took a hit. 2020 happened to be the final season of the five-year contract I had signed in 2015 and while the spread of the wage I was receiving was relatively even through those seasons, there was a bump in the payment I was to receive in the final year. That meant the impact was slightly greater for me and I really feel for the players whose contracts were back-ended heavily for that season and the next.

There was no real clarity in the information we were receiving from the AFL or the Players Association as to what the financial outcome would be for players, which added to the anxiety we were all feeling. Early on my teammate Josh Jenkins advised me things could become really serious financially, but at the start we were told in meetings our income might be cut by only 10 per cent. However, it was not long before others were saying it could be as drastic as 75 per cent before a 50 per cent cut in wages was agreed to.

To have an income is obviously important. But people tend to live to their means and our family was no different, with the cut putting real stress on our household. We were not living from pay cheque to pay cheque, but we did have significant commitments to meet. As an example, we probably over-extended when buying the farm a few years earlier because we loved it so much and the repayments on our dream property had to be met despite my dip in wage.

In the days after the announcement of the wage cut, Emma and I sat down to complete an exercise that I am sure was common across the world. We wrote down what was essential and what could be cancelled. Every cent needed to be accounted for because we did not know how long the pandemic would last. Of course, nobody knew the answer.

* * *

As the weeks went on, my mind began to wander, and a daunting prospect dawned on me: had I played my final game of AFL footy? Would a two-goal effort in that disappointing loss to the Giants be my last moments as a player?

Given the uncertainty, and with no prospect of the initial shutdown ending, the end seemed a realistic proposition, as I was now 31 and in the final season of my contract. Although I had been in the best form of my career, every player lucky enough to have their career extend into their 30s is mindful the end can come quickly. I had then played 14 seasons and although I felt as fit as I had ever been, the longer the season's suspension dragged on, the less time there would be for me to impress in order to convince the club to award me a new contract.

My mind turned to a recent example at Essendon when 34 players were rubbed out for the entirety of the 2016 season in the fallout from the supplements scandal. The circumstances in 2020 were clearly different, but I was aware some of the Bombers really struggled to find their best form when they resumed playing after spending so much time out of the game.

I was always hopeful we would return to playing that season, and we were told by Geelong's coaching staff to keep our fitness levels high to be ready to resume. But every prospect – even the possibility that my career would be over – had to be considered.

* * *

When the AFL announced on May 15 that we would be able to begin training within a few days, with a view to the season resuming on June 11, there was much relief. I was well and truly ready to get back into it and delighted to have the chance to play again. My confidence that I could have an impact in what would be an abridged 17-match season was also reasonably high because I had never been fitter.

Because we were confined to our farm near Geelong, a lot of my exercise consisted of running up and down the hills on our property or taking longer runs within the five-kilometre radius we were allowed to roam. As a result, I finished that shutdown as lean as I had ever been. Instead of lifting weights in the gym, I did a lot of weight exercises at home and the tweaks to my usual fitness regime helped me to maintain my interest in exercising.

When we were asked to play games off the shortest breaks of our careers, being leaner and fitter is something that enabled me to recover better than usual. My new leanness may also have helped extend my career as I felt lighter on my feet when moving around the ground.

The return to training in late May was strange. Initially we were not allowed any contact in training sessions, for example, which made for some unusual training techniques. We trained in small groups in order to minimise the impact of any outbreak and we were tested for the virus regularly for the same reason.

Perhaps the most onerous restrictions related to the protocols which prevented players and their families, along with match day staff and other key personnel, from attending places that might heighten any risk. Attending bars and restaurants was out, so too was sitting in cafes after Victoria reopened for the first time.

Those sacrifices had an impact on the social lives and the wellbeing of family members who had never signed on to be AFL players. I felt that restriction was particularly onerous.

But as unusual was training and living under the restrictions, nothing prepared me for just how strange it was to play matches inside empty stadiums. Our first experience of that was in round 2, when we hosted Hawthorn on a Friday night at Kardinia Park. The atmosphere for clashes between the Hawks and the Cats is usually incredible and because so many of those matches were thrillers, the crowd noise could be deafening. Players really do feed off that energy and excitement but now all we could hear was the sound of our own voices. It became a challenge to remain motivated and ready to perform at your best.

* * *

Chris Scott had been on the ball when he had stressed the impact the pandemic would have, and he was also spot on when it came to advising us of the importance of staying as fit as we possibly could. He forecast that an opportunity to be a competition leader would present if we were more than ready to go when resuming.

We had a number of senior players who were in their 30s, but there were also some exciting youngsters coming through. We felt that mix made for a talented and well-balanced combination.

There was a belief around the club that we had the maturity to handle any of the challenges thrown at us. What we did not realise was that there were plenty more to come. The reprieve from the pandemic did not last long, with a second wave of COVID hitting Victoria late in June. This forced the state back into lockdown and turned the competition on its head once again.

Our last game in Victoria for the year occurred in round 5 when we hosted the Gold Coast, with our 37-point win pushing us to third position on the ladder. But we were about to enter the unknown once again as the great exodus of the Victorian clubs began.

* * *

Playing a home-and-away game against Brisbane at the SCG is something I could never have imagined just four months before our 27-point win over the Lions in round 6. But at least there were some fans at the match – a handful, anyway, with the official attendance of 1311 the smallest crowd I played in front of during my career, not including those games when the stadium gates were shut.

The week in Sydney was the start of a journey that was supposed to go for a month but instead lasted for the rest of the season. After beating the Lions, we headed to Perth to join a new hub and played the Eagles, Fremantle and Collingwood at Optus Stadium over the next three weeks.

The prospect of being away from home for an extended period sat uneasily with a number of players, particularly those of us who had young families, and I was no different in that regard. I am well aware that people travel away from home for work for lengthy periods for all manner of reasons. It was an argument that was trotted out on talkback radio whenever concerns raised by the Players Association on our behalf were made public.

The difference for us is that it is not something that we had signed on for. Certainly, as a father of two young girls, I did not want to leave them or Emma for a long period during a time where there was such great fear everywhere. Exacerbating the difficulty of being away is that we were also unable to provide our loved ones with any certainty as to when we would be returning home.

The AFL had declared we would be away for no longer than 30 days but setting deadlines and making guarantees in a pandemic proved problematic. Balancing those concerns, every player also understood the importance of keeping the season going given what was riding on completing the season, ranging from our pay to clubs sponsorship deals, gate receipts and so much more. It must have been really hard on Gillon McLachlan and the AFL administration given the circumstances changed from state to state almost every day, and it is a credit to them that they were able to complete the season, as difficult as it was.

The longer the season went, the more we became aware that being able to watch games on television during the so-called 'Festival of Football' provided some entertainment, and a form of relief for fans unable to move far beyond their couches during the extended lockdown, particularly in Victoria.

Some of the decisions we faced during this time were quite difficult. We had to weigh up whether to bring our partners and children to the hub, mindful that we might only be absent for a few weeks if the virus was brought back under control in Victoria. We understood how difficult it was for those we left behind. It was not easy to turn to grandparents or friends for support with the restrictions imposed and such support was also not possible for some.

My family's wellbeing was my primary concern, but that was not the only responsibility I had. There are cattle on our property and Emma had to juggle looking after the herd as well as her day-to-day duties with our kids and her business. We shared some really tough phone calls. There were times when Emma would tell me that she needed me at home. I had committed to playing footy, but my priority will always be my family. The stress on both of us should not be underestimated. Emma was home alone, managing the needs of the farm, and two toddlers.

Mimi was one, and Belle 3. She also felt unsafe as everyone knew I was away and would be away for an unknown period. She was really struggling. Other players were heading home for personal reasons, which was completely understandable and there were times when I felt like I really should have done the same.

Thank heavens for FaceTime. At least I could see my wife and daughters via a screen whenever I wanted to or needed to, and it proved to be the smallest of mercies when we were in the hub. After our chats, although I wanted to go home, Emma would encourage me to stick with it and remind me that no matter what occurred, eventually we would all be back together again.

* * *

Our form was mixed in the first month we spent on the road. We had a shocker in our first match against Collingwood in Perth, managing to kick just one goal in the opening half before being beaten by 22 points in a scrappy match.

We did make some changes to the way we approached the introduction of shorter quarters and focused on our strength and adding power. As a rule during my time at Geelong, we prided ourselves on our stamina and ability to stay in games for long periods, mindful that if we were behind, we would continue to challenge. But burst footy became more important during this unusual period, because most teams had the ability to stay competitive for longer, given the reduced playing time – at least those who were still in contention in the latter part of the season; there was a significant drop in performance from those teams out of the race.

Since then, the merits of shortening matches is a topic that arises every now and then. The 2024 season is a case in point, with the reigning premiership coach Craig McRae among those advocating a change. I'm not a fan of shortening the actual playing minutes, but I have always thought that the amount of time at ground on match days can be reduced. Half-time seems to rattle by in the blink of an eye when you are a player, but I know that for fans sometimes that break can feel too long. If half-time was shorter, I'm sure players would adapt quickly, and I'm sure that seconds could also be saved between a goal being kicked and the ball being bounced in the middle. But, as a player, I like the length of the game as it is.

Being away from our home ground and our medical staff and missing regular routines was not ideal, but because we were all in it together, we quickly adapted. Our club doctor, Geoff Allen, was among the party who travelled with us during 2020 and the AFL made sure that we had access to everything we needed in terms of weights and training equipment, though we did have to abide by regulations that restricted the number of people using a weights room at the same time.

Once again it was a strange feeling. A clash against Collingwood at the MCG would normally draw at least 60,000 fans. But given our recent bizarre experience of playing before nobody in the stands, it felt good to play the Magpies in front of a crowd of 22,000.

We had a win over Fremantle and then a loss against the Eagles to finish our stint in Western Australia, but by then it was clear we would not be going home any time soon. With New South Wales now considered a hotspot as well, virtually the entire competition, aside from the Adelaide-based clubs, was heading to Queensland.

The organisation required to relocate more than half the competition to Queensland was a massive logistics challenge but somehow the AFL managed to pull it off. Teams were spread from the Gold Coast to Noosa. Sides would fly in and out of different capital cities on the same day in Adelaide, Brisbane and on the Gold Coast and at one stage, we were playing matches every fourth or fifth day. Despite the massive disruption, most clubs still found a way to cope, and some even thrived. I was blown away when the Saints, for example, got on a bus from Noosa to Brisbane before dawn, flew to Adelaide and somehow managed to pull off a win.

Being based in Queensland certainly seemed a boost for the Cats as we found form swiftly. Our mantra throughout the season was pretty simple, but also optimistic. We were well aware we would be challenged by the privations imposed upon us, as every club was. But the message from Chris Scott and the coaching staff was that the teams that handled those challenges the best would be in a position to challenge for the premiership. And so it proved. The coaches did an incredible job.

We were able to win seven of our final eight games in the home-and-away season, which included a victory in Adelaide over the Crows, to confirm a top-four spot. Despite the shortened games, another measure introduced to help players cope with the reduced breaks between matches, I was able to strike form as well in attack.

* * *

After prolonged discussions between the League and the Players Association, we received some positive news in the latter stages of our stint in Perth. We would not be able to return home to Victoria as the outbreak had worsened, but at least our families would be able to join us in Queensland after they served a fortnight of quarantine at a resort on the Gold Coast. More than 300 people came to the Gold Coast – AFL and club staff, players, umpires, and their families.

That was a really good thing. I have a lot of friends among those I have played with at Geelong, and those connections extended to their wives and kids, so to have all our families together again was a bonus in such a surreal season.

Being reunited with Emma and Arabella and Primrose was a massive relief. I was really lucky, also, that I was able to get some assistance at home with the property and cattle. My younger brother, Charlie, was then living in Geelong and was able to move out to the farm to lend a hand, while my sisters Jane and Edwina also provided great support. Without that assistance, it would have been far harder for Emma to be away for so long.

During our stint in Queensland, the Cats were based at a Quest Apartment complex adjoining the base of the Southport Sharks Football Club. There were times when I reckon every parent wondered whether the stress of having their kids in an apartment complex for a couple of months was worth it. Our family had two rooms next door to one another, and we left the door between the rooms open, but there were no open windows and admittedly those eight weeks sometimes felt like a slog.

While we were allowed out when those stuck in lockdown in Victoria did not have that option, there were still restrictions in place, and it was far from a normal life. Sitting inside cafes and restaurants and bars was off limits, so too other comforts that everyone takes for granted in normal times. For example, we could go to the beach but purely for exercise and were not able to spend extra time there relaxing.

Those who breached the rules were hit with massive penalties and had to deal with the negative publicity that inevitably followed. A couple of Richmond players were booted out of Queensland.

But other parts of the stint away were brilliant. As it was an experience that we never thought we would endure again, we all tried to make the best of it.

Our family lived next door to the Duncans and on the same floor as the Dangerfields and the Jenkins, among others, and all the kids basically ran riot with each other for two months. The bonds between our families and the broader group grew stronger as a result of the closeness imposed on us. But I have no doubt that the maintenance staff at Southport spent some time repainting scrapes on the wall, and probably had to rip up the carpets as well, after our departure. Incidental damage goes with the territory. As well as that the rooms were tiny.

So for the last four weeks of the season, through the finals, those with families moved to the RACV resort, which was more kid friendly. It was great to have our own community at Quest, but with so many kids at such young ages, the RACV resort gave us more space. What was remarkable was that the Richmond footy club was also there! So, for the entire finals series, several Geelong families would be sharing meals – breakfast and dinner – with the Tigers. As well as the Grand Final at the Gabba being unique, I am sure it will never happen again that players from the two competing teams would be having breakfast together on the morning of the decider!

* * *

On September 2, AFL chief executive Gillon McLachlin confirmed what was already apparent to the entire football competition – the finals would be played in Queensland and South Australia and the Grand Final would be held at the Gabba.

It was not a surprise to any of us given the hundreds of people associated with the AFL – from administrators to journalists and the families and partners of several players – who had arrived in Queensland a week or so earlier to enter hotel quarantine at a resort on the Gold Coast. McLachlan and Gary Ablett Jnr and Gary's family were among the contingent who exited Victoria on the final charter flight north.

Our players and coaches had guessed correctly that the AFL would not go to the expense that it did in setting up camps on the Gold Coast and Sunshine Coast if the decider was going to be held at the MCG.

For us, it was business as usual, though we were looking forward to the return of Gary once he had completed his quarantine. Gary, and a couple of other players including premiership Tiger Shane Edwards and Swan Dan Hannebery, were among those who quarantined with McLachlan and retained their fitness by training on a patch of turf about half the size of a soccer pitch. It was that kind of season!

* * *

Among the many sayings in footy is one that rings particularly true with me – bad kicking is bad football.

I entered the 2020 finals series in good form, having kicked 26.14 in the eight games when we were based in Queensland, a decent effort given the shortened match time, with an impressive accuracy of 65 per cent.

But in our qualifying final against the Port Adelaide in Adelaide, I had a nightmare in front of goal, kicking five behinds and not a solitary goal. Nor was I alone as we kicked ourselves out of the match, starting with 1.4 in the opening quarter and 5.12 for the match, losing by 16 points, ultimately beaten 9.4 (58) to 5.12 (42).

It is not always easy to pinpoint why some matches are better than others when it comes to accuracy. Conditions can play a role. So, too, fatigue or fitness. Some defenders are good at pushing forwards into more difficult positions when it comes to kicking for goal. Of course, if any forward knew the answer, they would never miss. My career accuracy hovers at about 64 per cent – a decent conversion rate. But there were occasions when it felt like I could not hit the side of a barn, let alone weave a ball through that vent back in Finley. That was one of those nights.

The loss left us with a difficult task to win the premiership, but we did have one thing in our favour. We were returning to Queensland, where our form had been strong. So it proved. The next week we ran rampant against Collingwood at the Gabba, managing to hold them to one goal until three-quarter-time as we skipped away to win by 68 points.

I had five shots that night as well, but this time I was able to kick 4.1. What a difference a week makes!

The next test was a big one: we would play the Lions on their home turf in a preliminary final.

Brisbane had been impressive all season and, with the chance to play in a historic Grand Final in their home state, clearly this was going to be a formidable challenge. The first half was tight, with our inaccuracy again an issue, but we were able to take a five-point lead into half-time. We managed to edge away in the third quarter before storming home in the final term win by 40 points. We would be playing in a Grand Final for the first time since winning the 2011 flag.

* * *

Nothing in a player's career compares to the thrill of Grand Final week when you are lucky enough to be involved. The crowds at training, the excitement of the Grand Final parade and the focus on winning the premiership makes it one of the most special experiences of your life. I was fortunate to be involved in four Grand Final weeks in my first five seasons at Geelong, the latter two as a senior player, and they produced some of my great memories. Those weeks were vastly different to the 2020 Grand Final week in Queensland, though it remained a remarkable experience to cap what had been an extraordinary year.

The 2020 decider was a historic event on a couple of fronts. Not only was it played outside Victoria for the first time, but it was also the first to be held at night. We would be playing off for a premiership certain to be remembered forever, given such unusual circumstances.

It did feel strange to be vying for the premiership when almost every Geelong fan was stuck at home and unable to travel more than five kilometres, let alone attend a training session or the parade or actually get to the game. Those things really saddened me and provided another reminder of the weird times we were living. We trained in relative isolation at Southport, walking distance from our lodgings.

My week started poorly after I fell ill with a virus. It was not the one everyone feared, though there was clearly a concern for a couple of days that I might have contracted COVID. In a sign of just how unusual the year was, the announcement that I had tested negative to the coronavirus was announced by the League's chief executive, Gillon McLachlan. But although not COVID, I had been sapped of strength and it left me bed-ridden just four days out from the Grand Final. It was a really nasty bug and flattened me for a couple of days. When I first fell ill, I thought, 'Oh no. Surely not. We have spent all this time away, and made so many sacrifices, and now I am going to miss the Grand Final.'

I was racking my brain, wondering if I had somehow managed to pick up COVID in our brief visits to the supermarket, even though the odds of that happening were astronomical because there were only a handful of cases in Queensland at the time. We were also taking major precautions and were only allowed into stores for a short time while wearing a mask. But it was hard to stop straying to a worst-case scenario and the severity of the symptoms did not help my uneasiness. I had a really sore throat and there is no other way to say it – whatever that lump was at the back of my throat, it was purple, painful and particularly ugly to look at.

On the Monday – Brownlow Medal night – I was sweating badly and had to spend the next day in bed, barely able to eat or drink given how sore my throat was. The virus also knocked Primrose around pretty badly, so we certainly had our concerns as a family.

I missed our initial training session and was isolated from my teammates early in the week for very good reason. It was definitely not something I wanted to pass on so close to the big match. Emma moved away as well. Not only did she not want to put my teammates at risk, she also wanted to be well clear of the Richmond players, given our unusual shared accommodation.

Clearly my preparation was hampered, but I was able to train on Friday and felt okay for the match.

* * *

It seems fitting that the most bizarre season the AFL has experienced almost ended up with the Grand Final being postponed due to an extreme weather event. Talk about surreal. After a near-perfect winter in Queensland, with scarcely a day of rain in the three months we were on the Gold Coast, a ferocious storm hit on Grand Final day. The rain absolutely bucketed down. It was so torrential that at times, visibility from the bus was almost non-existent as we headed to Brisbane.

We got to the Gabba three hours before the start of the game and I was feeling unusually nervous as we completed our final preparations. Of course, I had been nervous before the two premierships we had won in 2009 and 2011, but the presence then of so many senior players who had been there before had a calming effect.

Now I was the senior player and I was more aware that the opportunity to play in a Grand Final was far less common than it seemed when I was in the infancy of my career. Happily, by the time of the opening bounce, the weather had cleared and so too had my nerves. We were ready to deliver our best shot at Richmond.

* * *

The first moments of the game were as fierce and chaotic as any of the other deciders I had been part of. Gary Ablett Jnr badly injured a shoulder when he was crashed into the ground by Richmond captain Trent Cotchin and had to head to the interchange bench. That he returned to play out what would be the final game of his career carrying a crack in his shoulder while still managing to contribute, was a remarkable effort. I had never considered him a highly physical player – he did not need to be given the superiority of his skills – but that was a really tough, gritty performance and even though we lost, it was an exceptional way for him to finish such an incredible career.

Soon after Ablett was felled, Tiger Nick Vlaustin was knocked unconscious when colliding with Patrick Dangerfield in a brutal, though accidental, clash. A lengthy delay followed as Vlaustin was stretchered from the ground. The opening term was particularly tight and when the siren sounded for quarter-time, we led by one point.

We played our best football of the game in the second term and probably should have been further ahead given the chances we had. As it was, we had a very handy buffer until a late goal shortly before half-time changed the entire game. Although I had recovered from the illness that flattened me earlier in the week, I was not at my absolute best in the Grand Final. Playing at the Gabba at night can be tricky given the humidity and with the Grand Final a month later than usual, combined with the massive thunderstorm that hit south-east Queensland earlier in the night, the playing conditions were not great for key forwards. At the other end of the ground, Jack Riewoldt managed to kick a couple, while Tom Lynch snared one, but the conditions suited those closer to the ground. As the match started to get away from us, there was a moment where I felt exhausted. It had been a massive year for so many reasons and it was deflating to think we were not going to be able to clinch the premiership.

Despite our dominance in general play, Dustin Martin was able to conjure a goal out of nothing and our lead was reduced to 15 points at the main break. Martin did what champions do.

That goal hurt. It was not so much that it dented our confidence, because we had played well to that stage and had clearly shown our best could match the best of the Tigers, but I have no doubt that Martin's magic boosted Richmond's belief. That is the beauty of playing alongside a champion like Dusty. Great players give their teammates so much energy. I know this first-hand, having played alongside champions like Gary Ablett Jnr and Joel Selwood and Patrick Dangerfield. Richmond players certainly walked so much taller with 'Dusty' alongside them.

I have no doubt that we would have won that premiership if not for Dusty's phenomenal performance. He just did not miss at critical times, kicking goals from extremely difficult positions. He was dominant and that proved the difference in the end.

After half-time, Richmond played with more purpose, picking up the pace of their ball movement. It was still really tight, but the Tigers were able to score more freely in the third quarter and clinched a two-point lead just before three-quarter-time. Once the straw was broken in the last term, they were able to get away from us, kicking five goals to one, to win by 31 points, but I don't believe the margin does justice to how close the game really was.

* * *

There is little good to say about being beaten in any Grand Final, but this loss was particularly difficult to swallow. I felt extremely disappointed and upset when considering the season as a whole. I felt I had let Emma down given the sacrifices she had made, initially when shouldering responsibility for the kids and the farm, and then when packing up to move to Queensland. That we were unable to clinch the flag for all the Cats who had been left behind in Victoria, from the families of our coaches and support staff to the fans, added to this feeling. It really was a bitter ending to what had been a unique season.

One thing I was grateful for were the bonds that had developed through the season, particularly with younger Geelong players whom I might not have got to know as well, given the different stages of our lives. But once we had lost, I could not wait to leave Queensland and get back to the farm.

It was not that I was not grateful for what had unfolded. The AFL did an extraordinary job navigating the challenges posed during the season and Queensland was a wonderful host.

Some players did stick around to enjoy the sunshine for a few more weeks, but it was time for the Hawkins family to return to the peace and quiet of the farm. Having spent almost four months living out of a bag, and sharing meals and buses and apartment complexes, the comforts and quiet of home were calling.

We had a few beers at the Southport Sharks tavern after the Grand Final, the first time we had actually been allowed into an outside venue for months because of the AFL rules.

It was good to be able to debrief with each other about the loss, and also the weirdness of the season.

There is one aspect to Grand Final day that still makes me chuckle, namely the surprising thrill of realising that Dad had somehow managed to make it to the Gabba for the Grand Final. There is a great story to that which, now that the pandemic is behind us, I feel I can properly reveal. It involved a mix of good fortune and creative thinking.

Dad had contacted Brian Cook, the long-serving Geelong chief executive, who has since joined Carlton, to see if there was any prospect of being able to attend the match. Border restrictions had made it nearly impossible for family and friends to get there without a good reason, particularly from hotspots where two weeks of quarantine was still being enforced. But there were exemptions for truck drivers at the time to enable food and goods to be transported around the country.

What happened after Dad contacted Brian Cook remains a little vague. Brian received a phone call from a Geelong fan who happened to own Dimmeys, the discount retail chain. As it happened, this fan was due to deliver a truckload of goods to a Dimmeys store in Queensland and needed a reserve driver given the length of the trip. The timing of the trip, shall we say, was fortunate. Dad happened to have his truck driving licence and Brian Cook was able to put the pair in contact. The rest is history as they headed up the Newell Highway into Queensland a few days before the game. The reason for the trip was legitimate. They satisfied all the necessary requirements and had the paperwork that enabled them to enter Queensland.

Admittedly, I was not aware of any part of the plan and had no idea Dad was actually at the game until we were in the rooms after. It was a classic move by Dad, and it was great to see him given the family had been separated for so long because of the COVID restrictions.

Once again, this rammed home the most important lesson in life. Family comes first.

* * *

The immense disappointment of losing the Grand Final aside, I was proud to be able to claim the Coleman Medal for the first time in my career, and to gain a third All-Australian guernsey. When you consider the champion forwards who have claimed the Coleman, to have my name on the honour roll, among the best of my time, was something to celebrate. Lance Franklin is among the greatest and most exciting footballers to have played. Jack Riewoldt proved himself a champion with Richmond over my career, with his leap and straight kicking outstanding. West

Coast landed themselves an absolute ripper when they secured Josh Kennedy from Carlton in the trade that saw Chris Judd join the Blues. Josh was a monster of a forward and was extremely hard to defend against on either the lead or in the air and he is someone I admired from afar. Notably, those guys are all premiership forwards, which demonstrates how valuable a good key forward can be for a side in contention to win a flag.

Jeremy Cameron, too, is a deserving Coleman Medallist and I was absolutely delighted when he joined the Cats at the end of 2020. To be able to play alongside him at close quarters gave me an insight into the athleticism and brilliance that has made him a champion forward as well.

It was the first season since 2015 I did not manage to kick 50 goals in a season finishing with 49.36. But the reasons for that are clear. We played five fewer games than usual and the length of those matches was reduced to allow us to cope with the rigours of playing matches off short breaks once the season restarted in June.

24
On it goes

TIME ON THE farm and a few weeks' break in Sydney at the start of 2021 proved the perfect tonic to a return to footy. I was feeling refreshed and reinvigorated, but our sense of anxiety remained. It was clear that, despite the freedom we had felt through the summer, COVID storm clouds were looming on the horizon once again.

We had seen what had occurred in the United Kingdom through their winter and there were also cases in the Victorian community through January, even though we were living our lives freely again.

A successful career in footy requires sacrifice. Players miss a lot of the important milestones of family members or friends due to matches or travel. It is part of our sport. But when the freedoms you love, such as playing golf, or grabbing a beer with your mates, or enjoying a long lunch with your wife, are ripped away, it can make it even harder to switch off. That proved the case for a lot of Victorians throughout 2020 and I think everyone was hoping the following year would be different.

Because the Grand Final had been delayed until late October, pre-season training did not begin until January. The taste of the close-to-regular life we enjoyed over the summer was a welcome relief, but I also craved a return to the norms of footy through winter.

I have always loved the build-up to games, from the training sessions to the analysis of our rivals, the routine and rhythm that comes with match day and the nerves and anticipation that follow. The final siren is definitive. You know immediately whether you have succeeded or failed. There is no better feeling than when we are successful, particularly when victory comes on a Thursday or Friday night. A win then gives you the opportunity to celebrate over the weekend with your family and friends, knowing that all the work you have put in through the week has been worth it. I also follow a fairly set routine after matches and I missed those habits. A prime example was the freedom of being able to duck into a pub near a home game after a Saturday match to meet some mates for a quick beer or two. If we were not playing on a Sunday, my family would often head to one of the many wineries around Geelong and the Bellarine Peninsula for lunch.

* * *

We felt certain we could challenge for the premiership once again if fortune fell our way. We had landed a big off-season signing in GWS Giants' Jeremy Cameron, a fellow Coleman Medallist who grew up in western Victoria and was keen to move closer to home. There was much conjecture as to how we would partner with each other in the front end and what we could ultimately deliver, but having appreciated his talents from afar, I was confident that we would be able to complement each other well. But as I told reporters on our return to training in January, it would take the pair of us some time to gel and to maximise our partnership in attack: 'We're both very different players. He is more agile and leaner than me, but at the same time, he is really powerful. I'd say we will both get a look deep and we'll both get up the ground at stages.'

Jeremy was not the only mature-aged recruit we recruited in the off-season. Isaac Smith, an old rival who had played in three premierships with Hawthorn, and former Bulldog and Kangaroo Shaun Higgins, also joined the Cats. Isaac had just turned 32, and Shaun would be 33 when the season started. Between them they brought 447 games of experience to the club.

After we had come so close to winning a premiership in 2020, the arrival of a trio of such quality clearly boosted the expectation that we would be a contender again in 2021. 'We are well aware that bringing in some experience means there will be external pressure,' I told reporters. 'Internally we have not spoken about it yet, but the majority of the list arrived last Wednesday, and winning another premiership is our ultimate goal, so we will embrace the challenge that is in front of us.'

There was a widespread view that the Cats were signing too many older players, but that is not a viewpoint I accepted. My best footy has been played in my 30s and as long as players are performing, their age should not be a factor in their selection. I was also confident of the quality of the younger talent in our squad. Geelong had only missed the finals once in the previous 15 seasons and those given the task of ensuring we were competitive each year had a proven track record of getting decisions right.

* * *

As I feared, another wave of COVID had a big impact on the season, though there was less disruption across the competition. Some clubs certainly had it tougher than others, which was not ideal for them. It was a reminder to everyone about how fraught the situation remained. The Lions spent a few weeks on the road in the opening month of the year, then the Swans and Giants were forced to leave Sydney from July for the rest of the season. Although the restrictions had an impact on our personal lives, at Geelong we were fortunate to be able to spend the entire home-and-away season based in Geelong.

Our form early on was mixed. We lost to the Crows in Adelaide in round 1 and were lucky to beat the Lions at home by a point in a thriller the following week. Melbourne served us a warning that they were an improving team when they beat us by 25 points at the MCG in round 4. After another loss, this time to Sydney in round 7, we were in the eight on percentage only. A 63-point win over Richmond in our first meeting since the Grand Final boosted our confidence and sparked a surge of six straight wins. I managed to kick four goals against the Tigers at the MCG in what was my best game of the season to date. After that run of wins, by round 20 we shared top spot with the Western Bulldogs with 15 wins and had reason to be optimistic that we were well placed to challenge for the flag again.

* * *

I absolutely love milestone games. The ones involving my teammates are among the most treasured memories of my career and I was lucky to celebrate so many of them. The beauty of a milestone game is that you are able to invite your family and your friends, and they serve as a landmark in which to recognise certain achievements. In my time at Geelong, the club has placed a special emphasis on milestone matches, be it the first, 50th, 100th or 200th game, and so on.

It was always good in the lead-up to those matches to take note what a teammate had done and to celebrate their efforts in reaching that point in their career. We were not successful in these games every time, of course, but Geelong's strong win-loss record through my career meant that, more often than not, milestone matches would finish on a positive note.

When I was a young player, I wondered how many games I would manage in my career and thought it would be special if I managed to match or beat the 182 matches Dad had played. I'm extremely grateful to have been far more fortunate than that. My 250th game, which came against the Swans at the SCG in 2019, rates among the most special memories of my career. I was able, with Emma, to take Arabella and Primrose onto the ground and through the banner, which meant a great deal to me. It was a beautiful day in Sydney, and I had a ripper of a game, kicked five goals and gained two Brownlow votes, as we posted a 27-point win over the Swans after an even first half. When I marked deep in the pocket in the last term and snapped a left-foot goal from near the boundary, it was my first five-goal haul for the year and also a personal record against the Swans. This was the second time Arabella had been out on the ground for a milestone. Although she was only a baby the first time, it was a cool experience. That was in my 200th game against Adelaide at Kardinia Park, the match I was suspended for a jumper punch on Matt Crouch.

Milestone matches were a spur for me. I can remember thinking after playing my 250th that I should aim for 275. After that I thought, 'Let's get to 300!' Only a handful of Geelong players have managed to reach that mark and they are champions of the club. John 'Sam' Newman, who interviewed me on *The Footy Show* when I was 17, was the first, in 1980. Ian Nankervis reached the mark two years later. But from then there was a drought. It was not until premiership teammates Corey Enright and Jimmy Bartel reached the triple century in 2016 that Geelong had a third and fourth member of an exclusive club. Joel Selwood became the fifth in 2020 and I was about to make it a neat half-dozen.

My 300th game was one for the 'Zoom age' because that is how I ended up sharing one of the great milestones in my career with my wife and my daughters. The border restrictions in place precluded any of my family members from being able to fly to Adelaide for our qualifying final against Port Adelaide. That disappointment added to what proved to be a deflating experience.

Under South Australia's COVID regulations, we had to go into strict isolation on Tuesday evening before flying to Adelaide for the Friday night game. It really was a strange week and, as I said to reporters before the match, I was upset about not being able to celebrate the achievement with my loved ones. 'They're not going to be able to come across and I'm going to be away for a bit, which I am shattered about,' I said during a press conference – on Zoom. 'I would've loved to have taken my two girls out and Emma and have my immediate family and my friends come to the game. I take solace in the fact that I've got my teammates there, who are the other part of getting me to where I am today. That's life. I'm only going to play 300 games once, and I understand the situation, but it is a bit disappointing.'

Obviously, there were many people in more difficult situations, with so many people unable to travel interstate to see their families or return to Australia due to the border closures. But each person had their own unique disappointments from the pandemic and that was my flat spot. Making matters worse was the knowledge that no matter how we fared against the Power, with Victoria still in lockdown, we would be travelling to Western Australia for the remainder of the finals.

For the second year in succession in a qualifying final against Port Adelaide at the Adelaide Oval, things did not go to plan. Our form was a concern leading into the finals, for we had suffered losses to the Giants and Melbourne on our home turf in the last three weeks of the season. That loss to the Demons in the final round in the season, in particular, still stings. We absolutely dominated the second term that night, playing some of our best footy for the year, outscoring Melbourne by eight goals to one.

At three quarter-time we still held a 32-point advantage, yet somehow the Demons were able to reel us in in, courtesy of a Max Gawn goal after the siren; they headed into September brimming with confidence.

Port Adelaide were a strong team once again under Ken Hinkley, after being desperately unlucky a year earlier when beaten by Richmond in a thrilling preliminary final. The pandemic had marred their 150th anniversary celebrations in 2020, but they were determined to make up for it in 2021. With 17 wins and second spot on the table behind Melbourne, they had put themselves in contention to win the flag.

We were off the pace from the start, with inaccuracy again an issue as the Power kicked out to a 10-point lead at quarter-time. The second quarter was a nightmare as they moved well ahead with a four goal to one term, effectively ruining our hopes. I kicked a couple of goals, but we were well beaten. It was a rough end to a testing week.

But the message we received from the coaches before heading to Perth was similar to that when we had to travel to Queensland the previous year. If we handled the trip the right way, and adopted a positive mindset, we could still contend.

Thrust into another sudden-death semi-final, we performed well against the Giants, leading throughout and eventually winning by 35 points. I managed to boot five goals. That set us up for another clash against the Demons.

Heading into the preliminary final, we had reason for confidence despite that loss a few weeks earlier. We had played well against the Giants and had demonstrated we were capable of scoring heavily against Melbourne if the circumstances enabled it. The flipside was that coach Simon Goodwin had coached the Demons extremely well and they were full of belief with quality players stretching from full-back to full-forward.

Then disaster struck. Another virus swept through the Geelong group and this time it was not only me who was hit ahead of a critical final. The timing was far from ideal and did not help our chances. I woke up on preliminary final morning feeling half-decent, but midway through the day I was hit by a bout of gastro. Gastro floored at least six of us. There is not really a polite way to put this. I spend a significant portion of the hours before the match on the toilet, which is not the best preparation for a preliminary final. I also vomited in the race at half-time.

Despite that, I did not actually feel terrible early on in the game. I was so busy monitoring the action up the field and reacting to the situation that it distracted me from thinking about my illness. I was absolutely drained by the last term, which is not surprising given the nastiness of the bug.

Before the bug struck, I felt we could contend if fortune happened to fall our way. That wasn't to be, and it was not just about the illness that struck us on preliminary final day. We had also been stricken by injuries at the wrong time of the season and were too inconsistent in our performance. Our best was excellent, but ultimately, we could not produce it when it counted. For all that, Melbourne were deserving winners of the preliminary final and ultimately the premiers after their remarkable Grand Final victory over the Western Bulldogs.

It is one of the rare Grand Finals I have actually watched, and I only caught it because I was with a mate in Mortlake who is a Melbourne fan. Normally I do my best to avoid watching Grand Finals when we are not involved. It is the competitor in me. I always feel so disappointed that we have fallen short of our ambition and Grand Final day only reminds me of what we are missing out on. I absolutely hate them.

* * *

The drama of 2021 did not finish there, and again my timing was astray. The restrictions had started to ease in regional Victoria by the time we returned home, and we took the opportunity to head to the mountains for a family holiday. It was great to get a burst of late-season snow at Mt Buller, which the kids absolutely loved. But then we felt the earth shake, rattle and roll, for we happened to be on the mountain when an earthquake measuring 6.0 struck about 38 kilometres south of Mt Buller.

Talk about scary. The whole room was shaking and I froze, unable to move in my panic. Emma, to her credit, grabbed the two girls and dashed into the bathroom and jumped into the bath. We did have a laugh about that later, because that is what you are supposed to do in cyclones, not during earthquakes! But at least she had done something, which was better than I had managed.

There was some minor damage to buildings in Melbourne, but we were really relieved that we had escaped with only a big scare. After all that had unfolded in the previous two years, surely 2022 would prove a smoother ride. My fingers were well and truly crossed.

25

One hell of a ride

After our 10-point loss to St Kilda at Docklands in round 9, 2022, my confidence of featuring in another Geelong premiership side before my career ended was starting to slip away. Having been a leading contender in the two COVID-riddled years, we were again struggling for consistency.

Losses to a rebuilding Hawthorn in round 5 at the MCG, Fremantle at Kardinia Park in round 7 and then the Saints saw us sitting precariously in seventh spot, well behind the pacesetters. Melbourne were unbeaten and the Brisbane Lions had lost only once, though that was against us in round 4.

My form was strong, with the four goals I booted against the Saints taking my season tally to 27, an average of three a game. But our lack of cohesion overall was clear. We had tinkered with our game plan in the pre-season and added a couple of new faces, but things were not clicking consistently enough for us to feature among the frontrunners.

I've always been an optimist when it comes to footy, but the challenge we faced seemed a step too far. Perhaps those who had written us off as 'too old, too slow' were correct after all, though I was still confident that we could make finals if we could only play at our best. The prospect of finishing in the all-important top four seemed more remote by the week as the losses piled up. The challenge of winning four finals in succession should we get to September seemed a daunting prospect given the quality of some of the other leading sides. I never envisaged the winning streak that was about to begin, the challenge I would face later in the season, an individual acknowledgement that left me stunned, a third premiership to cap a career and the departure of a great mate. Emma was also pregnant and due to give birth to our third child in the middle of the year. It was one hell of a season.

So much for those mid-May blues after the St Kilda loss. I've never been more delighted to be proven so wrong.

* * *

Our optimism was high when we ran out onto the MCG in front of nearly 55,000 fans two months earlier to begin our season against Essendon. There was now a certainty that the worst of the pandemic was behind us. Victoria was back open, as were the borders around the country, and the prospect of having to leave our families behind and head off to a hub somewhere was now remote. Life was getting back to normal and it was great to know we would be back playing in front of big crowds.

We were enthusiastic about a change to our game plan. Conceived with input from assistant coaches Shaun Grigg and James Kelly, there was a strong belief that hastening ball movement from defence and backing our players to focus more on their strengths would make a big difference. With Jeremy Cameron entering his second season, and new recruit Tyson Stengle showing promising signs in the pre-season, we had an attack that should be potent. The trick was making sure the ball came down often enough, and at speed, to let us use our talents. Grigg, who had played in Richmond's 2017 premiership team and was considered an astute tactician, stressed that the Tigers were able to harness the best from Dustin Martin by using him in short bursts out of the middle while ensuring he was never too far away from goal. We still have nightmares about how destructive he was in the 2020 Grand Final.

Grigg believed that Patrick Dangerfield was capable of being similarly destructive if he was allowed to focus more on an attacking role. The plan was to enable him to roam from the centre through to half-forward given his ability to win the ball and sprint from a contest. The theory was that we did not necessarily need Dangerfield to be focusing too heavily on the defensive side of footy when we had players with exceptional defensive skills – like Tom Atkins, who I considered to be in the top 10 tacklers in the League – to cover that area. 'Danger' still had defensive tasks. We all did. But just as my role was to kick as many goals as possible while also setting up my teammates, we placed a premium on him running offensively forward of the centre.

There was also enthusiasm about the potential of some of the fresher faces in the team. Jeremy Cameron, of course, had already shown his wares with 39 goals in 2021, and Isaac Smith had shown in his 24 games with us that none of his gut-running had diminished. There was confidence that both of them would become far more influential in their second seasons having become more familiar with the traits of their teammates, and the Geelong way. Both were naturally aggressive players who covered the ground well and boasted exceptional skills, which we believed would assist the more aggressive system as well. Through the pre-season we were also encouraged by the development shown by several youngsters including Sam de Koning, Max Holmes, Brad Close, Jack Henry and Gryan Miers.

Tyson Stengle was the wildcard and we were all intrigued to see how he would perform. A nephew of former Sydney champion Michael O'Loughlin and a relative of former Carlton and Adelaide star Eddie Betts, he had shown talent as a small forward with Richmond and then Adelaide early in his career, kicking 15 goals from 16 matches over four years. His troubles throughout 2020 were well known after he lost his way in Adelaide, finding himself in trouble for a series of off-field incidents including drink-driving and possessing an illicit substance.

The Crows ultimately lost patience with him and he was delisted after the 2020 season, when he had played 14 games. But to his great credit he worked hard to turn his life around and returned to his original club Woodville-West Torrens, where he played 19 games, kicked 44 goals, made the South Australian team, and was named in SANFL's Team of the Year. To top that off, he kicked three goals in the Grand Final in Woodville-West Torrens' premiership victory.

The Cats' decision to recruit Stengle was supported by Betts, then our development coach, who had housed Stengle when he returned to Adelaide after being traded by Richmond for pick 62; Grigg also affirmed his potential after having played with him at Punt Road in 2017. Veteran list manager Stephen Wells and my former teammate Andrew Mackie, who was moving into a senior role in the footy department, were confident he deserved a second chance. It took only one game for Stengle to deliver as we kicked 20 goals to rout Essendon by 66 points, which provided fans with an early taste of the potency we were capable of. Stengle and I finished with four goals each, with Cameron kicking a couple as well in what was an encouraging start to the season.

A trip to the SCG a week later, which resulted in a 30-point loss, doused our optimism a little, but we were not overly perturbed given we had more scoring shots, with inaccuracy a factor in the loss. We bounced back to defeat Collingwood and Brisbane leading into the round 5 clash against Hawthorn, whose form has been up and down. At that stage the vibe around the club was entirely positive, but then came that frustrating period which led to those doubts. No matter how either club is travelling, matches against Hawthorn are always massive but after an inaccurate start, we never recovered in the Easter Monday clash.

After beating North Melbourne, the next week, we opened with five goals in the first quarter against Fremantle at home but managed only another five for the match to be beaten by three points. In hindsight it was not as bad a loss as it felt at the time, given the Dockers went on to play in the finals, but to manage only 10 goals at home given our talent was a below-par effort. It demonstrated the importance of Patrick Dangerfield, who was managing a corkie through the middle stages of the season and missed the match. We surely missed his run from the middle. We did recover to easily defeat the Giants before that loss to the Saints.

Unlike in 2007, there was no Paul Chapman-style burst delivered to the players. For starters, although the team was full of strong-willed competitors desperate to win another premiership, they were more measured and this was also mirrored in Chris Scott's approach. Among Chris Scott's strengths is the clarity in which he approaches any predicament. That skill is matched by the belief he has in our ability to overcome adversity. My faith may have been wavering but the message we received from Chris back at the club after the St Kilda loss was relatively optimistic. He told us that we 'were not too far off and just needed to tweak a few things'. He referred to our cohesion, our team defence and also our inaccuracy. There was no sense of panic at all. His points were strong. I was looking at our win-loss record, but those four losses were scarcely disastrous. We had kicked badly against the Swans (10.17) and lost the other three matches by a total of 25 points, while three of our five wins to that stage had been by 50 points or more. When we got it right, we were hard to beat.

We were also averaging more inside 50-metre entries than in previous seasons – up seven from a year earlier and the most since our most 2011 premiership – and the statistics also showed we were more efficient with our disposal, a by-product of our more direct style.

There was also clear evidence that those younger teammates were developing rapidly. Sam de Koning, for example, had played just one game leading into 2022 but was excelling in a key defensive post, while others including Max Holmes were showing great promise.

Confidence is a factor in footy, and it was stressed to us that a great opportunity was upon us to regain our momentum with matches against Port Adelaide and the Crows at home. As part of the message that year, Chris used an analogy based around swimming between the flags and stressed that if we wanted to become a great team, it would be worth exploring the territory beyond the flags, so to speak. Risks could lead to rewards. We were not to be mindless. Swimming outside the flags can be dangerous, after all. Turning the footy over in a reckless manner would allow the opposition the ability to hurt us on the scoreboard. But if there was an opportunity to swim in free water – namely, to take the game on and find space and keep the ball moving – it could be worth taking that chance.

Things did not click immediately against the Power, with our kicking for goal still ordinary (11.16), but we were able to hold them to just seven goals in a comprehensive 35-point win. Against Adelaide a week later, we straightened things up from quarter-time, scoring 13.3 in the last three quarters, and ran away with a seven-goal victory before returning to the Docklands to win for a tough 13-point triumph over the Western Bulldogs heading into the bye.

It is far better to be in contention for the finals heading into winter than out of the race and that hat-trick of victories made it easier to bounce out of bed for training. Our streak continued after the bye, with wins over the Eagles in Perth and Richmond at the MCG before we thumped North Melbourne by 112 points at home, a match in which I kicked a season-high six goals. That win took us to second on the ladder.

That run of wins set the stage for a defining match, at home, against Melbourne. After consecutive losses to Fremantle, Sydney and Collingwood leading into the bye, the Demons had bounced back to defeat Brisbane and Adelaide leading into our clash. Melbourne had beaten us in all three matches in 2021, and we still considered them the team to beat. But we had plenty of motivation to turn the tables. The adage about every game being worth four points is true and while coaches and players try to approach each match the same way, there is clearly a heightened value on some matches.

Matches against reigning premiers, at any time, are classic examples. So, too, are games against sides that have had success over you recently. It was also Isaac Smith's 250th match and while he was only in his second season with Geelong, he had already become a popular teammate. Add to the mix a battle for top spot and this was a significant match for us.

It turned out to be a match every bit as tough as we expected, with the result still in the balance midway through the final quarter. The defensive strength of Tom Atkins was on show as he proved a midfield dynamo with eight tackles. We were also able to limit the effectiveness of Max Gawn who, although he won the hitouts, failed to take a mark for the match in a battle against Rhys Stanley and Mark Blicavs.

Midway through the last term, with Geelong's lead reduced to seven points after Melbourne goals by Kysaiah Pickett and Christian Petracca, a Pickett shot hit the post and Bayley Fritsch missed soon after as we steadied. Although the margin ended up being 28 points, the result was not sealed until the 25-minute mark after goals by Mitch Duncan and Tyson Stengle. Our winning streak had now extended to seven, and we were now on top of the ladder.

* * *

Six days after our triumph over Melbourne – on July 13 – Emma gave birth to Henry Frederick. We were absolutely delighted. Emma had announced midway through January that she was pregnant, but we decided against finding out the gender of the new addition, preferring it to be a surprise.

We always wanted to have another child, but Emma had faced some challenges through the pregnancies of Arabella and Primrose with morning sickness and back and pelvic pain. The first and third trimesters were particularly difficult for her with the girls, so the decision to have a third child was not taken lightly. But we really wanted to add to our family. This was not driven by any wish to have a boy, though the arrival of Henry was a pleasant bonus, but simply because Emma and I come from families with four children and we had enjoyed really happy childhoods. We felt it was a case of the more, the merrier.

The girls are very outgoing with strong personalities and it was clear from the time we arrived home with Henry that they loved having him around and were very affectionate. Whether this remains the case in the years to come will be interesting, because if he turns out to behave in the manner I did towards my sisters when we were young, they will have their moments.

Emma was again amazing through the early stages of Henry's life. While it was great for me to be on the verge of playing in another finals series, it also meant I was going to be rather busy. Strategically, and sometimes forcefully, Emma allowed me to get some extra sleep and relaxation on my days off during our push to the premiership while she slogged through parenting a newborn along with our two extremely energetic daughters.

I'm a hands-on dad and probably would have worn myself out through this period, but Emma was really conscious of allowing me to try to stay as fresh as possible through the winter. We were both aware that the season was only a couple of months from finishing and that I would be able to assume more responsibility after that.

Henry's arrival means we now have three chances for the Hawkins name to continue at Geelong for at least another generation. There is no pressure, though. I'm very much of the opinion that the kids can do whatever they want as they grow up and we just want them to be healthy and happy, but wouldn't it be amazing to see Belle, Mimi and Henry playing for the Cats!

I suspect the Geelong recruiters will be keeping tabs on the Hawkins trio as they become teenagers, to see whether they will continue our family dynasty on the footy field.

* * *

Our roll continued with victories over Carlton, Port Adelaide and the Western Bulldogs to extend our streak to double figures heading towards the finals. The win over the Power at Adelaide Oval proved to be particularly satisfying after they kicked eight goals in the third term to seize the lead, putting our streak in jeopardy. We responded strongly in the last term to win by 12 points and I added another four goals to my tally for the season to move to within one goal of reaching the half century.

Things were almost too good to be true and, sure enough, a significant challenge arose in mid-August which cast into doubt my ability to finish the season as strongly as I hoped. After our round 22 win over the Suns on the Gold Coast, I started to feel pain under the second toe of my left foot. It was not unusual for me to experience tightness in the plantar fasciitis – and in both feet. It is something I have always had to manage. Right back to the issues that ended my second season in 2008, I have asked our club masseuses to put extra work into massaging the arches in my feet to alleviate pressure. But this was something different and it felt quite painful and certainly uncomfortable. It honestly felt like I was walking around with a rock pressing into the bottom of my toe. It was not ideal, particularly at this stage of the season.

I had the foot scanned when we were back in Geelong and it showed there was a partial tear in the plantar plate that connects the bones in the toes to the foot. The medical staff said there was a concern the plate could tear completely, but they also felt confident it was a problem that could be managed, and I would be able to play.

I kicked four goals in the last game of the season against West Coast, but the pain was worsening so the medicos decided it was best to give it a cortisone injection in the hope it would help to settle the pain before the qualifying final against Collingwood.

The challenge was being able to do enough work in training to retain my fitness and touch without overloading the foot and making the problem worse. This was difficult for me as I loved training and wanted to do everything possible to prepare for any match. With the prospect of another premiership now a real possibility, given our sparkling form, I was determined to make sure I did everything in my power to be fit enough to play.

* * *

My priority has always been team success but during the break between the regular season and finals series I was stunned by an individual accolade that came my way at the AFL's annual Awards ceremony.

All five of the Cats who were named in the preliminary squad of 40 for the All-Australian team, including me, made that year's side. I was thrilled with the recognition shown to Jeremy Cameron, Tyson Stengle, Tom Stewart and Mark Blicavs.

It was great to see Stengle's inclusion, in particular. I must say that when he arrived at the club, I did not really know too much about him, other than that his exit from Adelaide caused a stir due to the circumstances, but his talent was apparent immediately and the deeds that he managed throughout the season were indicative of just how outstanding a player he was. To kick 53 goals in a season as a small forward is extraordinary and he clearly established himself among the top couple of players in that position.

The All-Australian announcement came before the Grand Final, but there were moments in the decider when I was blown away by his talent. Of the four goals that he kicked, one in particular stands out to me. He had the footy outside the

50-metre arc and, thinking that he was going to struggle to make the distance, I worked hard to offer a lead. But he ran straight towards the man on the mark and kicked straight through the ball with the sweetest of timing, the ball soaring through the middle and ending up about ten rows back into the stands. He was like that around the club as well; to the point. We would always laugh because Tyson tended to be the last person to arrive for a club meeting, though it is worth noting he was never late. And we joked with him and he would look at us and tell us to relax. He had it all under control.

This was the fifth time I had been named in the game's best 22 and, as a mark of the consistency I found in my 30s, it was my fourth successive All-Australian honour. Since I turned 30, on the day we played Melbourne in round 18, 2018, I had kicked 260 goals in 99 games, an average of 2.6 goals a game, better than my career average of 2.2. What truly was a surprise was that I was announced captain of a side that also featured club leaders the calibre of Max Gawn, Patrick Cripps and Touk Miller. On the night I said I had never captained a side of any description before, but it had slipped my mind that I had co-captained Melbourne Grammar's First XVIII with Xavier Ellis.

I am aware that the decision to award me the All-Australian captaincy prompted some eyebrow-raising among fans given the presence of the outstanding skippers in the side. But the AFL had made it clear in recent years that the honour went to players for their broader impact on the game and as a celebration of their legacy. In the years before my captaincy, champions including Lance Franklin, Alex Rance and Patrick Dangerfield were named captain of the side when they were not their club's captain. Such chatter in no way diminished how grateful and honoured I was to be both named in the side again and also to be its captain. As I also said on the night, to be selected alongside some of the best players of my generation was truly cool.

There is another element to this. While I never officially held leadership roles at Geelong, I did my best to lead by example around the club once I had become a senior player. In part I tried to support Joel Selwood in any way I could, be it by taking additional press duties, when trying to lure new recruits to the club or making younger players feel welcome. I have been blessed to play under some outstanding captains in Tom Harley, Cameron Ling, Joel Selwood and Patrick Dangerfield but it was nice to have the (c) next to my name for once.

* * *

I always feel nervous leading into finals and despite the momentum we had built during our 13-match winning streak, this year proved no different. As well as we were playing, there was an unwanted record everyone at Geelong was familiar with – namely, our struggle to produce our best footy in recent finals series. After doing the hard work to secure a double chance, we had squandered the advantage when beaten by Port Adelaide in the first week in the previous two finals series while Collingwood had also beaten us in a qualifying final in 2019.

Only once since our 2011 premiership had we managed to win a final of any description in the opening week and that was against Hawthorn in 2016, but we then fell to the Swans in the preliminary final.

Playing Collingwood at the MCG always adds another layer of anticipation given the certainty there will be a big crowd, with the majority barracking for the Magpies. We were well aware they were a team capable of challenging. Under new coach Craig McRae, Collingwood had become a team that thrived under pressure. The tighter a game, the better they seemed to perform. The Magpies were considered miracle workers, with their seven wins in the final eight games of the home-and-away season all delivered by under 10 points. It must have been thrilling – and chilling – to watch as a fan, but it also signalled to us that it would be a tough and testing match that was likely to go down to the wire. And so it proved.

Our nerves were apparent from the opening siren as we struggled to move the footy with the same fluidity that had become our DNA in the second half of the season. That was also partly due to Collingwood's relentless pressure, and they kicked the first three goals of the match, to the delight of the Magpie army among the 91,525. It was not until Jeremy Cameron was able to find some room on his left foot with a couple of minutes left in the first quarter that we could score our first goal.

Given the Magpies inaccuracy – they had just 3.5 on the board – we were lucky to be trailing by only 14 points at quarter-time. But there was no real sense of panic because we knew we had not played well and believed we could bring the match back to level terms if we pulled it together.

I scored my only goal early in the second quarter when, despite being manned by Jeremy Howe, I managed to mark and kick accurately from a tricky angle. We kicked the first three goals of the term to hit the front before Will Hoskin-Elliott reclaimed the lead for Collingwood not long before half-time.

The third quarter was remarkably even. Ash Johnson kicked a great goal from the boundary line before Jeremy Cameron responded in kind. But after Jamie Elliott goaled right on the siren, the Magpies were able to take a seven-point lead into the final quarter. With Collingwood's record in tight matches, we now faced a significant test. When Jordan de Goey kicked the first goal of the last quarter to take their lead to 12 points, our task had become even tougher.

But then our stars rose to the challenge. Joel Selwood was brilliant out of the middle. Cameron kicked another critical goal. Gary Rohan took a superb mark and kicked an outstanding goal from outside the 50-metre arc, with just under five minutes remaining, to give us a one-point lead. A behind to Jack Crisp then tied the scores with under two minutes to play.

Despite heavy pressure, and plenty of fumbles, we managed to move the ball to our forward line, with Rohan able to handball to Max Holmes, alone in the goal square, for a simple goal. It proved enough. We had survived a thriller and broken the qualifying final curse without playing our best footy. Thankfully, we now had a week's rest after such a ferocious match.

That was especially true for me, because at some stage during the match – and I really have no idea when – my plantar plate tore completely. My challenge was getting bigger.

* * *

Another discussion with the medical staff followed: how best to treat the foot problem now that the plate was completely torn. The equation was straightforward. At most, I would have two more matches left in the season and we had a fortnight's break until our next outing against either Melbourne or Brisbane.

Remarkably, if anything, the level of pain I was feeling had reduced slightly as a result of the tear, but it meant there would be no option but to undergo surgery at some stage to repair the damage. Being assured that, in the short term, it was unlikely I would do any further significant damage was more than enough for me to agree to do everything possible to ensure I kept on playing.

The first course of action was to fashion a carbon-fibre plate that would sit in my shoes and boots in order to take some of the weight off the joint, near the second toe of my left foot. It was also decided I would need to train at least once leading into the preliminary final, which meant I would receive a pain-killing injection before the main session of the week. Naturally, I was extremely careful with the foot, trying to minimise risks, whether at home or around the club.

For the first time since winning a qualifying final in 2016, we had the luxury of sitting back in the second week of the finals and watching our prospective preliminary final opponents play. Melbourne was clearly the team to beat midway through the season, but by the time they reached September, it was clear they were not quite in the same touch as in 2021. The Demons dominated the first half against Brisbane at the MCG but were inaccurate and had no response to the Lions' surge in the second half and were beaten by 13 points.

Geelong had not played the Lions since a 10-point win in a tough match at Kardinia Park in round 4, but we had great respect for them, mindful they were clearly in a premiership window. Brisbane's midfield was outstanding and Lachie Neale, Dayne Zorko and Hugh McCluggage had been superb in the second half against Melbourne.

After our break we felt refreshed and my foot felt in reasonable condition when we stepped out for the preliminary final. Even better was the manner in which we started, in stark contrast to the nervous, uncertain beginning against Collingwood. Patrick Dangerfield kicked a goal in the opening minute and we never looked back, increasing our lead at every break to win by 71 points. It was one of those matches where almost everything went right and in the final stages, we were able to really enjoy the game knowing that we had an impregnable lead.

It also proved to be a massive confidence boost for me. Manned by Harris Andrews, I was able to checkside a goal late in the second term to give us a five-goal lead at half-time and I ended up kicking four goals for the night from 14 disposals. Most pleasing was the manner in which I was able to move. The injury did not prevent me from pushing off on the lead, or wrestling with Andrews when required or being able to pivot onto either leg, which was a real plus leading into the Grand Final. I knew I would be right to play in the decider.

The only negative from the night was the hamstring injury suffered by Max Holmes midway through the third term. He had been a revelation in his second season, playing 18 games, and was clearly in our best 22. It is never easy to see someone have their Grand Final dream torn away from them and it was no surprise to see how frustrated and disappointed he was on the sidelines.

The Swans entered the Grand Final on a nine-match winning streak, capped by their thrilling one-point victory over Collingwood in the preliminary final at the SCG, and were clearly a team to be respected.

We had not played Sydney since round 2 at the SCG when we had kicked badly to lose by 30 points, the heaviest defeat of the four losses we had for the year. We felt confident we had improved significantly since March and felt remarkably fresh going into the Grand Final following the easy victory over Brisbane.

* * *

The message from Chris Scott heading into Grand Final week was for us to make it one to remember. We were aware we had a job to do, but as we had missed the usual Grand Final week celebrations in Brisbane in 2020, Chris stressed the importance of enjoying the lead-in to the decider while ensuring we prepared properly.

On Sunday night, Emma and I sat down to work out the logistics for the days ahead. Although you try to approach it like any other week, it is never the case. The first thing to do was to consider ticket requests and make sure we could cater for those closest to the family who wanted to attend. A babysitter needed to be arranged for the Brownlow Medal function as both Emma and I would be attending. Even the finer details associated with our trip to Melbourne on the Thursday ahead of the Grand Final Parade, including Henry's sleeping routine, needed to be pinned down. From then on, the week seemed to go like a dream.

Everyone from the local postie to Belle's teachers and her friends at school were up for a quick chat to wish us well.

The atmosphere at the main training session was outstanding and so, too, was the crowd at the Grand Final Parade. There had been some criticism of the decision to float the players down the Yarra River on barges but to see the banks lined with thousands of people, with the city as the backdrop, made for a spectacular view. It's a sight I'll never forget.

Emma did an incredible job to navigate the crowd with our kids in order to meet me at the cars for the final parade to the MCG – my favourite part of the day. I was riding with Brandan Parfitt, who is great with children and someone our girls really like, and it was wonderful to see the crowd at the event after the trauma of the previous two years. The whole day really was a great thrill.

* * *

We were braced for a massive challenge from Sydney given the ferocious manner with which they attacked the contest all year, combined with their high level of skill. The Swans had emerged as an exciting team in 2022, with a legend in Lance Franklin and stars including Luke Parker, Isaac Heeney, Callum Mills and Dane Rampe, well supported by exciting youngsters Errol Gulden, Chad Warner and James Rowbottom.

They were extremely strong around the contest and, when not in possession of the footy, were a side that applied great pressure on the ball carrier in a bid to force a turnover.

As is the case with most Grand Finals, the initial stages were fierce, with neither side giving an inch for the first 10 minutes or so. It was how we had anticipated the entire match to unfold. Fortunately, I was able to break the arm-wrestle after nine minutes when, at a boundary throw-in deep in attack, I was able to edge Tom Hickey out of position and snap accurately after I had thrown the footy onto my boot. Five minutes later, a similar situation occurred, though this time on the half-forward flank about 35 metres from goal. Once again, I managed to edge Hickey under the ball and was able to turn and kick a checkside punt, which flew straight through the middle. As difficult as it was at the time, those boundary line throw-ins were perfect examples of the benefits of the education I had received from Bomber Thompson in 2010 when I was played in the ruck.

Those two goals helped settle any nerves while providing the side with a confidence booster. It was clear we had survived an early onslaught and were now finding our rhythm. Everything was going our way. Patrick Dangerfield and Joel Selwood were creating drive from the middle. Isaac Smith and Mark Blicavs drifted forward to score crucial goals and at quarter-time we had built a commanding 35-point lead.

My third and final goal for the day came midway through the second term from a tight angle about 35 metre out, after I received a free kick when Tom McCartin fell into my back. That put us seven goals in front, but the Swans were able to settle for the first time, with Isaac Heeney kicking a late goal to reduce our advantage to six goals at half-time.

The third term was a joy to be a part of as we put the match beyond doubt, kicking six goals to Sydney's solitary behind. Isaac Smith kicked another outstanding goal and Tyson Stengle demonstrated his All-Australian capabilities with a couple of magnificent goals as well.

* * *

With a 74-point lead at three-quarter-time, the premiership was well in hand when I made my way down into the rooms for what would be my last painkilling injection for the season. For the briefest of moments I pondered whether to sit out the match on the interchange bench but, while I was happy it would be the last time we would have to numb the joint, I wanted to spend the last quarter out in the middle, given how long we had waited for this moment.

Geelong's scriptwriter was clearly on song that day. With just under two minutes to go, Joel Selwood capped an incredible day and remarkable career with a superb goal, from 45 metres out, kicked with an unlikely checkside. That truly was a fairytale moment for Joel. For one thing, it was actually out of character, because I had never seen him kick that type of goal before. Usually he would try to pinpoint someone with a pass from that position. It reminded me of the goal Cameron Ling snapped at the end of the 2011 Grand Final. Just as it did for Lingy, this proved a fantastic finale to Joel's celebrated career.

As I was walking back towards the goal square after Joel's goal, my emotions got the better of me and I started to shed a tear. I simply could not believe that everything had come together so perfectly. Jeremy Cameron, whom I had edged out by two goals to claim the Geelong goalkicking award with 67 for the season – my eleventh in a row – could not stop laughing while standing nearby me. He came over at one stage and said: 'Mate. Stop bloody crying. We are about to win the Grand Final.'

I have always been emotional and am pretty quick to come to tears when I'm particularly moved, either by a tragedy or those moments in life where you are celebrating a great joy. And this was one of those moments. Jeremy had noticed, but I am not too sure Tom McCartin did. Or, if so, he chose not to make a point of it. He is a lovely man and a very good player and I'm sure, given the circumstances, he would have preferred to be anywhere else at that moment.

Would I have liked to know at that stage whether Joel was retiring? I am still not certain. It felt remarkably special to be able to celebrate another premiership with him given our history together and I doubt that me having certainty around it being his last game would have made any difference. After all, I was already swept up in the emotions of the premiership.

* * *

There was so much to be delighted about in the aftermath of our 81-point triumph. From my perspective, it truly felt like this premiership was the most special of all. Although I had kicked goals in each of our three winning Grand Finals, and also in the 2020 loss, there was a sharp difference in my role this time around. In 2009 I was a fringe player in a team of champions. In 2011 I played a really strong game, but for a period in that year I had spent time in the reserves. Now I felt like a true leader who had played a significant role from round 1 to the final siren of the Grand Final, which made the triumph sweeter than the other successes.

It felt like all our senior players led, by Joel but also including Mitch Duncan, Patrick Dangerfield, Zach Tuohy, Mark Blicavs, Tom Stewart, Gary Rohan, Cam Guthrie and Rhys Stanley had set the tone for a long time at the club and they could proudly claim responsibility for this premiership. The input of newer additions Jeremy Cameron and Isaac Smith was invaluable, with their leadership immense from their arrival in 2021. To be able to celebrate with so many younger teammates who were in the position I had been 13 years earlier made the celebrations even more special.

As is always the case following a premiership, the rooms afterwards were chaotic, but this time I was able to enjoy it with my children along with the rest of my extended family. We partied in good fashion, but with my age and role as a dad kicking in, I was no longer setting the pace. That made the Sunday gathering at the club in Geelong even more memorable and I'm so glad my kids were around to enjoy the party.

We gathered as usual for Mad Monday celebrations. It was the first time in 11 years where we truly had something to celebrate, but we could not resist a little dig at those who had written us off when suggesting we were too old and slow earlier in the season. A group of the more mature Cats raided our local op shops, and our grandparents' cupboards in order to dress like residents from a retirement village. We grabbed Zimmer frames and dressed in cardigans, baker boy caps and donned glasses with the thickest lenses. Joel Selwood had come up with the idea midway through Grand Final week and, in keeping with the light-hearted nature of the jibe, noted on social media that we had 'better make the most of today (because I'm) not sure if we'll make the 10-year reunion'.

* * *

The text message I was dreading came on the Wednesday, five days after the Grand Final, and it read: 'Mate. Are you around? I might just pop out to say g'day'. The sender? Joel Selwood.

I immediately knew what was about to happen. It probably shows how naive I am because while going out on a pinnacle as premiership captain is completely understandable, the way Joel had performed on Grand Final day – from the drive he provided through the middle to the goal he kicked to finish off the match – suggested he had far more to offer.

I was thinking, 'Why can't we do this again?' Geelong had been unable to defend a premiership in my time at the club but with the team we had and given our dominance in the final fortnight of the season, the prospect of achieving that feat was something we should consider.

There was also a part of me that really did not want him to go. He had been there alongside me every step of my career and provided the best friendship and leadership imaginable. I told Emma that Joel was coming to see me and when he arrived, he took me away from the living room, saying that he needed to tell me something.

I was thinking 'Oh fuck' but somehow, I managed to hold it together, which was strange given how significant the moment was and how emotional I had been throughout the week. My matter-of-fact reaction is something we have laughed about since. Joel said that when he was driving away to inform a couple of other teammates, he had sworn while telling his wife, Brit, that he had expected me to care a little bit more than I had shown.

But his decision truly left me feeling really hollow for a few days. After he left, I jumped into the car and went for a long drive around our property, contemplating the triumphs we had shared together and considering what his retirement could mean for me in the future. It was not as though someone had died, but I felt so flat, knowing that our time together on the footy field was at an end. But what a great ride we had enjoyed together.

* * *

This might sound strange but in terms of the plantar tear, it fell at a time in the season when I was able to manage it for long enough to survive in those last matches before requiring surgery. Had it occurred a couple of weeks earlier, it may well have reached a point where I needed to make a serious decision about whether playing on was worth the risk associated with making the injury worse.

A chance meeting with former Western Bulldogs midfielder Mitch Wallis while I was sitting on the beach in Noosa post-surgery rammed home just how fortunate my timing had proved. He asked me about the moon boot I was wearing and revealed that my injury was remarkably similar to what he had suffered against us in round 12 that season.

Out of contract at the end of the year, he tried to manage the problem for an extended period but ultimately it led to stress fractures and issues with his toes. He ultimately underwent a foot reconstruction and did not play at AFL-level again. That underlined just how lucky I was in terms of the timing, because if the injury had occurred a fortnight earlier, it is possible I could have developed similar stress reactions.

Clearly I had been fortunate to play in another premiership while not suffering a more serious injury, one that could have ended my career.

26

No joy

My emotions were in a whirl as I walked onto Kardinia Park for my first training session of 2023 after spending a prolonged period leading into Christmas wearing a moon boot. There was an obvious anxiety as to whether my foot had recovered properly. I had been cleared to resume training, but had to take it carefully because you never really know how well an injury has recovered until you can test it yourself, but I was really excited about being able to move properly again.

After our premiership success, I made the calculated decision to delay surgery for a few weeks to allow me to spend some quality time with Emma and the kids, and to celebrate our premiership success properly. The arrival of Henry midway through 2022 had been a blessing, but the previous three years had been intense given the stress associated with navigating COVID. Both the club and I were aware that the post-op rehabilitation on my plantar plate would take around four months, which meant my chance of playing in the opening round of our premiership defence, against Collingwood, was remote. But Chris Scott did not think that was a bad thing and told me that starting the season a little later could prove a positive.

In recent years, a conscious effort had been made at Geelong to manage the load of older players throughout seasons in order to keep them fresh, but I was an outlier in this regard, having played every match since I had missed the 2019 preliminary final through suspension. No matter the issue, from the viruses in the finals in 2020 and 2021, to the foot issue in 2022, I was able to find a way to make sure I was fit enough to play. Now in my mid-30s, and with nearly 330 games under my belt, a delayed start would freshen me up mentally and physically and allow me to flourish again in 2023.

* * *

Before the surgery, I was told that it was unusual for a player of my size and role to suffer the problem as it normally affects midfielders, who cover more ground. Without the supporting mechanism in place as a result of the rupture of the plantar plate, my second toe had become displaced and was quite painful in the weeks before the operation.

The surgery involved shortening my second toe by eight millimetres while also repairing the plantar plate. The surgeons also had to remove part of the fat pad from underneath the foot, which has been a life-changing experience. By that, I mean that I now wear shoes wherever possible because I realised soon after I started walking again without the moon boot that there was not much protection below my left foot now. Walking bare foot on the floorboards at home early one morning proved a sobering experience.

In all, I spent about seven weeks in the boot. While the technology has improved significantly during my time in footy, anyone who has used one will know they are an inconvenience. I was not allowed to put any weight on the foot immediately after the surgery, which meant I had to take a lot of baths instead of showers early in the recovery period. I was, however, able to fashion a way to sleep by finding a position to allow my foot to hang out of the bed. But not surprisingly, chasing after the kids was off the table for a period, which prevented me from giving Emma the support she deserved after such a busy year.

* * *

The weeks leading into the Christmas break went really slowly, though in the latter stages of the initial pre-season block, I was able to start doing some stationary boxing while exercising on non-weight-bearing fitness machines. But I didn't enjoy that time at all, and not just because I was limited in my training.

I was also missing my mates. For the first time in my career, aside from a few weeks when I was bed-ridden with that back complaint in 2013 and 2014, I was not on the training track and this surely contributed to the disconnect I felt during the rehab.

Footy moves very swiftly and when you return to the club to start a new pre-season, your focus shifts immediately to figuring out a way to win the next premiership. At the start of each pre-season, Joel Selwood and I would shake hands or give each other a fist bump and say to each other, 'Let's do this. We can win it this year.' It was a yearly ritual between us.

I missed that moment, but it was not just Joel I was missing. I felt the absence of some of the other experienced guys. Luke Dahlhaus and Shaun Higgins, who had arrived from the Bulldogs and North Melbourne, more recently, and were reliable on the field and excellent guys around the club had both retired at the end of 2022 as well.

The solution was clear. The sooner I was able to get back on the training track, the better. With the emphasis on being cautious, my training regime in January was very simple. The first week we focused on doing slow 50- to 60-metre stride-throughs in a straight line with a focus on my running technique and it gradually built from there. It was just over two months away from our first-round fixture against Collingwood on St Patrick's Day at the MCG, but for me, a return in early April had been pencilled in.

My main point of contact was Dr Ben Serpell, our senior strength and conditioning coach, but I also worked closely with Dr Sue Mayes, an experienced physiotherapist who has worked extensively with ballet companies around the world while also consulting with several other sports including cricket, tennis and basketball. I was not about to be gracing the stage in any production of *Cats*, nor would I be auditioning for a role in *The Nutcracker*, but her expertise was invaluable as I worked through techniques designed to ensure that my foot and toe were able to hold up under pressure.

At no stage did I feel a sense of urgency to try to return before early April, with good reason. I was now in my mid-30s, weighing 108 kilos and my foot had to be strong enough to handle the pressure of playing footy at the highest level for at least the next six months. With about six weeks to go until the start of the season, I was able to start running properly, which was a huge relief. I had followed the post-surgery rehabilitation programs diligently and to reach this point of the recovery without pain was encouraging.

At the start of March, I was still telling friends that I would not be back at the start of the season but out of nowhere, I started to feel unbelievable on the training track. I was able to run without any pain and I was not feeling fatigued after heavy sessions, which was a surprise. About ten days before the Collingwood match, I had another meeting with Ben Serpell and told him that I was feeling great during training. That matched with what he had been seeing and he told me he thought I was closer to playing than he had expected. I had the green light to play and trained at full pace and did a significant amount of footwork training without feeling any pain in my foot – or elsewhere for that matter – which boosted my confidence. Having played every game for the past three years, I was able to extend that streak into another year.

* * *

Driving to the MCG as we began our premiership defence, I felt a familiar sensation. I was nervous which, counterintuitively, told me that I was ready to go for another year. We were bracing for a significant test from Collingwood, mindful they were likely to be a leading contender again in 2023 after their bid six months earlier ended in that heartbreaker against Sydney.

I was also mindful of another fact: for the first time since 2011, we were again the team to be hunted by the rest of the competition.

Despite this, we were confident we would be more than capable of defending our premiership given our dominance at the end of 2022. The sentiment around the club was clear. Joel Selwood may not be around, with Patrick Dangerfield appointed captain, but our approach to the season was no different. Bring it on.

For the first three-quarters against the Magpies, we lived up to our lofty expectations in what proved to be a scintillating clash. We then hit the wall. Was this a pointer our flag defence might be in jeopardy? After kicking 16 goals to three-quarter-time and holding a six-point lead at the final change, we failed to kick another goal as Collingwood ran over us to win by 22 points. I was just average, kicking two goals, but I was at least able to get through the match without any issues with my foot.

If there was any doubt that sides were priming themselves to challenge us, a tight loss to Carlton at the MCG six nights later and then a poor loss to the Suns on the Gold Coast proved a reality check as we claimed a piece of unwanted history. We had become the first reigning premiers in the AFL era to start a flag defence with three straight losses – it was the worst start to a premiership defence since 1976 – and the first time we had lost three games in a row since 2017. As Chris Scott noted afterwards, it was not a great start to the new season. 'I won't be defensive if anyone says it is not the ideal start to the season. I get it. If you fall too far behind, you have to win more games in less time. But it is also true that if you win a lot of games in a row late, good things can happen,' he told the media. 'We could spend a whole lot of time thinking about what it means and referring back to last year, which I get why people do that, but it would be a mistake for us to do it.'

I was also a little confused about my own form, having managed only three goals in those three games. Although I felt physically fine, I was struggling for touch and was particularly quiet against the Suns, managing only one behind from five kicks.

* * *

Clearly things needed to change but the mood around the club, which has always been a strength at Geelong during my time, was not greatly different. Every time you walked into the club, it was to achieve something, and our poor start to the year should not affect that.

Thankfully, we were able to break the drought against Hawthorn on Easter Monday, winning by 82 points, starting a roll of five straight wins. My form also began to match the way I was feeling physically. I booted a couple of goals against the Hawks and then 17 in the next three matches, which included a bag of eight against Essendon in round 7 – a personal high. When it comes to playing against opposition teams, while I always treasured the antagonism that came with playing against Hawthorn and the electric atmosphere in matches against Collingwood, I was at my most potent against the Bombers. I have averaged just over two goals per match during my career, but that rate lifted to more than three per game against Essendon, a club that obviously had challenges during my career.

As a result of that run of wins, we jumped to sixth on the ladder, just two games behind the top-placed Magpies, and we had the third-best percentage in the competition. It appeared things were back on track, but that winning stretch ultimately proved a mirage.

The failure of our premiership defence came down to a combination of factors, though I do not believe that we had suffered a hangover or that we were too old. Continuity of personnel was a factor as we were rarely able to field our strongest team due to injuries to key players across the entire season. Cam Guthrie, a proper star in the midfield who had won his second Carji Greeves Medal in our premiership season, did not play after round 6 because of a foot injury. Mitch Duncan missed the first three matches of the year with a calf injury and then another three with a hamstring problem leading into the mid-season bye, when we had started to lose our way.

Patrick Dangerfield injured his hamstring in the win over Adelaide in round 8 and missed the next four matches, all of which we lost. He returned after the bye for the clash against Port Adelaide and showed incredible bravery to finish the game after suffering a partially collapsed lung and broken ribs after colliding with Dan Houston in the second quarter.

Mark Blicavs, who had proven remarkably durable through the first decade of his career, injured a hamstring against Fremantle in round 20 which forced him to miss the last month of the season, a period where our spluttering premiership defence finally ran out of steam.

We had played near-perfect football in the final 16 weeks of the 2022 season but were never to recapture the same form or momentum in 2023. I've never liked using injuries as an excuse, but we got them at the wrong time, which left us vulnerable. After our slow start to the year, it always felt as though we were chasing our tails. That can wear down the best clubs, regardless of their competitive spirit.

* * *

My own season followed a similar path to that of the club. A slow start followed by a promising burst of form before I truly hit the wall around round 8, as fatigue suddenly hit me.

It is probable the tiredness was caused by the reduced pre-season but after feeling as though I was running on top of the ground for the first couple of months, now I was just plugging away. Somehow, I managed to kick nine goals in the four games leading into the bye, but it was clear to me and the coaches that I was going to need a rest at some stage.

Unfortunately, the timing was never quite right for this to happen. It was partly due to the issues suffered by other senior players – as an example, I was due to take a break in round 16, but that was thwarted when Jeremy Cameron was knocked out in an accidental collision with Gary Rohan in round 15 against Melbourne.

My competitive spirits also kicked in. I was not at my peak but while we were still in contention to play finals, I should be doing all I could to assist. Ultimately, my body failed me. After an entire career where the joke around Geelong was that I was too slow to suffer from a soft-tissue injury, my luck finally ran out in the round 20 match against Fremantle at home. I managed to kick a couple of goals but as I was running early in the last quarter, I felt my hamstring grab and the shock of it pulled me up really quickly. It felt similar to the sensation if I accidentally touch an electric fence on the farm.

Adding to the embarrassment was that I was only running at about 60 per cent of my capacity. Black humour is always a factor at a club when things are not going right, and the fact that I had pulled a hamstring while running like a tortoise added to the mirth of my teammates. The injury brought an end to my streak of consecutive games but that was not the only disappointment as I finished the match sitting on the bench alongside Mark Blicavs, who had torn his hamstring earlier. To add insult to the injuries, Fremantle forwards Lachie Schultz and Michael Frederick kicked freakish goals in the final stages to snatch a seven-point win, casting us out of the eight.

With two rounds remaining, our hopes of defending the premiership were almost extinguished as we were now 11th.

After discussions with the medical and coaching staff, it was decided I could come back against St Kilda at the Docklands in round 23. While I would not be at 100 per cent I had been moving reasonably well at training. I managed to kick a couple of goals, but I wasn't able to move anywhere near the way I hoped. It was not to be for the Cats as we trailed at every break, by a widening margin.

I had been planning to play in the last game of the year, a match in which we were going to celebrate Isaac Smith's time with us at Geelong, but we had to ditch those plans, to my regret. Out of nowhere, my foot was once again sore and, given the problem of 12 months earlier, the medical staff immediately ordered a scan which showed big problems. The plantar plate had again torn and, as a result, my second toe had once again been dislodged. To say it was a flat week would be an understatement as I looked forward to another off-season in a moon boot. But that was a problem that could wait until after a break.

* * *

I was out of contract, and when it comes to negotiating a new deal, I was aware that doing so while on the injured list was not ideal. But to say I was unprepared for the lengthy struggle that was about to ensue between me, my agent Tom Petroro and the club, via my old teammate Andrew Mackie (who had replaced Stephen Wells as the list manager), would be the understatement of the century. Securing a new contract proved to be anything but a smooth process.

As was the case through the latter stages of my career, we had held contract discussions during the year with a view to settling something in the latter stages. In 2023 it was no different, at least initially.

Although it had been a difficult year for me on several fronts – from the reduced pre-season to the hamstring injury and finally the toe – the impact I was able to have on matches had still been clear. Some key indicators were down marginally compared with 2022 but I still managed to kick 49 goals for the season despite missing three games, which was only four goals fewer than Jeremy Cameron, who had played 20 games. I ranked first across the competition for marks per game inside the 50-metre arc, seventh in goals kicked per game and also finished in the top 10 in the Coleman Medal.

I was prepared for a slight dip in what the club would offer, but I was absolutely stunned with the initial package Geelong put before us given how I had performed and also because I believed I was capable of playing excellent football again in 2024. Yes, the foot was potentially an issue, but it was hardly a case of me limping to the finish line, as those statistics had showed. I also felt I had unfinished business given the way the season ended. We had missed the finals for only the second time in Chris Scott's tenure, but I had faith in our list and believed we could contend again in 2024.

Make no mistake, Geelong had been especially good to me over my career, but I also believed that I had provided years of good service on the field and also away from it with my mentorship of younger teammates and my work in the local community. I felt like this was something that should be valued.

Part of the reason the Cats were so strong throughout my time at the club was the fact that some of our best-performed players were prepared to play for less than what they could have made elsewhere. Although I never entertained any external offers, I am aware that rival clubs contacted Tom Petroro every so often, asking about my availability.

There were many reasons to stay, from the quality relationships and the camaraderie around the club in general to the lifestyle that comes with being able to live and play in Geelong. We also have enjoyed sustained success and that is something I will be forever grateful for. I never wanted to play for another club, though I'm sure Emma would have loved the opportunity to enjoy an adventure with the family in another state or in Melbourne. So to receive an offer so low given those factors was a gut-punch.

That said, Geelong quickly came back with another offer that was far closer to the mark, though not yet quite satisfactory, which led to further negotiations. When it comes to contractual matters, I have always preferred to leave it to my management. Part of the reason is that I struggle to say no, and I know that earlier in my career, when the club asked me to do something directly, I had been rather soft. In this case, I wanted to handle the key discussions myself, making it clear that the one-on-one conversations I had with Andrew and with Steve Hocking were not only amicable, considerate of both parties. In other words what was best for the club, and would I be part of that. The best fit for both. Did they need me in 2024? Could I take the pressure off them to make a decision? Given the problems I had with my foot, it was clear I didn't want to commit to another year and be on the sidelines. Steve was brave, back when I signed that long-term contract, and he was brave again in 2023.

As is the case in an industry where news related to contract negotiations and trades is eagerly reported on by journalists and consumed by fans, my negotiations became a story. It was reported that Geelong and I were at loggerheads but, as I pointed out, after the initial shock, we were quite close to a resolution. In the end, we haggled for a few weeks as we tried to reach a position that would satisfy everybody. I was prepared to meet halfway but did not want to give up too much ground, in part because I did not want it to affect my attitude when returning to the club for 2024.

It was reported at the time that other clubs were interested in the proceedings and while I never sought out any offers, Tom Petroro did receive queries. He has since told me that Melbourne and the Gold Coast would have been interested in talking to me if I decided to test the waters elsewhere, while I've heard Collingwood and Essendon were also keeping a close eye on happenings in case I could not reach an agreement.

But because my allegiance was always with Geelong, I asked Tom to keep those discussions to himself and ultimately, we agreed to terms on October 13, 2023. Due to the lengthy nature of the proceedings, and what I considered to be inaccurate reporting, I released a statement once a new deal had been signed:

> The choices we make in professional sports are not isolated. They ripple out and involve lots of other people in your life. That is why after each season and each contract, I always take time to sit and reflect with my loved ones to discuss our future and not only what is best for me but also for everyone who's on this journey with me. I was always motivated to continue playing with the Cats. Geelong isn't just where I work, it's home. It's the community that's given me so much and I feel privileged to have another chance to give back in 2024. The future looks bright from here in Geelong, I look forward to the young guys keeping me young and continuing to give my all to this club. My motivation, without question, is still there. I will continue as I was always taught, to try and leave this club in a better place than when I started. I'm really excited for the challenge that's in front of the team and myself moving forward into the future.

The contract was signed, but the deal was not quite complete in my heart and head. The way the negotiations had played out publicly is something that did not sit comfortably with me and I wanted to have a chat with Andrew Mackie to make sure that he understood there was nothing personal in me challenging the club's initial offer or in prolonging the negotiations. I'm very conscious that list managers have to juggle so many different priorities to ensure the club is in a position to challenge not just in the present but in the future. Footy is a business after all. He was as pragmatic in his dealings with me as he had proved as a masterful defender, which is why he is in the job.

A challenging season was at an end but there were no guarantees as we looked towards 2024 and what could be my last season.

27

More milestones

WHEN THE PROBLEM with my second toe first flared in the latter stages of the 2022 season, there were times where the pain was so significant that part of me wished I could cut it off. But as we assessed how best to treat the injury leading into what could prove my final season, I was astonished to learn that amputation was not just an option but was a realistic one should things go awry again. Again I stuck with the advice Matthew Egan had given me in 2008, and what my parents had drummed into me – I was determined to do my due diligence again.

While my contract talks had been progressing, albeit slowly, I was gathering as much medical information as possible in the hope that I would be able to avoid spending another off-season in a moon boot. As part of that process, I flew to Sydney to meet with two specialists, and then on to Brisbane later that day to consult with Dr Ben Forster, the surgeon who had operated on my foot the previous October. There were a couple of reasons why I chose to trust Dr Forster with looking after the injury. Part of it was his record. Being based in Brisbane, he had a lot of experience dealing with bigger athletes from Rugby League and Union backgrounds and with my bulk and height, I shared some of those attributes.

I also found him great to deal with. He had a great manner about him and was able to explain the process to me in a way that made sense. In the end, I only had one regret in my dealings with Dr Forster. As a result of the success of the operation on my foot, Geelong ended up sending at least five of my teammates to him for surgery. I really should have asked for a finder's fee or some sort of commission! Then again, he did enable me to extend my career, so that's payment enough.

It was an interesting exercise but at the end of the trip I was still not sure as to what the best course of action would, though the specialists had left me with options to consider.

The first was to leave it alone and let nature take its course. That would require rest where possible and to manage the problem should it flare again, as it had in the previous two seasons.

The second option was to have another operation on the plantar plate and the second toe, though this time the methodology would be slightly different. Once again it would require me to spend time in a moon boot, but if I took this course there was no certainty of success.

The third path was the gut-wrenching one – namely, to amputate the toe.

After discussing all this with Emma and Tom Petroro, along with the club's medical staff, we chose to roll the dice and see if I could manage the problem without resorting to surgery.

It was a tricky one; if the problem did arise in the middle of the year, it could prove an early end to my career. Something as simple as twisting it the wrong way or landing awkwardly could trigger it again.

I was also aware that should Geelong be in a position to contend in September, I might face an extremely difficult decision later in the year. Would I then chop off my toe to have a shot at a fourth premiership? That was a decision I feared having to make.

* * *

As a result of us failing to make the finals, we had the luxury of having our longest break since a similarly early exit in 2015. Given how chaotic the previous four seasons had been, when dealing with the pandemic, winning a premiership and then falling short in a difficult flag defence, it was felt a decent break would allow us to freshen up and find our focus again.

Despite the apprehension associated with the state of my toe, I was delighted to find that I was able to get through the pre-season without any real issues. Again, I kept in close touch with Ben Serpell and we continued to follow the advice Sue Mayes had offered a year earlier when I was recovering from surgery.

The priority was to ensure that I retained some function in the area and although I did not need to follow the extensive rehabilitation process of the previous year, some management was required.

I would work a band around underneath the toe, just to build a little strength in the region, and the club physiotherapists spent a lot of time working around the toe. They had my sympathy as

I imagine it was not much fun dealing with my feet for hours at a time.

It has been customary at Geelong to manage the loads of the more mature players in the pre-season, as happens across the competition. While it is imperative to reach a high level of fitness, senior players are coming off a higher base than younger players when it comes to strength and endurance, if not explosiveness. I was able to get through about 90 per cent of the program, felt good heading into a new season and was determined to live up to my end of that new contract.

* * *

There were some changes in personnel leading into the new year. Along with the retirements of Isaac Smith and Jon Ceglar, Sam Menegola was delisted and Esava Ratugolea was traded to Port Adelaide. In the coach's box, Shaun Grigg headed to the Gold Coast to join his old Richmond mentor, Damien Hardwick, and former captain Steven King returned from the Suns in what was effectively a straight swap, while champion AFLW player Daisy Pearce, who had been an assistant to Chris Scott in 2023, accepted the role as senior coach of West Coast's AFLW team.

There was also a major change at our home ground. After five years of renovations, a sparkling new grandstand was opened, fittingly named after Joel Selwood, the club's longest-serving captain. The stand's 14,000 seats took the ground's capacity to 40,000.

A near-capacity crowd of 39,352 attended our first match of the season – and the opening of the new grandstand – against

St Kilda, and the atmosphere was outstanding. It was a tense match as the hard-running Saints pressed us throughout. Despite our inaccuracy (10.16) we held on in a goal-by-goal last quarter to win by eight points.

The following week, against Adelaide at the Adelaide Oval, we celebrated Tom Stewart's 150th game. Tom was a mature-aged recruit who has blossomed into one of the finest defenders I have played alongside, which says something given the quality of former defensive stars Matthew Scarlett, Corey Enright, Andrew Mackie, and Harry Taylor.

There was some drama before the match, with Mitch Duncan having to rush back to Victoria to be with his wife, Demi, who had gone into labour shortly after we had arrived in Adelaide. Earlier that week we had discussed this prospect, and he and I were going to be on the first flight out of Adelaide the day after the match. Understandably, he dashed off early. Parker James Duncan, their fourth child, arrived on a night in which our positive results in milestone matches came to the fore again as we beat the Crows by 19 points. In a further boost, I was able to find my best form after a quiet match against the Saints, with a burst of three goals in the third quarter, after Adelaide had grabbed the lead, to help swing the match our way.

These early wins vindicated the faith I had in us being able to bounce back from the disappointment of 2023 while also giving me the confidence that I was still able to influence matches.

* * *

Milestone weeks are always special for me, and this was a season where it looked likely I would be able to celebrate some significant dates, provided all went well with my fitness and form. My first major milestone arrived in round 3, when we played our old rivals Hawthorn at the MCG in the annual Easter Monday fixture. This was to be my 350th game and it was a milestone I was determined to celebrate with all my family after the border shutdowns in 2021 prevented any of my loved ones from attending my 300th. That occasion proved to be a disappointment on many levels as we lost to Port Adelaide in a qualifying final.

One of the great joys about celebrating milestone matches at this stage of my career is that my children are able to attend and be a part of the fun. Belle and Mimi were old enough to be carried onto the SCG when I played in my 250th against the Swans in 2019, but this time around – aged seven and five – they could enjoy the whole week.

On the Tuesday before the game, Emma and the three kids came into GMHBA Stadium for a family photo and also to attend my press conference, alongside Chris Scott, in the club's theatrette. At one stage I noted they looked a little bored, to which Chris responded that at least they had not fallen asleep like Jeremy Cameron did on occasion, nor were their eyes as glazed as Mark Blicavs' were during strategy meetings.

While press conferences happen on a weekly basis, I particularly enjoy those around milestones as they enable players to discuss their total career and this was no different. I touched on my lengthy history at the club, how I had matured as a player, some of the challenges I have had to overcome, while also keeping the door open to continuing in 2025 if things went well through the season.

I was honoured that Chris not only attended the press call but was frank in the way he had seen my career unfold during his tenure. Chris's first game as my coach was my 80th, so he had seen close to 80 per cent of my career!

I was also touched by the tributes sent my way by my family, from some past and present teammates and some of the greats I had played against.

One of the things we do at Geelong before milestones is to put together a video tribute to the player and this proved no different, which stirred my emotions before the clash against the Hawks.

Emma and the kids, my old mates Cam Mooney, Steve Johnson, James Podsiadly, Corey Enright, Joel Selwood, Jeremy Cameron and Mark Blicavs, along with Jonathan Brown, Matthew Richardson and Jack Riewoldt and Channel Seven broadcaster Hamish McLachlan, who filmed his tribute while on a skiing holiday in the French Alps, all had their say on my time in the game.

Emma said that she 'always admired your love of the game and you are constantly thinking about your teammates while never taking yourself too seriously'. Blicavs suggested the next stand at Geelong should be named after me. Johnson was typically cheeky, stating I had 'come a long way since that first Mad Monday' and that his favourite memory 'aside from the cheapie (I gave him) in the (2011) Grand Final' was the kick after the siren in 2012 that toppled Hawthorn and gave new steam to the Kennett Curse.

Joel described me as 'the commander and the heart and soul of the footy club' while touching on something else that has driven me, namely that, 'He makes his games count, rather than counting his games'. It was a ripper of a tribute and I could not have asked for any more. There would be a lot more to come in 2024 and I was really looking forward to giving it my all.

* * *

My 350th game was always going to be memorable, but it turned out to be far more dramatic than anyone could have predicted, with a wild storm whipping up a chaotic finale.

Things could not have gone any better early in the match as we jumped Hawthorn with a seven goal to one opening term. Mitch Duncan zipped a perfect pass to me 11 minutes in and I was able to weave a 40-metre goal through from a difficult angle, with the ball fading from left to right in a fashion that has been familiar throughout my career. In the latter stages of the first quarter I kicked another while in heavy traffic on the goal line.

To their credit Hawthorn rebounded in the second quarter and reduced the margin to a goal early in the third term, but we were again able to seize the ascendancy.

With assistance from a clever kick from Tyson Stengle, I out-positioned Sam Frost in a marking contest, to kick my third goal. But the weather front was closing in. The storm had caused chaos elsewhere, with the famous Stawell Gift running race delayed for a couple of hours after a massive deluge soaked the Central Park Oval.

Holding a lead of 36 points, we had assumed our positions on the field for the final term but were then ushered off by the umpires. There was a serious threat that lightning would strike at the MCG.

As the fans were told to scamper for cover, we headed back to the rooms amid some confusion. To the credit of the AFL, they kept us well-informed and we were told it was likely the match would resume within the hour. It was a strange experience, but Chris Scott and the coaches told us to relax and take a rest as we awaited further news.

With that in mind, Jeremy Cameron and I headed into the tea room and enjoyed a cuppa, chatting away like a couple of old farmers as we chewed the fat about the price of cattle. I also managed to get myself in trouble, much to my surprise, for checking the weather radar on the mobile phone of one of the club's support staff. The AFL has a strict policy regarding the use of mobile phones during matches – for integrity purposes – and it is a rule I was aware of. But this was a spur of the moment act and something I did not give a second thought to until later. The incident sparked headlines stating Geelong was liable for a $20,000 fine but the AFL issued the club with a warning given it was such an innocuous act.

That said, we still had a football game to win. After going through the type of warm-up when readying ourselves to resume after the half-time break, we headed back out to the oval.

After a break of 43 minutes, the ball was bounced to start the fourth quarter amid torrential rain, but the threat of lightning had passed. The Hawks pressed initially but we were able to settle. Courtesy of an act of generosity from Jeremy Cameron, who handballed to me after he had marked directly in front, I snapped another goal to finish with four for the day in what was a memorable 36-point win.

The scenes in the room afterwards were jubilant with some similarities to our premiership celebrations given there were so many family members and also great friends from my years at Geelong filling the change room.

Harry Taylor had caught a 5.30am flight from Geraldton to Perth, and then another across the country, to surprise me and was among former teammates including Gary Ablett Jnr, Steve Johnson, Corey Enright, James Podsiadly, James Kelly, Isaac Smith, Steven King and Joel Selwood who gathered in the rooms for the song. In between post-match media commitments, legendary Hawk Dermott Brereton ducked in for a chat, while Melbourne Cup-winning horse trainer Danny O'Brien and his wife, Nina, who are friends of ours, were among the throng of what seemed like thousands in the room.

The Cats were unbeaten, my foot was feeling fine and I'd kicked nine goals from three matches to date. It was hard not to shake the sense that something special was again brewing.

* * *

Given my history, it is probably no surprise that I hit a flat spot which I described as a 'speed bump' as I went through the longest period of my career without kicking a goal.

We continued our winning ways with victories over the Bulldogs, North Melbourne and then Brisbane at the Gabba before losing a tight one to Melbourne at the MCG in round 8 to slip from top spot. I missed the clash with the Kangaroos as part of the plan to manage me through the season. I found myself in the midst of a drought, which created headlines leading into my 355th game, when I equalled the games record set by Joel Selwood in 2022.

I didn't feel I was playing too badly and was still influential during matches, with my score involvements at a similar level to my output in the first four weeks, even if I was not kicking goals myself. As an example, in the 13-point victory over Carlton in round 6, I was able to set up a couple of goals when getting the better of Blues ruckman Marc Pittonet, who was otherwise exceptional during the match, when he had drifted into our attacking arc for rucking contests.

There were other factors at play as well. My direct opponents through this period included quality defenders Carlton's Jacob Weitering, Lion Harris Andrews and Melbourne's Steven May. Our eight-point loss against Melbourne, after we had led at three-quarter time, ended our seven-game winning streak. It also continued a streak I was not happy with – it was the first time in my career when I had gone four matches without kicking a goal. There were reasons for that, although it's a streak I never wanted on my records.

With Geelong having a great spread of goalkickers led by Jeremy Cameron, Ollie Henry and Tyson Stengle, there were stages where I played almost as a decoy forward to drag the opposition's premier defenders away from play, as my coach Chris Scott explained: 'The last couple of weeks, we played well enough without 'Hawk' dominating on the scoreboard. What would we have in a perfect world? I think in a perfect world, we'd have four, five or six guys down there that are real threats. Over the years ... we've maybe been too conscious of Hawkins and he is a victim of what he has done in the past. It sounds a bit defensive, but of all the players I would have thought I might need to defend over the years, Tom would not have entered the top 50. So I'm not going to risk (that) by starting now and getting defensive. I'm pretty happy talking about this stuff because I'm just so supremely confident that when he has a couple of good days, which are coming, the conversation will look after itself.'

Aside from the queries about my form, which did not concern me too much leading into the record-equalling game against Port Adelaide on May 10 at home, there was a good mood around the club. Yes, our streak had come to an end, but it came after a narrow loss to the Demons and we were looking forward to bouncing back against the Power. There was also an air of celebration surrounding my feat, to reach this moment in my career. As the club had been in the week ahead of my 350th game, Geelong was superb in helping me celebrate the occasion.

On the Tuesday before the Friday night game, the club invited Geelong's other members of the 300-game club to an event in my honour. While John 'Sam' Newman and Corey Enright, who was working as an assistant coach at St Kilda, were unable to attend, Joel Selwood, Jimmy Bartel and the club's inaugural 300-club member Ian Nankervis, a teammate of my dad, were able to make it to the club alongside a couple of other good mates from my time with the Cats.

As I considered another milestone, there were elements that made me particularly proud, with my durability and consistency at the forefront. The milestone also felt like it was a celebration for everyone who had helped me along the way, from Finley to Melbourne Grammar – my own family and my 'work' family, as I called Geelong – while discussing the achievement at a press conference before the game.

'It feels a bit surreal and sits slightly uncomfortably. I make no bones about the fact I was an avid Geelong supporter who grew up watching the Cats through the 1990s and early 2000s, wanting to be here, wanting to call this place home. I have spent half my life here now in Geelong and I call it home. I refer to this environment that is work, as my home away from home. It has been incredible. I am sure that six-year-old boy who started Auskick (30 years before) would be pretty amazed. My grandfather Fred, on my mum's side and who played 20-odd games here at Geelong, always used to say to me in my junior footy, "Head down. Arse up". That is something that always sticks with me. He messages me before every game, so he has racked up a hefty phone bill over the journey, but he always says that to me. That is probably something that always sticks with me in a football sense.'

I added that Kardinia Park will always be a home away from home, when my playing days are over. 'I'm happy just for a seat next to Joel Selwood in the Joel Selwood Stand. If I can find myself a seat somewhere, that would be more than enough, because once my time is done here and I am no longer a footballer, I can't wait to come here and watch Geelong for a long part of my life.'

The highlight of that 355th game did not occur during the match, but rather at half-time when Belle stepped out for her first game on the oval. She was among dozens of kids with the chance to play during the break in an AFL Auskick grid game on the ground and she demonstrated all her skills.

She managed to complete a cartwheel, get a stitch and also kick a goal in ten minutes of footy! Even better is that we got to pose for a photograph on the ground. Unfortunately, that was where the celebrations came to an end as we lost to Port Adelaide at home for the first time since 2007, my first year with Geelong.

The Power shone early with an eight-goal opening term and led by 49 points midway through the second quarter. We managed to respond but our charge came too late and Port Adelaide held on to win by six points in a match where I had been manned by my old teammate Esava Ratugolea. He had promised to spoil the party and played a really good match restricting me to seven possessions. He later said his familiarity with the way I played and also the manner with which Geelong players kicked to me helped him on the night.

I was able to end that four-match drought when I finally kicked a goal in the second quarter, but I missed everything with another shot which may well have changed the result. But it was not to be.

I was rested for a trip to Darwin to play the Suns the following Thursday night. This meant that I established a new games record against GWS Giants on May 25, which came just four days after my dad Jack celebrated his 70th birthday.

* * *

Dad is my great mentor when it comes to working the land. Which raises the point. Just as Dad spent decades involved at club and league levels in coaching and administration after returning to Finley following his career at the Cats, I'm certain when it comes to my time to retire, I'll remain involved in footy as I still love the game. It will be good to be able to enjoy a beer or two with mates at a nearby pub after Geelong games as we discuss the match and a new generation of Cats or to attend Carji Greeves Medal nights and reminisce about our glory days.

With all I have learnt in football from my coaches Bomber Thompson and Chris Scott, there may come a time when I'm able to pass on a tip or two to aspiring key forwards and ruckmen about how best to use their bodies, among the other tricks of the trade over my journey. Whether that's in clubland or in the commentary box, who knows?

As I write this, and with the end near, I think back to that time back in 2015 when I wondered how my footy would be considered. Then, as I wrote, it was something like this: 'Tom Hawkins? He was a good player, but he could never quite put it all together for a long enough period to be considered a champion.' Now, I think back on something Mum always told me: to be patient. Often, I was slow at doing things, but when I did them I would do them really well, and I think of that as something of a metaphor for my career. Geelong people had to be patient too, but I think ultimately the end product was worth the wait.

But now, watching the kids muck around on the farm, wearing the blue-and-white hoops of Geelong, my mind often drifts to the future. Future footballers? From the Brushfields to the Callans and Le Deuxs, and through to the Hawkins' clan including Dad, my uncles and me, my family has been involved in some capacity with Geelong for more than 100 years.

Most of all, though, I'm looking forward to seeing Belle, Mimi and Henry grow up. As long as they are healthy and happy, we'll be delighted with whatever they do.

Milestones and statistics

Tom Hawkins

Date of birth: 21 July 1988
(Statistics to 9 June 2024)

Draft: No. 41 (Father-Son), 2006 national draft
Debut: round 2, 7 April 2007, Carlton v Geelong, Docklands

ORIGINAL TEAMS

Sandringham Dragons (TAC Cup)/ Melbourne Grammar (APS)/ Finley Football Club (NSW)

HONOURS AND ACHIEVEMENTS

Team

AFL Premiership (Geelong): 2009, 2011, 2022

McClelland Trophy (Geelong): 2007, 2008, 2019, 2022

2009 NAB Cup Premiership

2007 VFL Premiership

Individual

All-Australian team: 2012, 2019, 2020, 2021, 2022 (c)

Coleman Medal: 2020 (equal second 2012)

Carji Greeves Medal (Best and Fairest): 2012
(second in 2014 and 2020)

Geelong leading goalkicker: 2012, 2013, 2014, 2015, 2016, 2017, 2018, 2019, 2020, 2021, 2022

Tom Wills Medal 2023

Geelong FC Tom Harley Award for Best Clubman 2021

2020 All-Stars

Geelong FCCommunity Champion Award 2019

AFL Army Award 2009

AFL Rising Star nominee 2007

AFL Under-18 Championships 2006

Larke Medal 2006

Under-18 All-Australian Forward 2006

NOTABLE RECORDS

Record-holder of most games played for Geelong FC (exceeding the previous record of 355 games, held by Joel Selwood)

Member of four AFL Grand FInal teams: 2009, 2011, 2020, 2022

305 games played as teammate to Joel Selwood

Most Goal Assists in season: equal second in 2020, fourth in 2022

Most goals in a match: 8 goals Geelong v Essendon Round 7, 2023

Average goals per match: 2.2

Goal-kicking accuracy: 63.9%

MILESTONES

Games

50th game: round 7, 9 May 2010, Geelong v Sydney, Kardinia Park

100th game: round 23, 1 September 2012, Geelong v Sydney, Kardinia Park

150th game: round 4, 26 April 2015, Geelong v North Melbourne, Kardinia Park

200th game: round 11, 2 June 2017, Geelong v Adelaide, Kardinia Park

250th game: round 19, 28 July 2019, Sydney v Geelong, SCG

300th game: QF, 27 August 2021, Port Adelaide v Geelong, Adelaide Oval

350th game: round 4, 1 April 2024, Hawthorn v Geelong, MCG

Goals

50th goal: round 21, 21 August 2009, Western Bulldogs v Geelong, Docklands

100th goal: round 24, 2 September 2011, Collingwood v Geelong, MCG

200th goal: round 13, 23 June 2013, Brisbane Lions v Geelong, Gabba

300th goal: round 10, 6 June 2015, Essendon v Geelong, Docklands

400th goal: round 4, 17 April 2017, Hawthorn v Geelong, MCG

500th: round 1, 22 March 2019, Collingwood v Geelong, MCG

600th: Semi Final, 10 October 2020, Geelong v Collingwood, Gabba

700th: round 14, 18 June 2022, West Coast v Geelong, Perth Stadium

796th: round 3, 9 June 2024, Sydney v Geelong, SCG

Acknowledgements

Footy has given me some great memories, and not just the trio of premierships. More importantly, it has given me a brother for life in Joel Selwood, along with the many other great mates who I had the fortune to play alongside at the Cats. When I passed Joel's games record in 2024, I was so honoured to have so many of those players who came to the game: Harry Taylor, James Podsiadly, Cameron Mooney, Matthew Scarlett, Brad Ottens, Joel, Steve Johnson, Mathew Stokes, and Bomber Thomson were all such influences on me. They showed me the way and I will be forever grateful to them.

Throughout 18 seasons with Geelong, my teenage sweetheart and now my wife, Emma, has been with me. She is my greatest supporter and my backbone. We now have our own family – two daughters, Arabella and Primrose, and a toddler, Henry. Emma has a flourishing business – Homegrown – creating clothes for kids, and we have our own farm, a place where I am looking forward to spending a lot more time working while cheering on the Cats from afar. I have no doubt I will be busy chasing my kids and my cattle. But I'll love that.

Playing for the Geelong Football Club has been a truly great experience. The journey was made all the more amazing by the remarkable people who have been such a big part of my life. I am forever grateful.

I want to thank the Geelong Football Club's coaches and support staff, the AFL and my manager, Tom Petroro and his team.

Thanks too to Courtney Walsh and the team at Hardie Grant Books.

Lastly I want to thank not just the Geelong fans but all the fans who make the game what it is, for coming out rain, hail or shine to support their teams and to cheer on the players.